THE
LATE ROMAN
ARMY

THE
LATE ROMAN ARMY

PAT SOUTHERN
&
KAREN RAMSEY DIXON

Yale University Press
New Haven and London

For J.T. and co., who all helped
(P.S.)

To the memory of my father Michael Scott Dixon
a deeply missed dad
(K.R.D.)

Published in the United States by Yale University Press and in
the United Kingdom by B. T. Batsford Limited.

Typeset and designed by David Seabourne and printed in
Great Britain by Biddles Ltd, Guildford, Surrey.

Library of Congress catalogue card number: 96-60156

ISBN 0-300-06843-3

A catalogue record for this book is available from
the British Library.

10 9 8 7 6 5 4 3 2 1

CONTENTS

FIGURES

PLATES

PREFACE AND ACKNOWLEDGEMENTS

The study of the late Roman army is rather like trying to grasp the soap in the bath. The available information is about as slippery, promising much but not yielding enough to create a continuous picture of the development of the army from the end of the second century to the beginning of the sixth. This book aims to bring together the evidence concerning the history, organization and fighting methods of the army, in a form accessible to students, utilizing both primary and secondary sources which are not readily available to the general reader.

The subject has been covered by several authors in the past, but most of the works cover only one or two aspects of the late Roman army, and many of them are in a foreign language. Most are out of print, including the eminent A.H.M. Jones's superlative work on the later Roman Empire, without which no one can proceed to study the late Roman army. In particular, there is no synthesis covering the transitional stages whereby the army of the late second century was gradually transformed onto the twofold field and frontier armies that emerged in the fourth century. Furthermore, illustrations of equipment, and plans and reconstructions of fortifications, tend to be omitted from some published works, and those that are available are scattered among several different publications.

We would like to record our thanks to Kemmis Betty of B.T. Batsford Ltd (who wields the fastest Biro in the West) for prompt attention to queries. Messrs Crow and Daniels, and Drs Greene and Rushworth at the University of Newcastle upon Tyne have been long-suffering listeners and have given hints and useful advice. Professor John Mann, Dr Roger Wilson, and Dr Jochen Garbsch are gratefully acknowledged for their invaluable help. The 'Cedar Road Triumvirate' of Richard Underwood, Ian Stephenson and Philip Clarke were of inestimable help throughout the writing of this book, sometimes offering more advice than was actually wanted.

Mrs Wendy Young typed at olympic speed, and Graeme Stobbs produced drawings and plans at the same pace. Richard Underwood is gratefully thanked for producing the scales for all the drawings in the equipment and siege warfare chapters.

The staff of Newcastle University library and in particular the Inter-library loan desk deserve especial thanks for ready co-operation. We would also like to acknowledge the following museums for providing photographs: Museum der Stadt Worms; Germanisches National Museum, Nürnberg; Vojvodjanski Museum, Novi Sad; Rijksmuseum Van Oudheden, Leiden; Römisch-Germanisches Museum; Cologne; Musée d'Art et d'Histoire, Geneva; Parrocchia di S. Giovanni Battista Museo del Duomo, Monza; Koblenz Museum.

Omissions, errors of judgement and misunderstandings remain firmly our own property, but we are perfectly willing to share them, or to hear reasons why we may be mistaken.

LIST OF EMPERORS

Undivided Empire			
Date AD	Emperor	Reigned approx.	Death
177–92	Commodus	15 years	Assassinated
193	Pertinax	2 months	Assassinated
193	Didius Julianus	2 months	Assassinated
193–211	Septimius Severus	17 years 9 months	Natural causes
198–217	Caracalla (with Severus 198–211)	19 years	Assassinated
209–12	Geta (with Severus and Caracalla)	2 years 3 months	Assassinated
217–18	Macrinus	1 year 2 months	Assassinated
218–22	Elagabalus	3 years 9 months	Assassinated
222–35	Severus Alexander	13 years	Assassinated
235–8	Maximinus	3 years 3 months	Assassinated
238	Gordian I	3 weeks	Suicide
238	Gordian II	3 weeks	Killed in battle
238	Balbinus	3 months	Assassinated
238	Pupienus	3 months	Assassinated
238–44	Gordian III	5 years 6 months	Assassinated
244–9	Philip I	5 years 7 months	Killed in battle
247–9	Philip II (with Philip I)	2 years	Killed in battle
248	Pacatian	? weeks	Assassinated
248	Jotapian	? weeks	Assassinated
249–51	Trajan Decius	1 year 9 months	Killed in battle
251	Herennius Etruscus	1 month	Killed in battle
251	Hostilian	4 months	Natural causes
251–3	Trebonianus Gallus	2 years	Assassinated
253	Aemilian	3 months	Assassinated
253	Uranius Antoninus	?	Assassinated
253–60?	Valerian	6 years	Captured in battle
253–68	Gallienus (with Valerian 253–60)	15 years	Assassinated

Undivided Empire (cont.)

Date AD	Emperor	Reigned approx.	Death
259	Saloninus (with Gallienus)	? weeks	Assassinated
268–70	Claudius II Gothicus	1 year 5 months	Natural causes
270	Quintillus	3 month	Suicide
270–5	Aurelian	5 years	Assassinated
275–6	Tacitus	7 months	Natural causes
276	Flavian	2 months	Assassinated
276–82	Probus	6 years	Assassinated
282–3	Carus	10 months	Killed in battle?
283–5	Carinus	1 year 8 months	Assassinated
283–4	Numerian	1 year 2 months	Assassinated
284–305	Diocletian	20 years 5 months	Natural causes
286–305	Maximianus (with Diocletian)	19 years 1 months	Suicide
305–6	Constantius Chlorus	1 year 2 months	Natural causes
305–11	Galerius	6 years	Natural causes
306–7	Severus II	8 months	Executed
309–11	Maximinus II	4 years 9 months	Natural causes
306–12	Maxentius	6 years	Killed in battle
308–24	Licinius	16 years	Executed
307–37	Constantine I	30 years	Natural causes
337–40	Constantine II	2 years 6 months	Killed in battle
337–50	Constans	12 years 6 months	Assassinated
337–61	Constantius	24 years 1 month	Natural causes
360–3	Julian	3 years 3 months	Killed in battle
363–4	Jovian	7 months	Accidental
364–75	Valentinian I	11 years 8 months	Natural causes
364–78	Valens	14 years 4 months	Natural causes
367–83	Gratian	16 years	Assassinated
375–92	Valentinian II	16 years	Assassinated?
379–95	Theodosius I	16 years	Natural causes

Divided Empire

EASTERN EMPIRE

Date AD	Emperor	Reigned approx.	Death
383–408	Arcadius	25 years 3 months	Natural
408–50	Theodosius II	48 years 6 months	Natural
450–7	Marcianus	6 years 6 months	Natural
457–74	Leo I	17 years	Natural
474	Leo II	1 year	Natural
474–91	Zeno	17 years 2 months	Natural
491–518	Anastasius	27 years 2 months	Natural
518–27	Justinus I	9 years	Natural
527–65	Justinian	38 years 3 months	Natural

WESTERN EMPIRE

Date	Emperor	Reigned approx.	Death
393–423	Honorius	30 years 7 months	Natural
423–55	Valentinian III	29 years 4 months	Assassinated
455–6	Maximus	2 months	Assassinated
455–6	Avitus	1 year	Deposed
457–61	Majorian	4 years 4 months	Executed
461–5	Severus	4 years	Natural
467–72	Anthemius	5 years 2 months	Executed
472	Olybrius	? weeks	Killed
473–4	Glycerius	1 year 3 months	Deposed
474–75	Nepos	1 year 2 months	Assassinated
475–6	Romulus Augustulus	10 months	Deposed

OUTLINE OF
SIGNIFICANT EVENTS

Reigning emperor	Reigned	Date	Events
Severus	193–211	193	Revolts of Pescennius Niger and Clodius Albinus
		194	Severus defeats Niger
		195–6	Invades Parthia
		197	Defeats Albinus
		197–9	Parthian War
		208–11	War in Britain
Caracalla	211–17	212	*Constitutio Antoniniana*
Macrinus	217–18		
Elagabalus	218–22		
Severus Alexander	222–35	234	War on Rhine
Maximinus	235–8		
Gordian III	238–44	238	Civil war
Philip I	244–9	248	Civil war
Trajan Decius	249–51	251	Civil war
Trebonianus Gallus	251–3	253	Civil war
Valerian	253–60	259	War with Persia. Shapur I captures Emperor Valerian
		260–1	Usurpers Macrianus, Quietus, Regalianus
		260–7	Odenathus of Palmyra recognized as *dux* and *imperator* by Gallienus
Gallienus	253–68	267–74	Palmyrene Empire
		259–73	Gallic Empire forms breakaway state
			259–68 Postumus
			268 Laelianus
			268–9 Marius
			269–70 Victorinus
			270–3 Tetricus
Claudius II	268–70	267	Goths sack Athens
Aurelian	270–5	271	Aurelian builds walls of Rome
		273	Reconquest of Gaul by Aurelian

Reigning emperor	Reigned	Date	Events
		274	Reconquest of Palmyra and the East
Probus	276–82		
		282–4	Civil war
Diocletian	284–305	293	Tetrarchy founded; Diocletian and Maximian as Augusti; Constantius and Galerius as Caesars
		286–93	Revolt of Carausius in Britain
		293–6	Allectus in Britain
		296	Reconquest of Britain
		297	Persians invade
		301	Diocletian's Price Edict
		303–4	Edicts against Christians; persecutions begin
Constantius Chlorus	305–6	305	Abdication of Diocletian and Maximian
Galerius	305–11	306	Revolt of Maxentius
Constantine I	307–37	311	Edict of Toleration; persecution of Christians ceases
		312	Battle of Milvian Bridge; Constantine defeats Maxentius
		313	Edict of Milan
		316	War with Licinius
		320	Crispus defeats Alamanni
		324	Constantine defeats Licinius. Constantinople founded
		325	Council of Nicaea
Sons of Constantine	337–61	330–2	Dedication of Constantinople which becomes Imperial residence
		350	Revolt of Magnentius
		351	Battle of Mursa. Constantius defeats usurper Magnentius
		357–9	Julian's campaigns in Gaul; Battle of Strasbourg 357, Julian defeats Alamanni
Julian	360–3	360	War with Persia under Constantine
		361–3	Pagan revival under Julian
		363	Julian invades Persia and is killed
Jovian	363–4	363	Jovian makes peace with Persia

Reigning emperor	Reigned	Date	Events
		367	Raids by Picts, Irish and Saxons in Britain Conspiratio Barbarica
Valentinian I	364–75	376	Visigoths settle in Balkans
Valens	364–78	378	Battle of Adrianople, Valens and Eastern Roman army defeated
Gratian	367–83		
Valentinian II	375–92		
Theodosius	379–5	380	Settlement of Visigoths in Moesia
		382	Theodosius I makes treaty with Visigoths
		383–8	Revolt of Maximus
		391	Closing of pagan temples
		392	Revolt of Arbogast
		394	Battle of Frigidus. Theodosius defeats Arbogast and reunites the Empire

Eastern Empire	Reign	Western Empire	Reign	Date	Events
Arcadius	383–408	Honorius	393–423	395	Division of the Empire under Honorius and Arcadius
				395–408	Ascendancy of Stilicho
				395–6	Revolt of Alaric and Visigoths, defeated by Stilicho in Greece
				397	Revolt of Gildo in Africa
				399–440	Revolt of Gainas at Constantinople; massacre of Gothic soldiers in Eastern army followed by recruitment of indigenous troops
				406	Vandals, Alans and Sueves cross the Rhine
				406/410	Roman garrison leaves Britain
Theodosius II	408–50			408	Stilicho murdered, Alaric invades Italy
				409	Vandals, Alans, Sueves invade Spain
				410	Alaric sacks Rome. Death of Alaric
				412	Visigoths enter Gaul
				415–18	Visigoths move to Spain, and eventually settle in Aquitania
		Valentinian III	423–55	427	Aetius becomes *Magister militum* in the west
				429	Vandals invade Africa
				430–53	Ascendancy of Aetius in the west; employs Hunnish troops against Goths
				437–8	Theodosian Code published
				439	Vandals take Carthage
				440	Huns invade Balkans
Marcianus	450–7			451	Huns invade Gaul. Aetius employs Franks and Visigoths against Attila. Battle of Mauric Plain. Attila retreats across Rhine

Eastern Emperor		Western Emperor		Date	Event
				453	Attila dies
				454	Aetius murdered
		Maximus	455	455	Vandals sack Rome
Leo I	457–74	Avitus	455–6	456–72	Ascendancy of Ricimer as *Magister militum* in the west
Leo II	474	Majorian	457–61		
Zeno	474–91	Severus	461–5		
		Anthemius	467–72		
		Glycerius	473–4		
		Nepos	474–5		
		Romulus Augustulus	475–6	476	Odoacer King of Italy
				488	Theodoric and Ostrogoths invade Italy
Anastasius	491–518			493	Ostrogothic kingdom in Italy
				481–511	Clovis reigns in Gaul; origin of Frankish kingdom
Justinus I	518–27			507	Clovis defeats Visigoths
Justinian	527–65			533–4/5	Justinian reconquers Africa
				534	Franks overthrow Burgundian kingdom
				535–54	Wars in Italy. Justinian reconquers Italy
				543–8	Berber revolt in Africa
				565	Death of Justinian

I

SOURCES

There has been a vast increase in the publication of secondary source material on the Roman army in recent years. Various aspects of Roman military history have been discussed by a growing body of scholars, such as Luttwak (1976) who examined the broader issues of frontier strategy, and more recently Whittaker (1994) who reassessed frontier policy in general. Intelligence gathering and the use of diplomacy in the Late Empire have been studied by Lee (1993) and Austin and Rankov (1995). Precisely because these authors have discussed these specialist fields, this book does not aim to go over the same ground. Rather, it is intended to document the physical presence and appearance of the army from an archaeological and historical point of view. Lack of space precludes any in-depth discussion of methods of warfare or the tactics of particular battles.

A large part of the ancient source material concerning the army is of an administrative nature. The relevant sections of the two great law codes, the *Codex Theodosianus* and the *Digest* of Justinian, illustrate the problems faced by the military authorities over the changing years of the late Empire. The *Codex Theodosianus* was published in the reign of Theodosius II. Many of the problems of using any ancient source material prevail, in that the compilers were themselves using sources already about a century old, which may not have been totally reliable. The *Codex* is arranged by subject groupings, but military affairs can be found under more than one heading; perhaps the greatest value of the *Codex* lies in the provision of firm dates. The laws clearly concern a situation that the emperors wanted to achieve, rather than the situation as it actually was, and the repeated reiterations of laws, sometimes listing penalties of increasing severity, reveal that the law was not supreme in the Empire and that the will of the emperors was not enough to ensure good behaviour. The *Digest* contains less information about military matters, but yields a wealth of social detail.

A document that has been discussed by modern authors for many years is the *Notitia Dignitatum*, which is literally a list of civil and military officials, and their staffs, listed by title or rank, complete with an enumeration of the commanding officers and the names of the units in garrison at various forts and military establishments. This sort of official and authoritative document promises much in the way of reliable information, but ultimately creates more questions than answers. The most important fact to remember is that such a document would need constant revision, and although the *Notitia* can be said, broadly speaking, to represent the army of the late fourth century, the complete text is composed of elements of different dates, and therefore it is not representative of the whole Empire at one time. The version that has come down to us is the western one, in which the information for the eastern Empire probably predates that for the west. Furthermore it is not a complete record of all the forts, garrisons, units and military establishments of the whole Empire. Used with caution, however, the *Notitia* is invaluable, simply because there is nothing to match it for the study of the late army.

Ancient authors who were concerned directly with the army include Vegetius, Ammianus, Procopius and the Anonymous. Vegetius was not a military commander, but a civilian official with a sense of history, who at some uncertain date compiled a lot of disparate information drawn from many different periods into a book designed to encourage the Emperor of his day (perhaps Theodosius I, alias Theodosius the Great) to improve the army. The work is not reliable as a portrait of the late army, but only of what was wrong with it and what had been lost, but since this is a matter of Vegetius' personal opinion, it is also a matter for debate, and so his writings must be used with caution.

Ammianus Marcellinus is the supreme authority for the fourth-century army. He was a military man, born at Antioch c. 330, who saw active service, and incorporated into his history accounts of events that he had witnessed or had lived through. The first thirteen books of his narrative are lost. In these he documented the history of the Empire from 96 to c. 350, for which he would have used older sources. Books 14 to 31 concern the history of the Empire from the mid-fourth century to the battle of Adrianople. Ammianus is generally considered to be reliable and, compared to some writers, remarkably free from religious or personal bias, save for his extreme partiality to Julian. The work of the Anonymous is a fantastic collection of ideas for improvements to the army, addressed to the Emperors Valentinian and Valens. Some of this unknown author's suggestions seem plausible to the modern scholar, and reveal a few of the defects of the late fourth-century army, but the more ambitious machinery which he describes leave something to be desired in the practical sense. Procopius was a sixth-century author who wrote the *History of the Wars*, about the campaigns of Justinian. Like Ammianus, he described contemporary events, incorporating details about the army and how it operated. His alternative work, the *Secret History*, is so vituperative that it cannot be used with any confidence.

The military manual attributed to Maurice, called the *Strategikon*, was probably written at the end of the fifth century or the beginning of the sixth, and therefore its use in connection with the army of the fourth and fifth centuries is anachronistic. But the information contained in this work is of such an eminently practical and sensible nature that it seems more relevant than the speculations of the improving authors such as Vegetius and the Anonymous.

A large amount of Latin and Greek literature survives with sporadic or fragmentary relevance to the army. The *Historia Augusta* purports to document the events of each emperor's reign, but the work is neither carefully researched nor systematically presented. Recent scholarship has established that there was only one author, rather than several different ones as named in the work (Syme 1971; White, 1967). The date of composition is also disputed (Baynes 1953). In some instances, the information is little better than gossip, and reliance upon any statement would be ill advised. Similarly, the various panegyrics addressed to the later emperors cannot be taken at face value because of their overt and pronounced bias, and staunchly positive outlook. Nevertheless, they cannot be completely ignored, and do provide a broad general background against which to evaluate military events.

Letters, poems, essays and speeches occasionally reveal useful information about the army. Ausonius, born at Bordeaux c. 310, wrote optimistically of the state of Gaul around the last three or four decades of the fourth century. Sidonius, bishop of Clermont-Ferrand, provided the same sort of information for the mid-fifth century. The speeches of Symmachus, a pagan orator (c. 340–402) and Synesius, a Christian (c. 370–413) provide differing views on the state of the Empire and what should be done about the barbarians.

The fourth-century *Orations* of Themistius strike a more reasoned note on the subject of the barbarians. The Christian/pagan bias in the literature of the late Empire distorts to varying degrees the value of the sources. The life of Constantine was well documented and the literature survives by dint of its extreme value to the Church authorities, but it was not only Christian writings that survived. It is refreshing to note that as well as sickening panegyrics, hostile narratives were also preserved, regardless of the religious convictions of the victim. The Christian author Lactantius blamed Diocletian for all the ills of the Empire, while Zosimus, the pagan, blamed Constantine instead.

Epigraphic evidence for the late Empire is perhaps less abundant than for the earlier Empire, but is still vast, covering a wide range of provinces and a broad time-scale. The great builders, such as Diocletian, Constantine and Valentinian, are better represented epigraphically than most others. The information about some Imperial decrees survives only in epigraphic form, such as Diocletian's famous price edict, by which he attempted to stabilize the economy. Many inscriptions were reused as building materials, and although this means that they are no longer *in situ* and cannot reveal much about the buildings they came from, they are still useful and can supplement the written sources by documenting the details which were not considered important or interesting by the literati.

There is a fairly extensive body of papyrological evidence for the late army. The duty rosters of *Cohors XX Palmyrenorum* stationed at Dura-Europos in the third century reveal that bureaucratic documentation had not diminished, but the detail about routine procedures is perhaps more applicable to the army of the early Empire than it is to the late army. The correspondence of the commanding officer at the fort of Dionysias is more relevant, and has been published as *The Abinnaeus Archive* with translation and commentary.

Archaeological remains include military equipment, coins and pottery, and skeletal finds, all of which have been made to yield considerable evidence about the late army, its appearance, and to a lesser extent its movements. Military equipment is perhaps the most exciting aspect of archaeology of the late army, imbued as it is with the ideas of both living personality and military glory. Skeletal evidence speaks for itself, revealing much information about the height, state of health and often cause of death of the person concerned. Coins are useful indicators of Imperial propaganda, as well as being helpful in providing dating evidence on archaeological sites. Pottery is also used as dating material, and can illustrate the quality of mundane daily life. Finally, buildings themselves are important documents if considered from the point of view of geographical location, architectural history and archaeological remains. Study of them can augment our knowledge derived from literary and epigraphic sources, and if taken in conjunction with this supplementary information can fill in some of the gaps in understanding of the late army. Unfortunately the degree of investigation of late Roman buildings has not been as intense as it has for the early Empire, so that the internal arrangements of forts is as yet little understood, and since the supposed standardization of earlier forts (now proving rather more elusive than hitherto expected) was abandoned in the late period, it is not possible to draw definite conclusions about the organization of the units in occupation, nor even about their relative strengths. As for the mobile army, it is not in abundant evidence on the ground; neither buildings nor documents nor archaeological finds can pin it down sufficiently to enable scholars to produce a complete picture. There are only glimpses of it here and there and from time to time.

II

CRISIS
AND TRANSITION

The late Roman army was ultimately a product of the reforms of Diocletian and the more far-reaching measures taken by Constantine, but a discussion of its origins must begin in the late second century in order to illustrate the background to the reforms of these two emperors. There are certain landmarks in the origins of the late Roman army, conventionally placed by modern scholars in the reigns of Marcus Aurelius, Severus and Gallienus. Any evaluation of the development of this army must take these landmarks into account, but with this proviso: that it is important to realize that the successive remodelling of the army that occurred between the reigns of Marcus Aurelius and Constantine was not undertaken as part of a steady progression by logical stages towards an established goal. The benefit of hindsight enables scholars to discern, in the changes in military organization made by Marcus, Severus, Gallienus and Diocletian, the embryonic forms of the later army, with the result that it seems that there are definite links in the chain of development connecting the armies which Marcus Aurelius assembled on the Danube, with the later field armies of Constantine. This is not, strictly speaking, the case, and has been the subject of debate for nearly a century.

Changes which were made at any time in the command structure of the Roman army and in the organization of troops must of necessity have been related to the problems faced at that time, or more specifically to problems most recently faced and overcome. At no stage could the Roman high command be expected to make long-term predictions as to the nature of future threats and accordingly take in advance the necessary preventive measures. It goes without saying that if there are links in the chain between the army reforms of the late second or early third centuries and those of the fourth, they are retrospective and empirical, based on experience of what had gone before and what had proved most effective in dealing with threats from different sources. The task of the archaeologist and the historian is to try to assess at what point, if any, can it be said that the changes in the army are truly unrelated, unprecedented and original.

The Roman Empire reached its greatest territorial extent during the reign of Trajan, who conducted major offensives in Dacia and in the East. His successors, the less warlike Hadrian and Antoninus Pius, made adjustments to the frontiers resulting in some further gains of territory, but these were not major additions and can be seen more as a rationalizing process whereby frontier defence was facilitated. Hadrian fell into disfavour by abandoning some of Trajan's conquests, probably because he did not think that the Empire's resources were sufficient to hold them. For several years the Empire was, on the whole, peaceful, and the orator Aelius Aristides waxed enthusiastic about Rome's frontiers. But this peace was not long maintained.

Tomlin (1987, 107) points out that the first signs of strain on military resources occurred during the wars in the reign of Marcus Aurelius. The Emperor dealt with the situation by brigading together vexillations and whole army units from different parts of the Empire, to create field armies distinct from the provincial armies already stationed in the threatened areas. This use of vexillations was not a new idea, but the size of these armies and the duration of the wars foreshadow the adaptations which future emperors made to their armies in order to defend the Empire. One important development which can be traced to Marcus' reign is the promotion of military commanders on the grounds of their suitability for the tasks to be performed, regardless of their social origins or whether they had passed through all the relevant progressive stages of the traditional *cursus honorum*. Thus the rudiments of two of the important changes in the organization of the army were already apparent at the end of the second century.

A great number of writers are of the opinion that the true beginning of Rome's decline is clearly recognizable in the reign, and sometimes in the personality, of Septimius Severus. Gibbon acknowledged that Severus brought peace to the Empire, albeit ruthlessly and at great cost, and in the end the long-term effects were disastrous, so that while contemporaries of Severus excused his methods, 'posterity ... justly considered him the principal author of the decline of the Roman Empire.' Rostovtzeff (1957, 710, n. 10) went even further, and attributed the beginning of the end of the Empire to the 'ambition and unscrupulous policy of Septimius Severus'. Boak (1955, 19) dates the beginning of serious manpower shortages to Severus' reign, and MacMullen (1963, 156) and Walbank (1969, 68; 77) both consider that Severus' reforms of the army laid the foundations for most of the problems which occurred later on.

It is apparent, then, that in this Emperor's reign there are detectable changes which seem to foreshadow the development of the late Roman army. It is debatable, however, whether the measures taken by Severus are to be seen as the nascent stages of the process which culminated in the Diocletianic and Constantinian reforms, or whether they were adaptations to the needs of the moment, with little or no bearing on later decisions.

Severus' Army Reforms

It is necessary to describe the Empire as Severus found it, paying particular attention to the military establishment, before discussing the changes which he made to it. This brief survey is merely intended to set the scene, highlighting the broad details of the late second and early third-century army, and therefore does not enter into the finer arguments about various points which merit much lengthier treatment.

At the end of the second century, when Severus fought his way to supreme power, Rome was still the capital of an undivided Empire, the administrative nerve centre of an agglomeration of provinces and the seat of the Emperor's authority. The Senate still exercised a somewhat curtailed influence. Political and military advancement went hand in hand, and was achieved by following the various stages of the *cursus honorum*, a blend of both civilian and military posts of more or less graded importance. Legionary legates and most provincial governors were senators. There were limited opportunities for the middle classes or *equites* to rise to high rank, but there were already certain avenues by which they could rise to power; the governors of Egypt, for instance, were always equestrian prefects.

The frontiers of the Roman Empire were of several different types. Some of them were completely open with scarcely any boundary definition, others were provided with only a road as boundary, yet others followed the lines of rivers, and some of them were closed off by physical running barriers. These barriers were not of uniform design, except that most were accompanied by one or more ditches. Hadrian's Wall in England is extremely elaborate, composed of three separate features: a ditch to the north, then the wide stone wall with turrets, milecastles and forts strung out along it, and finally the larger ditch to the south, known as the Vallum. It has been justifiably described as overkill. Other frontiers were not so complex. In Germany, Hadrian built a timber palisade fronted by a ditch, replaced sometime later by a bank of earth, on a slightly different alignment. In Britain, Hadrian's Wall was replaced for a short time by the Antonine Wall, built not in stone, but in blocks of turf. In Raetia a stone wall was constructed, not so wide as Hadrian's Wall, and in Africa stretches of stone walls have been found marking sectors of this very long frontier, other sectors of which were left open, but not necessarily unguarded.

In most frontier provinces the legionary fortresses were situated in the interior, some distance behind the frontiers. On parts of the Rhine and Danube, along the sectors where the frontiers were marked by the rivers themselves, the legions were stationed at strategic points close to the river banks, sometimes so close that the fortresses were washed away and had to be rebuilt further back from the rivers. The auxiliary troops were stationed in forts on the frontier lines, actually attached to them as on Hadrian's Wall and the Antonine Wall, or some short distance (1–2km; 110–220yd) behind them, as in Germany and Raetia. Most frontiers were equipped with smaller fortlets like the milecastles attached to Hadrian's Wall, or the free-standing German Kleinkastellen. In between these there were usually watchtowers. To label these towers signal stations begs the question as to their function. It is not at all certain that signalling was one of their primary purposes, nor how, if this was the case, the signals would have been transmitted. The way in which the fortlets and towers were operated and manned is unknown. The soldiers most probably came from the nearest auxiliary forts.

Legions were about 5500–6000 strong, and were composed, theoretically, of Roman citizens. This does not imply that all legionaries came from Rome itself, for citizenship extended over most parts of the Empire. Auxiliary units, composed of non-citizens, were of three main types: *alae* consisting solely of cavalry, *cohortes peditatae* consisting solely of infantry, and mixed units of both foot soldiers and horsemen, called *cohortes equitatae*. In size, the auxiliary units were usually about 500 strong (*quingenaria*) or 1000 strong (*milliaria*). Roman citizenship was a privilege granted to them after 25 years' service. Recruitment to both legions and auxiliary units was for the most part from the local population living around the forts, except in the case of specialized units such as the oriental archers, which seem to have continued recruiting from their original provinces, most likely in order to retain the standard of expertise in the use of their specific weaponry. Recruitment *en masse* of tribal contingents was sometimes carried out after the conclusion of a war. The troops raised in this manner were either distributed among exisiting units, or if kept together they would normally be removed to a distant province, where they would be organized and trained as a regular unit under the command of Roman officers, even if they continued to fight with their own weapons and accoutrements.

The changes in army organization introduced by Severus have been much discussed by both his detractors and his supporters. Probably in an effort to make service in the army more attractive and thereby to encourage recruitment, he allowed the soldiers more privileges. Until his reign, marriage was forbidden to soldiers, but in legally sanctioning such marriages Severus was merely giving official recognition to a situation which had already existed for some time. More important, and with more far-reaching consequences, Severus increased army pay. He has been censured for this by writers of his own times and those of the present. Jones (1966, 19) doubted very much whether such an increase was at all justified. Others consider that the increase only just caught up with inflation. Severus clearly thought of the payment of the soldiery as a high priority, and his advice given on his deathbed to his sons is probably one of the most frequently quoted passages from ancient literature. It is redolent of common sense or cynicism, depending on one's point of view: 'live in peace with one another, enrich the soldiers and ignore everyone else' (Dio 77.15.2). Cash had always proved one of the most effective means of coercing the army and winning it over. Military revolts could be put down or deflected by large donatives, and it must have seemed to the inhabitants of the Empire, whose taxes went towards these payments, that the soldiers on whom they depended for their defence were holding them to ransom. Dio (75.2.3) and Herodian (3.8.5) both accused Severus of bleeding the Empire dry to provide the cash for the soldiers' pay and donatives. In turn, a modern author accuses these writers of wilfully misunderstanding the needs of frontier defence, and also of wanting effective protection at a very cheap price (Smith 1972a, 493). The adage probably held true in the third century just as it does today: you only get what you pay for, a fact of which Severus seems to have been only too aware.

As well as granting privileges and more pay to the army, Severus also paved the way for easier promotion. This may have provided an additional incentive to enlistment, in that it was made possible for soldiers to rise from the ranks to officer status, and from there to the Praetorian Guard and even to the equestrian posts of the civil service, or further still if ambition and the right circumstances coincided. The career of Triccianus illustrates how the path to high office was open to anyone. According to Dio (79.13.4) this man began his military service as a private soldier in Pannonia, and by 217 he had worked his way up to become commander of a legion. Full of righteous disapproval, Dio records a further example of this sort (80.3.4). A certain Comazon rose from a very lowly position to the post of commander of the Praetorian Guard, and then to *praefectus urbi*, 'a thing that had never before happened in the case of anybody else'. Dio's distaste for this unprecedented event has lost nothing of its strength over the centuries.

Severus showed a preference for equestrians, though not to the complete exclusion of senators, in his choice of military commanders. He appointed equestrians to the command of the three new legions which he raised, and as governor of the new province of Mesopotamia, he installed an equestrian prefect of high rank, comparable to the governor of Egypt. Some authors interpret the rise of the *equites* in the third century as a deliberate attempt by Severus to exclude senators from military commands and from the provincial governorships. It is unlikely that he planned a wholesale removal of all senators, however. Even if he secretly harboured a wish to rid himself altogether of the waning power of the Senate, it would have been difficult to achieve such a plan, except in the very long term, not least because of the immediate lack of trained manpower. It is much more likely that Severus appointed military commanders on merit, the principal merit, after demonstrable military competence, being loyal support for himself.

The rise of the *equites* and the increasing powerlessness of the Senate cannot be laid wholly at Severus' door. Already in the reign of Marcus Aurelius, *equites* had risen to important posts and eventually become senators. Pertinax, of humble birth, rose to the command of a legion; for his services in the wars of Marcus' reign he was rewarded with the consulship. He later became emperor, surviving for three months before he was murdered (*CIL* VI 477; Herodian 2.2.9; Dio 73.5.2–4). Valerius Maximianus was another equestrian who reached senatorial rank during the wars of Marcus. Inscriptions survive documenting his progress (*CIL* III 13439 = *ILS* 9122; *AE* 1956. 124). He undertook a variety of special tasks, usually in charge of mixed troops brought together for a specific purpose. Eventually he became a legionary legate, and further promotions followed.

The employment and personal advancement of non-senators was therefore not an innovation of Severus' reign, but the influence of the Senate was progressively weakened, and the appointment of equestrians to military and civilian posts became more formal and more frequent in the course of the third century. In most cases where an equestrian was put in command of troops or made governor of a province, the post was usually a new creation, and the officials were given new titles, usually phrased so as to give the impression that the post-holder was acting merely in a temporary capacity (Arnheim 1972, 32–3). The senatorial title *legatus legionis* for instance, was exchanged for the equestrian title *praefectus legionis agens vice legati* indicating that the post-holder in question was serving in place of the legate, with the connotation that this was a temporary arrangement. This legal fiction was maintained for some time, as the influence and power of the Senate gradually declined and equestrians were appointed to high office.

The Praetorian Guard had always been a privileged body, stationed in Rome instead of in the provinces, better paid, and serving for a shorter term than the legionaries. On his accession, Severus dismissed the old Guard and reconstituted it by enrolling men from all parts of the Empire. Previously, only Italians and Roman citizens from a few provinces had been eligible for the Guard, and by opening its ranks to any suitable legionary soldiers, Severus democratized it. He has been accused of barbarizing the army, deliberately excluding Italians from service in the Guard in particular and in the army in general. Feeling against him was strong among his contemporaries. Dio (75.2.5) talks of the youth of Italy reduced to banditry because they were denied the opportunity of serving in the Guard, and he bemoans the fact that the city of Rome was full of uncouth provincial soldiers, looking like savages, and terrifying in their rough speech. This is hyperbole. Dio thought it was bad enough, but perhaps fortunately he could not know that barbarization had not yet begun. Later on, whole groups of barbarians were settled within the Empire and employed as its protectors. The exclusion of Italians will not stand investigation, since inscriptions (*ILS* 1180; 1332; 9014) show that Italians still served as officers in the army (Parker 1935, 83–4).

The most important change which Severus made was to increase the size of the army. Marcus Aurelius had already recruited two new legions, *II* and *III Italica*, during the wars of his reign, but Severus went much further. He may have raised extra auxiliary units, such as *Cohors I Septimia Belgarum, Ala II Septimia Syrorum milliaria*, and possibly *Cohors XX Palmyrenorum milliaria* (Birley 1969, 67–8). Better attested are the three new legions which he raised, called *I, II* and *III Parthicae*, presumably for one of the eastern campaigns. The exact date is disputed, but the date does not closely concern this discussion so much as the fact that whilst *I* and *III Parthicae* were left in garrison in the newly organized province of Mesopotamia, *II Parthica* was placed in garrison at Alba, only about twenty miles from Rome itself. In addition, the Praetorian Guard and the Urban Cohorts were increased in size, and with these augmented troops and the new legion it is estimated that Severus had at his disposal in Italy a force of 30,000 men. This figure is from the calculations of Durry (1938, 86) and has been accepted by most scholars. The major dispute concerns the use of this large force, and whether or not it should be seen as a direct forerunner of the later mobile armies.

Field Armies

During the wars of the early Empire, it was common practice to assemble troops from one or more provinces and move them to another, either as part of an offensive, or to provide defensive assistance in times of crisis. Troops collected together for either of these purposes would be additional to the legions and auxiliary units already stationed in or near the area to be fought over. The Latin term for such groups of soldiers was *vexillationes*, which derives from the name of the military standard, or *vexillum*. Detachments of various different units could not be given the title *legio*, *ala* or *cohors* because they were operating outside their parent bodies, and in normal circumstances it was intended that eventually they should return to them. There are only a very few examples of the word *vexillatio* in its singular form, indicating that the bodies of troops so constituted were commonly drawn from more than one unit. These vexillations could comprise either purely legionary or purely auxiliary troops, or more often both kinds of troops would be brigaded together, operating as an individual army. Saxer (1967, 119) concluded that even when vexillations consisting only of legionaries are mentioned on inscriptions, it is almost certain that auxiliary troops would be present as well. There was no standard formula, and no standardization of vexillation size. Each special body of troops of this kind would be put together from whatever manpower resource was available at the time, and employed in whatever manner circumstances dictated.

After the conclusion of the war, the fate of the vexillations differed. They could be disbanded and returned to their original provinces either immediately or after a lapse of time. On occasion, as part of the reorganization of the territory either defended or won, the extra troops could be retained, becoming in some cases permanent units, such as the *vexillatio equitum Illyricorum*, which was drawn from the auxiliary units of Illyricum to fight in Trajan's Dacian wars. It was never returned to its original province, and was not split up in order to distribute the soldiers among the other auxiliary units of Dacia. Eventually it was formed into a regular *ala* (Saxer 1967, 124–5).

The important point to note is that there was no permanent standing field force which could be taken to threatened areas whenever attacks were made on the frontiers. The extra troops needed for such wars had always to be assembled and removed from the armies of other provinces. If the wars were prolonged or unexpectedly fierce, then new units had to be raised to provide the necessary manpower. In Marcus' reign, both expedients were employed, and in addition to the vexillations of troops which he brought to the war from other provinces, Marcus was forced to raise new legions in Italy, hitherto a largely unprecedented measure. When the wars finally ended, these legions were placed in fortresses in Raetia and Noricum, on the frontiers.

Severus' new legion, *II Parthica*, stationed at Alba, has been described as a mobile reserve (Smith 1972a, 487), and also as the strong nucleus of a field army (Birley 1969, 78). There is probably more truth in this than in the list of ulterior motives which have been read into Severus' actions, such as the despotic intention to subdue Italy by reducing it to the level of the other provinces. That may have been the result as the Italians saw it, and as Dio lamented, but it was probably not the primary purpose. It has also been suggested that Severus needed a force loyal to himself to counter the power of the Praetorians. This may be so, but he had already countered their power in the first place by dismissing them, and then recruiting a new Guard. Besides, legions and Praetorians could be bought and influenced with money, and rather than each providing a check on the other, their potential power if united would have been formidable.

Since no one can ever know what was in Severus' mind, it is permissible to question whether he intended to use *II Parthica* and the other troops in Rome as a mobile reserve. To quibble about these points might seem mere pedantic hair-splitting, but in order to assert that the development of the field armies of the fourth century can be traced back to the use of large vexillations and to Severus' new legion, it is necessary to prove the purpose behind the creation of such an extra force, and continuity of its use. Neither of these criteria can be substantiated from the evidence available. Once established at Alba, it seems that *II Parthica* did not accompany Severus on his later expeditions to Egypt or to Parthia (Birley 1988, 129). There is as yet no firm evidence that it was brought to Britain during the wars in Scotland from 208–11. It is possible that Severus did not intend to employ the legion as a mobile reserve, but as a support for his throne while he was away from Italy.

The description of *II Parthica* as a mobile central reserve is capable of some refinement. On a journey from Rome to any threatened area, the legion would make no better speed than troops from the Rhine or the Danube. It has been estimated, for instance, that it would take sixty days for the march from Rome to Cologne (Ferrill 1986, 46). Whilst this would seem to be a conservative estimate, and troops have been known to march faster, absolute accuracy is not the point at issue. Mobile the legion may have been, but the speed of its mobility is questionable. Centrality is therefore also questionable. If Rome had been central, or at least conveniently placed to counter the threats of the fourth century and later, then Rome would have remained the capital and Constantinople would have remained Byzantium. Milan is a much more suitable location for a mobile central force. 'Reserve' is therefore the most apt title for *II Parthica*, and in this capacity, the successors of Severus certainly employed the legion, or part of it, on various campaigns. *II Parthica* was with Caracalla, when he was murdered on the road between Carrhae and Edessa (*SHA* Caracalla 6.7), and immediately afterwards it was at Apamea with Macrinus as emperor. The legion is next heard of in Germany, under Severus Alexander, then at the siege of Emona under Maximinus, and with Gallienus at Milan in 258 or 259 (the date is uncertain) when he inflicted a crushing defeat on the Alamanni (*CAH* 12. 71; 80; 155).

From the death of Severus Alexander until the temporary establishment of peace under Diocletian, there was an expeditionary army permanently in the field. It was not always exactly the same army, consisting of exactly the same units. Successive emperors commanded armies composed of vexillations from various different legions, *alae* and cohorts of the provincial armies, the choice of troops depending upon the location of the almost perpetual wars and the availability of manpower. More than ever before, the presence of the Emperor was necessary at the scene of the fighting, and so major cities within the provinces, with good communications with the affected zones, were used as bases. Cologne, Trier, Milan, Verona, Aquileia and Sirmium all became, among other places, the headquarters of the Imperial armies at different times during the disturbances of the third and fourth centuries. Maximinus Thrax wintered at Sirmium in 235, and for the next two years he campaigned in Dacia, returning to Sirmium in 238. Throughout these years he kept together his army, the nucleus of which was presumably the expeditionary army which Severus Alexander had taken to the Rhine, and with which Maximinus had inflicted a defeat on the Germans. There is probably little reason to doubt the specific statement to be found in the *Scriptores Historiae Augustae* that the army which Maximinus led to Germany was Severus Alexander's. It is described as powerful and an excellent war machine, and Maximinus is said to have augmented it (*SHA* Severus Alexander 61.8; the two Maximini 11.7–9). In addition to his field army, Maximinus recruited large bodies of German cavalry, perhaps raised by the terms of a treaty after his victory, or perhaps by accepting volunteers. Cavalry was becoming increasingly important in the defence of the Empire and the struggle against rebels and usurpers. In both cases, mobility was essential. Roman armies could no longer choose the time and place for their battles and mount a campaign with the advantage of time and planning on their side. The days of overt imperialist conquests, pre-emptive strikes to check threats, or punitive expeditions were over. Now the battles were all too often sprung upon the Roman high command, by barbarians or by other Romans, and often both at the same time.

Gallienus' mobile cavalry

At some indeterminate date, probably about 255 when he was defending the Rhine frontier, there was a desperate necessity for rapid movement, Gallienus created a cavalry army (de Blois 1976, 26), which he may have employed within the conglomerate army hastily gathered together for the battle against the Alamanni in 258 or 259. This army was probably quite small. Gallienus assembled legionaries from the Rhine, Pannonia and Noricum, and brought *II Parthica* and the Praetorians from Rome, but he probably had only detachments of each of the various legions rather than whole units. The distribution of coins supports this composition (Okamura 1991, 388 and refs) and has been used to suggest that the vexillations remained loyal to Gallienus even after their parent units had broken away from his control under various usurpers, successful or otherwise (Tomlin 1987, 108). This collection of soldiers may possibly have been amalgamated into a standing force; it seems certain that at least the cavalry elements remained together and were used to good effect against Ingenuus when the latter revolted against Gallienus. From about 259, this cavalry was based at Milan under its single commander Aureolus, whose task, according to Zosimus (1.40.1), was to prevent the Gallic usurper Postumus from invading Italy. The threat posed by the breakaway Gallic Empire may not have been Gallienus' sole concern, however. A much more pressing reason for occupying Milan in considerable strength, with an emphasis on mobility, was the presence of the Alamanni in Switzerland.

Little is known about Gallienus' cavalry. One certain fact is that the Emperor could not have assembled an effective cavalry force by gathering together raw recruits and untrained horses. A rider, even a good one, is not a cavalryman until he and his mount have undergone some training (Dixon and Southern, 1992). This process is not impossible to execute, but it takes time, and this was the one commodity which Gallienus could not afford to squander unnecessarily. It is likely, therefore, that he recruited his cavalry from existing units of proven ability and skill. Besides the regular *alae* and cohorts of the provincial garrisons, there was probably a considerable body of trained, effective cavalry available to Gallienus, which he could use as the nucleus of a mobile army without removing too many troops from the frontiers. The Mauri and Osrhoeni recruited by Severus Alexander in the East were brought to Germany for the Rhine campaign (*SHA* Severus Alexander 61.8; the two Maximini 11.1; 11.7; Herodian 7.2.1). If they had enlisted for 25 years, they would probably have had a few years left to serve when Gallienus was seeking for extra horsemen. They do not seem to have been placed in permanent bases as part of any frontier garrison, and were therefore probably to be counted as supernumerary. Their numbers are not known, but were probably not very large, and there would probably be a need for additional cavalry to make the force effective. Gallienus augmented his forces by extracting men from the mounted troops of Dalmatia, the *equites Dalmatae*. Opinion is divided about the nature of these troops. Some scholars argue for an ethnic Dalmatian origin, while others aver that recruitment of indigenous tribesmen is not implied, and that the title simply denotes a collection of soldiers gathered from units already in Dalmatia. These troops and the Mauri and Osrhoeni were probably all brigaded together, but it is not known how they fought together on the battlefield. They seem to have employed different, specialized fighting techniques, the Moors being armed with javelins and the Osrhoeni with bows and arrows. Individual sections may have been used for different purposes, but the cavalry had only one commander-in-chief, and this unity of command presumably implies unity of operation. It also facilitated potential usurpations, since the commander of the cavalry had an excellent power base at his disposal, similar and possibly superior to the position of the praetorian prefect. Aureolus did not resist the temptation to rebel against Gallienus, but he did not succeed to the throne; he merely cleared the path to it for Claudius Gothicus, before being murdered himself.

In many discussions of Gallienus' cavalry, it is usually stated that the mobile force contained some detachments of legionary *equites*, the probable ancestors of the *equites promoti* and *scutarii* of the *Notitia Dignitatum*. This is not proven, but remains a strong possibility. Gallienus already had vexillations of legions under his immediate command, and it is possible that he separated their cavalry contingents from the main bodies, using them in the mobile force together with the other units. This should not imply that Gallienus based at Milan all the available legionary horsemen from every single legion. The notion that the *equites legionis* could be split off from their parent bodies was not new, since there were already precedents for using the legionary cavalry separately in battle or on campaign, just like any other mounted units. But from the reign of Gallienus, the cavalry was separated from the legions more or less permanently, and this had important consequences. Some authorities affirm that it was Gallienus who increased the numbers of the legionary cavalry from 120 to over 700. This is a separate measure, nothing to do with the central cavalry force based at Milan.

The question of the survival of the mobile cavalry and whether Gallienus is really the innovator behind the later mobile field armies is probably unanswerable. A Byzantine chronicler, George Cedrenus, states quite firmly that Gallienus was the founder of the first mobile cavalry army (*Compendium Historiarum* 454 in Migne vol. 121, 495). Not all modern scholars would agree with his judgement. The Byzantine writers had the benefit of hindsight and were accustomed to the use of cavalry armies from the time of Constantine onwards, therefore it is natural that any army composed purely of horsemen, which was moreover not part of any provincial garrison but answerable via its commander to the Emperor alone, would seem to be a direct forerunner of the later mobile cavalry field armies. In order to be certain that this was the case, it is necessary to trace the history of this cavalry force, but unfortunately there is insufficient information to demonstrate its continuity as a separate force for many years after the murder of its creator. As de Blois points out, the cavalry was no longer at Milan after about 285 (1976, 28). By this time, the Gallic Empire had been recovered and united under the central Imperial command, thus rendering redundant the once precarious border between Italy and Gaul. De Blois takes the view that the cavalry army which Gallienus assembled was not unlike the vexillations employed in other wars, brought together temporarily for a specific purpose and disbanded when that purpose had been fulfilled. This view is shared by Ferrill (1986, 32) who thinks that Gallienus had no permanent policy in mind.

One minor point may possibly contradict this and could be used to rehabilitate, in part, the opinions of older scholars. Coin evidence shows that the title given to this body of cavalry was simply *equites*, rather than *ala* or the less permanent *vexillatio*. This use of the non-specific title possibly signifies that the troop was not intended to function after the fashion of the provincial *alae* and was somewhat different from the cavalry which was based in the frontier forts, but at the same time it was not intended to function as just another vexillation. An inscription (*ILS* 569), dating to the year after Gallienus' death, preserves this distinction, whatever it may mean, by listing *vexillationes adque equites* side by side.

Another point concerns the strategic location of Milan. Some authors maintain that it was not important after the reclamation of the Gallic Empire (de Blois 1976, 29). Ferrill (1986, 32) describes Milan as almost a frontier outpost in Gallienus' reign, with Postumus to the west and the Germans to the north. Some writers compare Milan to the other strategic points of the Empire, such as Cologne, Verona, Aquileia, Poetovio and Sirmium, where large armies were stationed for the duration of wars or merely to deter external threat. In this case, the cavalry army based at Milan can be interpreted as an ordinary vexillation, no different to the other vexillations gathered together at any of the temporarily occupied strongholds. Indeed, some scholars consider that the army at Milan was not made up purely of cavalry, and that it must have had some infantry attached to it, which would make it even more similar to ordinary vexillations in composition and perhaps also in function (de Blois 1976, 30, n. 33).

Whilst this is true up to a point, it should also be acknowledged that Milan, to a much larger extent than Verona or Aquileia, is the strategic centre of northern Italy, and the independence or otherwise of Gaul cannot alter this fact. It is in an excellent position for obtaining supplies, both because of the fertile lands around it and because of the ease of transporting goods, surely two factors of overriding importance to the well-being and survival of a military force dependent on horses. Milan is also well placed for surveillance of the Alpine passes, and for journeys through them; it is possible to reach Gaul, the Rhine and the Danube from Milan rather more quickly than from Rome. The Tetrarchs chose Milan as one of their Imperial residences, and the Emperor Honorius, aided and advised by Stilicho, based his court there at the end of the fourth century, before he finally withdrew to Ravenna. Its use as Imperial residence lends some weight to the arguments as to the importance of Milan. Gallienus' choice of this city as the base for a mobile army cannot have been accidental, and it is possible that he did in fact intend his cavalry to be a permanent force, stationed in the best location from which to organize rapid intervention at threatened points. Intention, however, is not sufficient to ensure the actual event.

It is not possible, given the current state of the evidence, to refute or endorse the theory that Gallienus' cavalry was intended to form the first permanent mobile cavalry force, the consciously planned precursor of the *comitatenses*. Gallienus originally developed the cavalry force in answer to his need for mobility on the Rhine, and then adapted the use of this force to the multiple desperate situations facing him in the ensuing years. Permanent survival of the cavalry could have been almost accidental at first, and then regularized by custom afterwards. It could be argued that the cavalry's disappearance from Milan is a possible indication that after 285 it was permanently in the field with the current reigning Emperor, employed in similar fashion to the *comitatenses*. Archaeological traces of such a mobile force would be almost non-existent, but lack of evidence does not prove the discontinued existence of Gallienus' cavalry army. It may have been used by Claudius Gothicus against the Alamanni, who invaded Italy through Raetia just after Gallienus' death. After initial defeats, Claudius appointed Aurelian 'commander-in-chief of the cavalry' (*SHA* Aurelian, 18.1). There is no proof that this command embraced the cavalry of Gallienus, but it is at least likely that remnants of it formed the nucleus of Aurelian's troops. There were Dalmatian and Mauretanian cavalry units in his army, just as there were in Gallienus' cavalry, and Aurelian used them to defeat the heavy-armed Palmyrene horsemen (Zosimus 1.50.3–4; 52.3–4). Beyond this event it is impossible to demonstrate the survival of a central mobile cavalry reserve with any certainty, and it is not recorded whether the use of such a force set the example for later emperors, or whether they arrived quite independently at the same solutions to the need for mobility and self-preservation.

The *Protectores*

Perhaps as part of his efforts to ensure the loyalty of the army to himself, Gallienus bestowed on his high-ranking officers the title of *protectores divini lateris*. This was a distinction, not strictly a rank. The *protectores* were usually legionary prefects or praetorian tribunes, and the holders of the title were usually men of established military experience who had a close bond with the Emperor. Later on, the title was given to selected centurions and was regarded as the starting point for a good career (de Blois 1976, 85; 106). The *protectores* were not simply members of the Emperor's bodyguard; perhaps the best interpretation of the word as it was used in Gallienus' day, is that the holders of the title formed a staff college, loyal to the Emperor who fought off more usurpers than any other (Parker 1935, 180; 220). By Diocletian's time there was a corps of *protectores* who accompanied the Emperor, and indeed when he became emperor, Diocletian himself was a member of the *protectores domestici*, but this use of the title is anachronistic, since the description *domestici* was not added until much later (Jones 1964, 53–4).

The reforms of Diocletian

Seston (1946, 305) suggests that the mobile cavalry was deprived of its single commander to prevent his power from becoming too great, and that it was either Carinus or Diocletian who took this step. This may be so, but it is not certain if at this stage Gallienus' cavalry still existed – after 25 years, it would hardly be the same cavalry, and it is unknown whether its numbers had been kept up by recruitment into its ranks. It may already have disappeared, in which case Diocletian simply did not bother to recreate it, or perhaps, if it still existed, he disbanded and dispersed it by placing detachments along the frontiers, which it was Diocletian's policy to restore. He strengthened the defences of the Empire by rebuilding forts and garrisoning them, probably dispensing with a large central mobile reserve. This innocent phrase is highly emotive and opinion is still divided as to whether Diocletian laid the foundations of Constantine's field army, or whether the latter was the sole creator of the *comitatenses*. There is an impressive body of scholars who readily affirm that Diocletian already had a *comitatus* or central reserve army (Mommsen 1889; Baynes 1925; Parker 1935. 272–3; Ensslin in *CAH* XII 1939, 398–9; Jones 1964, 54; Hoffman 1969, 2; 258). Others see Constantine as an innovative genius whose system of defence owed nothing to, and differed from, that of Diocletian. In a long article, Nischer (1923, 10–12) expressed the opinion that Diocletian introduced a general system of reserves but it was Constantine who created the true mobile armies. This article provoked two more by Baynes (1925) and Parker (1933), who refuted the ideas expressed in it.

According to Seston (1946, 305–7) and van Berchem (1952, 106–8; 1977, 542) the chief obstacle to the continued existence of any large central mobile army, cavalry or infantry, was the fact that whoever commanded it was in a very good position to usurp the throne, and Diocletian, like Severus a century before him, was concerned to prevent this occurrence. Seston and van Berchem maintain that Diocletian had only a central bodyguard, rather than a reserve army of any great strength. Williams (1985, 93) gives a further reason for the lack of a central force: the division of the Empire into four units each under its own Augustus or Caesar, chosen by Diocletian himself, reduced the likelihood of civil war, and therefore the presence of a field army clustered around the Emperor was not necessary. This view is not without its opponents, since it could be argued that the splitting-up of the Empire into four individual parts, each with an army under its own Imperial commander, could only lead that much more easily to revolt. In practice, as always, the strongest man won, even though in the first instance he may not have intended to seize power. It could be said that, at first, Constantine was a victim of circumstance, though once launched on his path to the throne, he pursued it tenaciously, not to mention vigorously and on occasion viciously.

The argument about Diocletian's *comitatus* hinges on the evidence from a papyrus and two inscriptions. The information from the papyrus concerns the composition of an expeditionary army which Diocletian took to Egypt in 295. Alongside the ordinary cavalry and the *vexillationes* a body of cavalry is listed as *comites*, as though to indicate that these horsemen are to be distinguished from the others (*P. Oxy.* 1.43, col. 2, 24–8). An inscription from Troesmis records a soldier of *Legio XI Claudia* who was *lectus in sacro comit(atu) lanciarius*, indicating that he was chosen to enter the Imperial guard (*CIL* III 6196 = *ILS* 2781). The *lanciarii* were men chosen from the legions and formed into a specialized force within the legion, probably as early as the reign of Severus (Casey 1991, 10–12). Their status improved as time went on, and they became Imperial guards when the Praetorian Guard was dissolved in 312. They occupied an honoured position in the *comitatus* of Constantine. By association, therefore, the presence of a *lanciarius in sacro comitatu* in Diocletian's entourage lends some support to the theory that he had a mobile army. Another inscription (*CIL* III 5565 = *ILS* 664) records the building of a temple by the *praepositus* of a Dalmatian cavalry unit which is also styled collectively *comit(es)* or *comit(atenses)*. The abbreviated Latin makes it possible to argue for either restoration of the complete word. Hoffman (1969, 257–8) is certain that *comitatenses* is the correct reading.

Diocletian's *comitatus*, whatever its size and nature, probably consisted of a mixture of different troops. Among the horsemen were units such as those in the expeditionary forces taken to Egypt, and there were probably special cavalry units like the *equites Dalmatae*, and the legionary cavalry or *equites promoti*, physically but not administratively separated from their legions. Among the infantry there were units such as the *lanciarii*, and probably the legions of *Ioviani* and *Herculiani* formed from *I Iovia* and *II Herculiana* stationed in Scythia. In addition Diocletian may have created units of *protectores*, using the title which Gallienus originally conferred on his officers, without forming them into troops. The *scholae*, or personal bodyguard of the Emperor, may have been instituted by Diocletian. The earliest evidence for the *scholae* is Constantinian in date, but Jones (1964, 54) traces their origins back to the Tetrarchy.

While it seems that there is no room for doubt about the existence of Diocletian's *comitatus*, there is, however, room for doubt about what the word actually meant at this date, a point which is discussed by van Berchem (1952, 108). In the Republic and early Empire, the members of the entourage of a magistrate or provincial governor were styled *comites*. The Emperor's immediate circle of friends and advisers were *comites Augusti*, who were said to serve *in comitatu principis*. In the reigns of Marcus Aurelius and Severus the term took on more official meaning, denoting the body of officers and men who accompanied the Emperor on campaign. From the Severi onwards the *comitatus* was always *sacra* as efforts were made to distance the Imperial court from the populace. The *comitatus* was not purely military in function or make-up, consisting of both bodyguard and also representative elements of the administrative machinery of the Empire and the personal household of the Emperor, much like the peripatetic court of a medieval king.

Those scholars who prefer to deny that Diocletian had a mobile army usually insist that *comitatus* should be understood in its older sense of bodyguard and companions of the Emperor, and that the meaning changed over the years as the word became identified solely with the field army. Others argue that there was no change in the meaning of the word and that the *comitatus* of Diocletian provided the nucleus of a field army, which Constantine merely altered slightly and augmented substantially.

The problem will probably always remain unresolved. The eminent Jones usefully sythesized the differences of opinion (1964, 54–5). It cannot be denied that Diocletian had a *comitatus*, which Jones declared was a small mobile reserve army, much smaller than that of Constantine. It is unknown whether the other three co-emperors each had a *comitatus* of their own. Jones thought that Maximian, as the second Augustus, must have possessed at least equal forces to Diocletian. Hoffman (1969, 155–8) assigns an important role to Maximian and traces back to him the creation of the first of the infantry units later known as the *auxilia palatini*. It is perhaps significant that some of these units are entitled *Iovii*, which has strong Tetrarchic overtones.

Though Maximian's role may have been almost as important as Diocletian's, and perhaps both *Augusti* had a *comitatus*, it is less certain if each Caesar commanded a central reserve. This may be what Lactantius, a Christian openly hostile to the persecutor of Christians, implies when he accuses Diocletian of wastefully quadrupling the size of the army, so that each of the Tetrarchs continually tried to outdo the others in increasing his numbers of troops (*De Mort. Pers.* 7.2). Most modern scholars reject the idea that the army was increased fourfold, and put this statement down to spiteful hyperbole. Diocletian quite definitely did increase the size of the army, introducing conscription, sometimes commuted into money payments, to furnish the necessary manpower (Jones 1964, 615), but there is still not enough evidence to vindicate Lactantius' judgement. It is possible that Lactantius wilfully misinterpreted Diocletian's creation of several new legions and the splitting of some of the older ones, so that it seemed that many more army units existed than ever before. It may be worth pointing out that Diocletian increased the number of provinces by splitting them up into smaller administrative units with new names, but no one would go so far as to suggest that by this means he increased the size of the Empire.

The most telling factor against acceptance of Lactantius' accusation is the fact that during the Tetrarchy, whenever expeditionary armies were needed for frontier wars, they had to be assembled as they had always been assembled in the second and third centuries, from the existing units posted on other frontiers. Jones endorses the opinion that Diocletian was mainly interested in reconstituting the frontiers, and that in order to strengthen them, he probably even broke up the field armies assembled for major wars, replacing them in their forts (1964, 55–6).

The famous passage from Zosimus (2.34) may therefore contain a germ of truth, in so far as he is full of praise for all that Diocletian had achieved, for the frontiers were secure and no barbarians could infiltrate through the strong defences which Diocletian had built up around the Empire. According to Zosimus, Constantine took men away from the frontiers and put them into cities which did not need defending, and the sorry state to which the frontier provinces were reduced was all his fault. A note of caution should be appended to this judgement, in that Zosimus was a confirmed pagan, indignant at Constantine's encouragement of the Christian religion.

The reforms of Constantine

When Constantine made his bid for the throne, his position was very similar to that of Gallienus, precariously maintained in the face of multiple and hostile opposition forces. He put together an army of troops from Britain, to which he added Gauls and Germans from the Rhine frontier (Zosimus 2.15). He could not afford to strip the north-western frontier of all its troops and thereby leave it open to attack, and so the army with which he marched into Italy was probably quite small. According to the figures which Zosimus gives he was outnumbered by 100,000 men, so that his defeat of Maxentius at the Milvian bridge was justifiably termed miraculous.

The Constantinian field army is not heard of officially until 325 when in a legal document (*Cod. Th.* 7.20.4) it is distinguished from the *ripenses* or frontier army, and clearly ranks higher than the latter. After the elimination of Maxentius, Constantine was left with his own and the remnants of his rival's armies, all of the available troops being immediately under his personal control. It seems unlikely that he would disband these troops and send them back to the frontiers; his position was too precarious for that. He probably kept most of the army together, using it to defeat other rival contenders for the throne. Unfortunately not much is known about the composition of his mobile forces. It cannot be ascertained how many men he commanded at any one time, nor how they were organized. Indeed, the early organization may have been flexible, so that it could be changed on an ad hoc basis to meet the needs of the moment. Lack of evidence makes it impossible to decide categorically whether this emperor was an innovator of genius, or whether he adopted and adapted some of the measures of his predecessors.

The truth is possibly that he was both innovator and adaptor, for it is fairly certain that his reforms could not have been carried out overnight. Some accounts give the impression that the late Roman army sprang up, fully fledged and instantly operational, on the morning after the battle of the Milvian Bridge. The changes no doubt took much more time than that, but the process is not clear. Some measures probably had antecedents which are obscure, and after Constantine there would be further changes, rather less obscure perhaps, but still not sufficiently well documented to provide a chronological sequence. Crump (1973, 93–4) points out that as the fourth century progressed, modifications were probably made to the Constantinian system to meet different threats at different times, so that the late Roman army as depicted in the major sources such as Ammianus and the *Notitia Dignitatum* had no doubt undergone some transformations, and may have been considerably altered since its original conception. The unfortunate fact is that very little is known for certain about Constantine's army, and those who attempt to reconstitute it in theory, by extrapolating backwards from the slightly better documentation of later periods, can produce widely divergent results, mostly because so much guesswork is necessary to fill the gaps in our knowledge. The army evolved continuously, but the successive stages are not fully documented.

Nischer (1923) attempted to discern the original components of the Constantinian army by analysing the names of units in the *Notitia*, but Baynes (1925) objected to this, pointing out that between Constantine's reforms and the compilation of the *Notitia* there had occurred the disaster of the battle of Adrianople, which caused the loss of too many troops to allow for precision when trying to draw up a list of Constantinian units from a much later document.

With regard to the field army of Constantine, a distinction should be made between the mobile units of the *comitatenses* and the Imperial bodyguard. The latter, called *scholae palatinae* may have derived from units formed by Diocletian, but Hoffman (1969, 281) thinks that it was Constantine who was responsible for their creation, pointing out that since Constantine abolished the Praetorian Guard after the battle of the Milvian Bridge, he would immediately require a new bodyguard. Significantly, the *scholae palatinae* were under the direct command of the Emperor, thus removing the possible accumulation of power that the praetorian prefects had been able to excercise in the past. Henceforth the praetorian prefect lost his military powers, but remained in charge of the administration of supplies to the army. The strength of the Constantinian units of the *scholae palatini* is unknown; at a later period they were 500 strong.

The *comitatenses* were divided into cavalry, commanded by the newly created officer called the *magister equitum*, and infantry, commanded by his equally new counterpart the *magister peditum*. These men may have ranked as highly as the praetorian prefect, but since none of the Constantinian *magistri* is known, nothing can be deduced about their rank or their previous careers, so their military experience and expertise, and therefore their suitability or otherwise for their posts, cannot be estimated.

The existence of a single mobile army centred around the Emperor was not sufficient to keep the peace in all parts of the Empire at once, and so inevitably, at an unknown date, regional field armies were formed in different areas of the Empire, in particular in Gaul, Illyricum and the East, each with their own commanders, most often entitled *magistri*. In part these field armies were formed by extracting troops from units of the *limitanei* or frontier armies. The sections of the regional field armies derived from the *limitanei* were the *pseudo-comitatenses*, not so well paid nor so elevated in status as the central *comitatenses*. The regional mobile armies did not replace the mobile army of the emperors, and in order to distinguish the Imperial *comitatenses* from the regional forces, the title *palatini* was bestowed on them. This title is not recorded until 365 (*Cod. Th.* 8.1.10) but may already have been in use before that date. In the same way, the *magistri* in command of the *palatini* added the words *in praesenti* or *praesentalis* to their titles to indicate that they served directly under the Emperor.

The numbers of men in the original Constantinian *comitatenses* may not have been large. The size of the mobile army was no doubt gradually increased, or even on occasion decreased, as circumstances demanded and manpower sources dictated. There may never have been an established paper-strength such as we are led to believe was the case for the legions and auxiliary units of the early Empire. Besides, a mobile central reserve is not identical to an expeditionary army, and for major wars the mobile reserve was no doubt supplemented from other sources. According to Zosimus (2.22) Constantine collected 120,000 infantry and 10,000 cavalry for the final battle against Licinius. Even allowing for tremendous exaggeration in these figures, it seems unlikely that this army represented the mobile central reserve and nothing else.

Initially, Constantine's mobile force would no doubt have been constituted from whatever units were available to him, and may have included the Diocletianic legions of *Lanciarii*, *Ioviani* and *Herculiani*, which were taken over more or less intact. There would also be cavalry vexillations immediately to hand which could have formed part of the mobile army. Constantine brought troops from the Rhine to fight for him at the Milvian Bridge, and he would most likely have kept these with him too. It may have been from the Rhineland where he, or possibly his father, raised the new units called *auxilia*, which certainly formed a part of his mobile army. These units were all infantry and were nothing to do with the old-style auxiliary *alae* and cohorts of the early Empire. They seem to have been completely new formations, possibly raised from volunteers or from tribesmen provided by the terms of a treaty, or by both methods. Hoffman (1969, 156–7; 172–3) credits Maximian with the creation of some of these units, but in general their orgins are obscure, and there are no clues as to their dates and areas of recruitment to be gleaned from a study of their names: the titles *Cornuti*, *Bracchiati*, *Iovii* and *Victores* reveal nothing. The consensus of opinion is that they were probably raised in Gaul and the Rhineland, as their use of Germanic war cries possibly indicates (Tomlin 1987, 111). It is significant that they were given a title which distinguished them from the old-style auxiliary units, a distinction which they preserved throughout their later history, revealing that they were not distributed among the existing units and lost to view.

Some of the units of the field army share names in common with those of the frontier units, and this has been taken as an indication of the fact that the field army was at least in part made up of troops withdrawn from the frontiers, just as Zosimus says. It is impossible to discover precisely from which units Constantine may have taken troops because the sources are all of a later date and do not elucidate his reign sufficiently. There can be no doubt, however, that from the time of Constantine if not before, the field armies and the frontier armies were for ever separated in function and status.

Frontier Armies

The system of frontier defence inherited by Septimius Severus at the end of the second century has already been described (above, pp. 5–9). It is a tribute to the effectiveness of the frontiers, or at least to the value placed upon them by the Roman high command, that Severus expended so much time and effort on repairing them. In Britain, his restoration work on Hadrian's Wall was so extensive that in the nineteenth century it used to be thought that Severus had actually built the Wall, and that Hadrian had merely been responsible for the ditch known as the Vallum. In Germany, the Hadrianic palisade was replaced by a bank and ditch on more or less the same alignment. It could be argued that as part of the rationalization and better protection of the frontiers, Severus expanded the Empire by taking in new territory in Africa. He may also have remodelled the frontiers of Dacia, but the date of the Alutanus and Transalutanus frontier lines in this province are disputed.

Following the reign of Severus, in the first half of the third century, the frontiers held out against attacks without undergoing permanent destruction. Some of the forts on the Rhine and Danube suffered damage in the 230s, but the damage was repaired and life went on as usual. On the Taunus and Wetterau frontier in Germany, forts such as Kapersburg, Saalburg, Butzbach and Echzell were rebuilt (Baatz *et al.* 1982, 213). In the reigns of Philip the Arab and Decius, the occupants of several forts in Germania Superior were actively dedicating altars to their various gods and confidently placing milestones along the roads (Filtzinger *et al.* 1986, 92). Sometime between 244 and 249 the fort baths at Jagsthausen were being rebuilt (*CIL* XIII 6562). There is no sign here that the Roman army had diminished in its activity, nor that the high command had foreseen the crisis of the mid-third century.

The evidence is similar for the African provinces. Some destruction that had occurred in the 230s was repaired and readjustments were made. While some posts, for example *Castellum Dimmidi*, were abandoned, some forts were either rebuilt or newly founded, for instance an inscription records building work at Doucen in 242 and at Ausum in 247, though both these forts may have had Severan, or even earlier, predecessors. Smaller posts called *centenaria* were added to the frontier between 244 and 246, such as Gasr Duib and possibly Gasr Uames. The loss of territory in the third century was not so extensive nor so alarming in Africa as it was in Europe (Daniels 1987, 256 and 260).

Less than 20 years later the Empire was on the verge of breaking up. The upheavals of the mid-third century affected almost the whole of the Roman world, and were not brought under control until the reign of Diocletian. Destruction was widespread, reaching far into the hinterland of the frontier provinces and sometimes even further into areas which had experienced no external threat for many years. The situation was compounded by rebellions against the central authority, thinly disguised in some cases as a bid for self-help in the face of renewed attacks which the legitimate Emperor was not capable of fending off. The motives for rebellion may on occasion have been noble, but the results were destructive in that troops which could have been more usefully employed in fighting the real enemies of the Roman Empire were more often wastefully employed in fighting each other.

Various theories have been put forward to explain the reasons for the barbarian attacks on the frontiers, the most common being that the removal of troops to fight in other areas so weakened the now vulnerable frontiers that the tribes took immediate advantage of the absence of Roman troops to lay waste and plunder. This may have been the reason in some cases, but infiltration did not always take place when troops were removed for wars elsewhere, and even if it did, the raids were not always successful. Some authors have therefore disagreed with the explanation that the barbarians were induced to attack because the frontiers were only weakly defended. Alternative theories have been advanced to account for barbarian raids, such as food shortages and pressure from other barbarians in the rear of the marauding tribes. It is possible that all these factors had a part to play. A classification of the attacks on the frontiers has sometimes been attempted, distinguishing the ordinary hit-and-run raids at one end of the scale from – at the other end of the scale – the more serious invasions for the purpose of taking over lands for permanent settlement. One other reason for barbarian attacks which has not been suggested is simply a penchant for fighting, which on occasion may have been the only motive for raiding. The late twentieth century has witnessed enough senseless violence, spontaneous or otherwise, for this possibility to be considered.

The reasons behind the barbarian unrest are without doubt complex and incapable of complete elucidation. In any case they are not so important to a study of the Roman army as the clearly attested results of the invasions, and the Roman response to the threat of further raids. It is certain that the Franks and the Alamanni caused more damage in 259 and 260 than ever before. The Franks had already appeared in Lower Germany in 257, destroying and raiding their way into Gaul. Two years later the Alamanni raced through the Alps to Ravenna. In 260 they crossed the Rhine and wasted Gaul.

In this year, one of the darkest in Rome's history, the fragmentation of the Empire began. On the Rhine, the fort at Niederbieber was destroyed, and the forts of the Taunus and Wetterau abandoned (Baatz *et al.* 1982, 217). The lands on the right bank of the Rhine opposite Cologne were entrusted to a German chieftain who had entered into an agreement with Gallienus, and some of the Marcomanni were settled by the same emperor inside the province of Pannonia, foreshadowing the frequently used procedure of *receptio* whereby tribes were taken into the Empire *en masse* and given lands on which to settle. Forts of the upper Danube were abandoned, and Raetia was lost. The Romans held only the right bank of the middle Danube with troops at Eining, Regensburg and Passau (Filtzinger *et al.* 1986, 95). There is evidence of devastation in Noricum and Pannonia from about 255 to 260, when towns and villas were destroyed, and people buried hoards of coins which they never recovered (Alföldy 1974, 170). The distribution of the coin hoards and the pattern of destruction reveals that the Alamannic invasion was not limited to the north of the province. Further east along the Danube in east Pannonia and Upper Moesia, the picture is not quite as clear, but the greatest crisis seems to have occurred in these areas in 260. It is certain that Gallienus took steps to stem the flood of destruction, and as part of these measures he seems to have abandoned the northern part of Dacia (Mocsy 1974, 205–7).

Persian attacks on the Roman eastern frontier began in the early 250s, resulting in the loss of some forts. Dura-Europos was destroyed in 256–7 and never recovered. In 259 the Emperor Valerian was captured and many Romans were taken prisoner. It was left to the Palmyrene ruler Odenathus to attack the Persians on their way home, and after defeating them he extended his power over a large part of the east. As a later author described it, looking back with disdain on the recent past, 'the ruler of Palmyra thought himself our equal' (*Pan. Lat.* 8.10). To all intents and purposes, this was what Odenathus was. Gallienus was not in any position to oust him, and recognized him officially as ruler of the east.

This official recognition was not extended to Postumus, who seized power in Gaul, setting up a separate Gallic Empire which was not reconciled to the main Empire for several years. Thus in 260, Gallienus had to contend with two breakaway states, while he fought to keep the parts of the Empire which were under his control free of barbarian invaders and usurpers who threatened to seize what was left of his authority.

The history of the frontiers as the third century progressed into the fourth shows the transition from defended running barriers to a different system, using fortified strong points along the roads or rivers at the edges of Roman territory. The boundaries of the late Roman Empire incorporated the older established frontiers only in part. In some areas the frontier was completely redrawn, notably the Danube–Iller–Rhine *limes* joining the two rivers by a string of fortified posts guarding the passes through the Alps. There was no artificial running barrier here, nor elsewhere, except in Britain. Where appropriate, the frontiers in Europe were marked by the great river lines of the Rhine and Danube, except for a short stretch of the upper Danube which was now outside the Empire. In the east and in the African provinces where rivers were not so conveniently placed, it was more usual to mark the frontier by means of a road defended by fortified posts.

It is virtually impossible to discern what was happening to the frontier armies at this time. Many units had probably been split up and never reunited. Vexillations initially detached for service in a war had in some cases become permanent additions to the garrison of the provinces in which they had served. A vexillation of *Legio XIII Gemina* from Dacia was permanently stationed at Aquileia (*CIL* V 808). The distinctions between an expeditionary army and a permanent field army are probably blurred in the latter half of the third century, because of the long duration of the wars which succeeded each other all over the Empire. There had been an army in the field somewhere in the Empire for many years. Once an uneasy peace reigned, some units or parts of units may have gone back to their original provinces, though not necessarily to their original forts. Any endeavour to locate such units in the quarter century separating the reigns of Gallienus and Diocletian would be well nigh impossible.

Next to nothing is known about the methods used to keep the legions and auxiliary troops up to strength during the frequent wars. In some instances, heavily depleted auxiliary units may have been allowed to disappear from the record, and the survivors, if any, may have been redistributed among other *alae* and cohorts. Some units may have been combined with one or more different units, the resultant amalgam being given a re-used title, or possibly a completely new title. Such a procedure would give the impression that there were more units in existence than was in fact the case.

There were energetic attempts to pull the Empire back together from the 270s onwards. Aurelian campaigned against Queen Zenobia, the successor to Odenathus, and won back the east, following this success with a victory over the troops of the Gallic Empire at Chalons. Elsewhere he was not so successful. The Goths in Dacia had caused so much damage that reconquest was rendered impossible, so Aurelian abandoned this province altogether, reorganizing the frontier along the Danube, and placing the two Dacian legions at Ratiaria and Oescus. To garrison the east he raised two new legions, *I Illyricorum* and *IV Martia*. Probus continued his work, driving the Franks and Alamanni out of Gaul, and settling many barbarians on land inside the Empire in return for service in the Roman army. Next he repelled the Vandals from Illyricum. For all his energy and success he met the same end as the other emperors. The soldiers killed him at Sirmium. Three years later, after the reigns of Carus, Carinus and Numerianus, the soldiers hailed Diocletian as emperor. All the measures taken by the emperors from Gallienus to Numerianus to restore order and secure the provinces from attack were at best piecemeal and localized, and usually not permanent. It is not until the reign of Diocletian that there emerges a systematic, comprehensive endeavour to reconstitute the frontiers.

The frontiers under Diocletian

Diocletian's reconstruction of the frontiers was not undertaken in isolation. From necessity, the Emperor set in motion a thorough reorganization of the whole state. Much of the fabric of the Empire was restructured, primarily to meet the needs of defence and ultimately to ensure the survival of *romanitas*, though it emerged in an altered form at the end of the proceedings. The provinces were divided into smaller units, the command structure of the provincial armies was revised, civilian and military careers were progressively separated, financial affairs became more rigid and were linked very firmly with recruitment and the payment of the soldiers. Though these measures are all administrative, it could be said that almost the whole of the administration was now geared to the needs of the army.

The full extent of the damage which Diocletian inherited over the whole Empire cannot be assessed in detail, nor can this Emperor's work of reconstruction be distinguished in all cases from that of his predecessors or his successors. For this reason many scholars review the work of Diocletian, the Tetrarchs and Constantine as one continuous development, surveying the situation in retrospect from its fourth-century appearance, with much help from the *Notitia Dignitatum*, even though the information contained in this document dates from the century after Diocletian.

Literary and epigraphic sources for the Diocletianic frontiers are not as abundant as one would wish. A vague reference (*Pan. Lat.* 9.18.4) to the rebuilding of forts for *alae* and cohorts along the Rhine, the Danube and the Euphrates does no more than inform us that such work was carried out. The writer Eumenius probably composed his work in the years 296 to 298, so he was at least a contemporary of Diocletian, which ought perhaps to lend more weight to his statement than can be found in the brief notice of the Byzantine author John Malalas (*Chron.* 12.38), who informs us that Diocletian built forts on the *limes* from Egypt to the Persian frontier. Zosimus (2.34) confirms the impression that the frontiers were everywhere secured by Diocletian by means of forts and fortresses 'which housed the whole army'. It is a pity that Zosimus' discussion of Diocletian's frontier policy is lost along with the end of Book One and the beginning of Book Two of his work.

It is not in doubt that Diocletian repaired various frontiers and in some cases inaugurated new buildings, but it is difficult to produce even a minimal catalogue of the structures that should be attributed to his reign and that of the Tetrarchs. Evidence for rebuilding comes from Africa, the Eastern frontier, the Rhine and the Danube, and by studying these diverse frontier systems, scholars have been able to discern some general trends of the Diocletianic and Tetrarchic periods. 'With Diocletian and after, we are in a new world' (Fink 1971.2), and so it is perhaps rewarding to pay considerable attention to the developments of the late second and early third century. Despite the lack of dating evidence and the obvious gaps in knowledge of all the sites where building or rebuilding took place in Diocletian's reign, it is clear that from now onwards, forts changed their appearance. In Britain and Gaul, the forts of the Saxon Shore, begun under Probus, had already departed from the conventional types of fortifications of the first and second centuries. These were for the most part new foundations; many other forts in the Empire were restructured. Entry to many military fortifications was reduced to only one gateway, the others being blocked off or converted into towers projecting from the walls. In the Danube region, interval towers were often U-shaped, while corner towers were distinctively fan-shaped, to allow for better supervision of the defences. No dating evidence has yet come to light connecting this type of fortification with Diocletian, but it is probably not mistaken to view them as part of his reorganization of the Danube frontier (Johnson 1983a, 253).

The use of watchtowers and *burgi* strung out along the roads, and of bridgehead forts and fortified harbours on the great river frontiers, was not a new phenomenon in the late third century, but all these methods of defence were now exploited much more fully, a process which continued into the fourth century and after. Strengthening of the frontiers was not sufficient protection in itself, for now the interiors of the frontier provinces were also threatened to a much greater extent than ever before. Roads had to be watched and food supplies guarded. Undefended cities were given walls, from the mid-third century onwards, to preserve them against the double threat of incursions of the barbarians and the ruinous effects of internal lawlessness. In many cases the size of these cities was drastically reduced, perhaps because the population had declined, and definitely because there was a need to reduce the circuit of the defences. This extra fortification went hand in hand with the defence of the frontiers.

Seston, full of admiration for Diocletian, attributes the reconstruction of the frontiers to the Emperor's direct and energetic personal intervention, declaring (1946, 298) that 'no other Emperor played so great a part in the construction of the frontier', a point with which the shade of the second-century Emperor Hadrian may be excused for wanting to take issue. Nevertheless, no one can deny Diocletian's energy and grim determination. He was in Raetia when it was reconquered, in Pannonia when the Sarmatian wars were waged, and in Antioch when the Syrian frontier was re-established. Though Diocletian provided the directing force behind all the work of restoration, he did not perform all of it single-handed. Maximian undertook the defence of Gaul in 286 to 288, first clearing the Bagaudae, usually described as landless peasants who had taken to earning their living by banditry. Next, in June 286, Maximian went to Mainz, and from then till 288 he waged war against the Alamanni and Burgundians, the Chaibones and Heruli. He seems to have mounted an expedition or expeditions across the Rhine and carried the war into the territory of the barbarians. He restored the frontier to the satisfaction of his pane-gyricist, who declared that 'the Rhine seems to have been made by nature to protect the Roman provinces from the ferocity of the barbarians' (*Pan. Lat.* 10.7). This is possibly true, but only if the river is lined with troops watching for invaders and then moving out to meet them.

Little evidence has come to light for Diocletianic rebuilding along much of the middle Rhine. As for the upper Rhine, a new frontier was drawn, running from Strasbourg via Basel and Lake Constance to Gunzburg on the Danube. In modern parlance, this frontier has acquired the name of the Danube–Iller–Rhine *limes* (see **fig. 7**). It was established when increasing disturbances forced the Romans to abandon parts of the erstwhile provinces of Germania Superior and Raetia. If the line of towers is correctly interpreted as a frontier, all the territory to the east of the Rhine, as well as a stretch of the upper Danube, were outside the Roman Empire, but not necessarily outside Roman control. There may be outposts awaiting discovery, and the army may have sent out patrols in advance of the so-called frontier.

The Emperor Probus may have been responsible for the foundation of some of the forts and towers along this new line, which may have been established in stages and completed by Diocletian and Maximian, then repaired by Valentinian (Drack and Fellman 1988, 279). An inscription dated to 294 (*CIL* XIII 5256) records building work of some kind at Burg bei Stein am Rhein (*Tasgaetium*), where a fort of 91m x 88m (99 x 96yd) guarded part of this frontier. Another building inscription of the same date comes from Oberwin-tertur (*Vitudurum*), south-west of Stein am Rhein. It is possible that the forts at Zurzach (*Tenedo*) and Kaiseraugst, and the roads through Irgenhausen (*Cambiodunum*), Pfyn (*Ad Fines*) and Arbon (*Arbor Felix*), were all repaired by Diocletian (Drack 1980, 3).

On the Danube, there is evidence of Diocletianic rebuilding at Regensburg (*Castra Regina*) (Johnson 1983a, 253), and at Lorch (*Lauriacum*), Mautern (*Favianis*), Tulln (*Commagena*), and possibly Zeiselmauer and Vienna (*Vindobona*) (Genser 1986). In Pannonia, Diocletian's policy seems to have been not merely defensive, but quite aggres-sive (Soproni in Lengyel and Radan 1980, 109–10). This part of the Danube frontier came under attack from the Sarmatians, who were themselves probably threatened by the Vandals, Gepids and Goths to their north and north-east (Mocsy 1974, 267). Diocletian was at Sirmium from 289 to 294, campaigning probably beyond the Roman frontiers as Maximian had done across the Rhine. To assist him in 293, Diocletian appointed Galerius to the command of Illyricum. Numerous battles of which we are ill-informed took place in those five years, culminating in a special victory celebration in 294, when it is likely that territory to the east of the Danube was occupied by Roman troops. A documentary source (*Chron. Min.* i p. 230) records that forts were built in Sarmatia in that year (*castra facta in Sarmatia contra Acinco et Bononia*). This passage may refer merely to the bridge-head forts constructed on the left bank of the Danube opposite Aquincum and Bononia, but Mocsy (1974, 269) draws attention to the two corroborative entries in the *Notitia*,

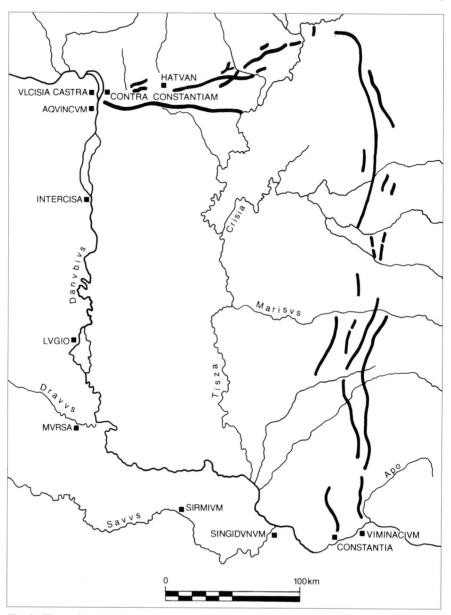

Fig. 1 *The earthwork defences, possibly built by Diocletian or by Constantine, east of the Danube. (Redrawn by G. Stobbs from Mocsy 1974.)*

referring to forts *in barbarico*, a phrase which is never applied to the other bridgehead forts known to be occupied and listed in the same document. The troops under the *dux Provinciae Valeriae* include a unit styled *auxilia vigilum* which is located *contra Acinco in barbarico* (*Not. Dig. Oc.* XXXIII 48). The description of the troops under the *dux Pannoniae Secundae* is more specific: *auxilia Augustensia contra Bononiam in barbarico in castello Onagrino*, indicating that this unit is not stationed at the bridgehead fort, but at some other fort further into Sarmatia (*Not. Dig. Oc.* XXXII 41). The whereabouts of these fort sites *in barbarico* has so far eluded archaeologists.

Several authors have related the earthwork fortifications known as the Devil's Dyke to the period after Diocletian's Sarmatian wars (**fig. 1**). This feature can be dated only very broadly and not very helpfully to some time between the third and the ninth centuries. The earthworks were in use for a long time, since certain sections were repaired and even realigned on more than one occasion. The earthworks probably enclosed the territory occupied by the Sarmatians in the third and fourth centuries, and would have served more as lines of demarcation than defensive frontiers. Their connection with Diocletian or Constantine is by no means proven (Mocsy 1974, 269).

Further along the Danube, the fort at Drobeta may have been reconstructed by Diocletian. The rebuilding changed the appearance of the fort both externally and internally. North of the Danube, another series of earthworks, no more closely dated than the Devil's Dyke, runs from west to east, more or less parallel with the river. These lines may have demarcated territory occupied or patrolled by Roman troops in the same way as that suggested for the Devil's Dyke, but there is no implication to be gleaned from documentary sources that troops may have been located here in the third or fourth centuries, and no fort sites have been found by archaeological means.

The boundaries of Egypt were rationalized when Diocletian gave up territory south of the First Cataract of the Nile, probably because the maintenance of troops there was costly compared to the meagre returns yielded from the land, which he gave to the Nobatae (Procopius *History of the Wars* 1.19.29–34).

The small, roughly square forts of the African frontier, known as *centenaria*, were already in existence before the reign of Diocletian. Their name implies that they were garrisoned by a *centuria*, nominally 100 men (in practice only about 80), but the internal areas of the centenaria vary considerably, which may or may not mean that in proportion to their size, their complement of soldiers also varied. Some of these small forts may have been rebuilt by Diocletian; an inscription (*ILS* 689) records rebuilding at *Aqua Frigida*. Other *centenaria* are dated by inscriptions to the reigns of Diocletian or Constantine (*CIL* VIII 8712; 9010; 20215; 22763). Excavations at Mdoukal (*Aqua Viva;* **fig. 2**)

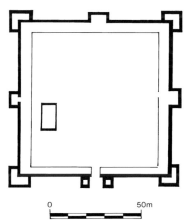

Fig. 2 Centenarium quod Aqua Viva appellatur, *the small square north-African fort at Mdoukal, built in 303. (Redrawn by G. Stobbs from Lander 1984.)*

revealed that the building was completed in 303. The inscription describes the work very specifically as *centenarium quod Aqua Viva appellatur* (van Berchem 1952, 46).

Small square forts, similar in size and shape to the African examples, are known on the eastern frontier, and whilst they cannot be dated firmly to Diocletian's reign, an inscription of 306 from one of the Syrian sites (*CIL* III 14380) can be taken to imply that the building of such installations began under this emperor (Johnson 1983a, 253). On the Euphrates, Diocletian fortified *Circesium*, attested by both Ammianus (23.5.2) and Procopius (*History of the Wars* 2.6.2.4), who adds three more Diocletianic forts, naming one of them, *Mambri*, but none of them can be identified with certainty (*History of the Wars* 2.8.7).

Perhaps the best known study of any Diocletianic frontier system is van Berchem's work (1952) on the *Strata Diocletiana* (**fig. 3**), which may have extended, as Malalas affirms (*Chron.* 12.308), from Egypt to the Euphrates, though it has not been traced over this

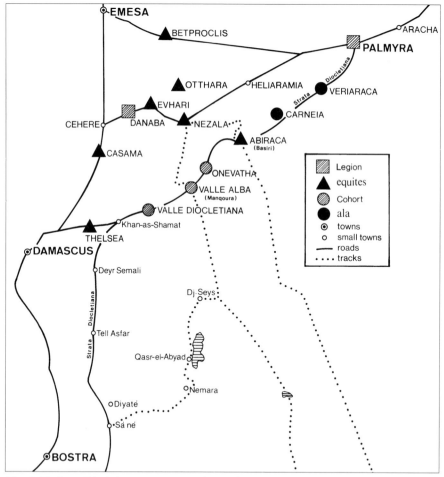

Fig. 3 *The* Strata Diocletiana *as reconstructed from documentary and archaeological evidence by van Berchem (1952). (Redrawn by G. Stobbs.)*

great distance. Roughly a hundred miles of it are known, and the structures along the frontier road are dated epigraphically to Diocletian or the Tetrarchy (Isaac 1990,164). There was no running barrier along this frontier, only a road guarded by forts and fortlets situated at relatively close intervals, backed up by more fortifications in the rear. Van Berchem was able to assign units to the forts along this road, by first studying the place-names on the several milestones found in the region, then by marrying these names to the known forts and fortlets with corroboration from the place-names in the *Notitia*. From van Berchem's researches, it can be seen that there were two legionary bases, one at Palmyra, an important city and road junction on the frontier itself, and another some distance behind the *limes*. The *equites*, élite mounted units distinct from the *alae*, were all in the rear, except for one which was stationed at an important road junction. The infantry cohorts and cavalry *alae* were all stationed on the frontier or very close to it.

This disposition of troops may not reflect precisely the state of affairs of Diocletian's day. The information about troop locations is drawn from the *Notitia*, and should not be used as a template for Diocletianic or Tetrarchic frontier policy, usually labelled, in recent publications, 'defence in depth'. This classification presupposes that there was a unified, predetermined master plan for the whole Empire. Apart from the overriding need to repair the widespread damage in virtually every province, and to ensure their future safety, probably no such master plan ever existed, in either Diocletian's mind or in that of any other emperor, before or after his reign. Modern terminology cannot sufficiently elucidate Roman intentions; argument about the meaning of the word *limes*, and whether or not certain routes constitute proper frontiers, does not help at all in deciding how the Roman high command perceived the threats facing them nor how the army was meant to deal with those threats. Archaeology reveals hardly any evidence for patrolling and police work, or the way in which troops were employed. Contemporaneity of all the fortified structures, confidently placed on maps, cannot be demonstrated, nor can the actual numbers of men stationed in any of these sites be definitely known, despite the calculations that can be made from the size of the forts in question. As a result, frontiers which seem to have been elaborately defended may in practice have been only lightly manned, and, vice versa, frontiers where there seems to be only a few defended points may have been more strongly garrisoned. Furthermore, a plethora of fort sites on any map reveals much more about the amount of archaeological work performed in that particular region than it does about the nature of the Roman defences, and similarly a dearth of sites may only represent a dearth of archaeologists with an interest in the area.

It is not possible to discern with any accuracy what Diocletian's frontier army was like, nor how it operated. Apart from the uncertainty as to the nature and size of the Diocletianic *comitatus* (above, pp. 15–17), the overall size of the army at this period is not much clearer than at any other, but in the light of Lactantius' statement that Diocletian quadrupled the size of the army, it is of particular interest to historians and archaeologists to attempt some estimation of the numbers of units in the army, and the numbers of men in these units.

The frontiers could not be strengthened merely by rebuilding forts and founding new ones. It is self-evident that these structures would have been useless without soldiers to man them, but unfortunately so very little information is available about the internal buildings in most forts that it is difficult to estimate the numbers of men who may have been in garrison. Overall size alone is no real guide, because it is hardly ever known what proportion of the fort's interior was given over to barracks and what proportion was filled with administrative buildings, workshops, storage of food and equipment, and possibly animal shelters. The *Notitia* is virtually the sole source from which it is possible to reconstruct Diocletian's army. The dangers and difficulties of using a document of about a century later than the period being studied cannot be stressed too many times; it is comparable to using the payroll of Cromwell's army to reconstruct the Elizabethan military establishment, or in an American context, comparable to studying the army of the War of Independence via a document dating from the Civil War. Since nothing surpasses the *Notitia* as a source, historians are forced to use it, but with the necessary caveat. As Jones points out (1964, 56) the *Notitia* shows only those units that had survived from Diocletian's army, and the losses are unknown.

Auxiliary units in Diocletian's army were probably not much different from those of the early Empire, and were most likely still either approximately 500 or 1000 strong, but this is a nominal paper strength. Some of the units may have been reduced in size as a result of the civil wars, and may have recovered their original numbers only very slowly. As Jones (1964, 56) points out, there is no contemporary evidence to tell us in what state Diocletian found the armies on his accession, nor is there any documentation on how he dealt with deficiencies during his reign. At a later date, it seems that auxiliary units were either much reduced in size, or were divided up and stationed in more than one fort (Duncan-Jones 1978, 549). In some cases, forts of a known size can be identified in the *Notitia,* for instance on the *Strata Diocletiana* (see **fig. 3**), where some of the small square forts have been linked with those listed under the command of the *dux Foenicis* (*Not. Dig. Or.* XXXII). The units in question are *alae* and *cohortes,* which in the early Empire comprised about 500 men. The small forts on the *Strata Diocletiana* could not reasonably have accommodated so many men, and the discrepancy between the supposed numbers of men in garrison and the space available for their accommodation leads to the conclusion that at some time between the latter half of the third century and the end of the fourth there had been a drastic reduction in unit strength, but the date at which this may have occurred is not established. The troop dispositions of the *Notitia* do not necessarily reflect the arrangements made by Diocletian, so it cannot be stated categorically that it was he who reduced the numbers of men in the old-style auxiliary units. Furthermore it cannot be ascertained whether this conjectural reduction in numbers, whatever its date, applied to all the frontier provinces of the Empire. Archaeology has not yet brought to light every single fort in all provinces and, to complicate matters even further, the *Notitia* probably omits several sites from its lists, not least because the document probably records only those forts which constituted the administrative headquarters of each unit. Outposts and small forts may not have been listed at all.

The cavalry vexillations stationed on the frontiers may also have been about 500 strong (Jones 1964, 56). Probably since the reign of Gallienus, the legionary cavalry had been employed separately from their parent legions, and towards the end of the third century they acquired the name of *vexillationes,* which had been used earlier to denote temporary detachments of mixed troops assembled for a campaign. In legal documents, the *vexillationes* are equated with the legions and enjoy the same privileges, but they are listed as formations in their own right, usually by the formula *legiones vel vexillationes* (*Cod. Just.*

7.64.9; 10.55.3). The optimum paper strength of both auxiliary units and cavalry vexillations may have remained comparable to those of the high Empire; there may have been less standardization than is usually supposed. Actual numbers may have varied according to time and place, affected by the needs of the moment and subject to the availability of manpower.

Legionary strength is a different matter. On this subject scholars are presented with that most dangerous of tools, a little knowledge, inevitably of a disputed nature. It is certain that Diocletian increased the number of legions, though the exact figure is unknown. Seston (1946, 298) suggested that between 280 and 305 the number of legions rose from 39 to a total of 59 or 60. Jones (1964, 59–60) estimated that nearly all 34 of the legions of Severus' day survived, and Diocletian added about 35 new ones. The number of men in a legion clearly holds much interest for those who try to compute the overall size of the army. The addition of 35 new legions, if they were only 1000 strong as some scholars have suggested, is not such a strain on manpower, but if they were still 6000 strong, the task of raising so many new legions becomes monumental, especially when it is remembered that there was probably a similar increase in the number of auxiliary units, and coupled with that there would be the need to recruit men to fill the gaps in existing units, caused by the retirement of time-expired soldiers, by desertion, and by deaths from military action, disease and accidents.

The fourth-century author Vegetius declared that it was proving difficult to recruit sufficient men to keep the legions up to strength (2.3). He informs his readers that the two legions recruited in Illyricum before Diocletian's reign were 6000 strong (1.17; 2.2), a figure which, as Duncan-Jones concludes (1978, 553), was presumably abnormal in Vegetius' day. Statements of this sort in Vegetius' work are unreliable, because he was concerned with optimum standards of the past rather than the harsh reality of his own era. Thus Mommsen could ignore him and advance the hypothesis that Diocletianic legions were only 1000 strong (1889, 229; 254). Mommsen was followed by Grosse and other scholars. The point is debatable, but even if it should prove to be true that Diocletian's new legions were smaller than the earlier ones, this should not be taken to mean that all legions were permanently reduced to this low figure. Jones (1964, 56; 68) reiterated the argument that the older legions were still 6000 strong, but more importantly, he suggested that the legions of Diocletian were of the same size, since later on, both old and new legions contributed detachments to the *comitatus*, and according to the *Notitia* they were split up into several detachments on the Danube frontier and in Egypt, which would hardly have been possible had they numbered only 1000 men. Jones accepts that later legions were smaller, but he puts the blame for the reduction in their size uncompromisingly on the successors of Diocletian.

Seston's opinion (1946, 299) was similar to Jones's, in that he considered that the older pre-existing legions, which were able to furnish detachments to other frontiers, remained approximately 6000 strong, otherwise they would have been have been dangerously weakened by such a drain on their manpower. He differed from Jones on the matter of the new Diocletianic or Tetrarchic legions, suggesting that they would have been much smaller, probably not more than about 1000 men. This would seem to be supported by the excavations at a site whose name is redolent of the title 'legion' – El Lejjun (Parker 1987), where the legionary fortress is only one fifth of the size of the fortresses of the early

Empire (Kennedy and Riley 1990, 131). It was founded in the Tetrarchic period along with the new foundation, or reoccupation and refurbishment, of a series of smaller forts on the *limes Arabicus* (Parker 1987, 455). The fortress probably held only about 1500 men at the most, yet it possessed its own Tetrarchic *principia*, which implies that this was the headquarters of the entire legion, if not the base designed to hold the entire legion. According to the *Notitia* (*Or.* XXXVII 22) the fortress was the headquarters of the *praefectus legionis Quartae Martiae*. This legion is not listed anywhere else, but there remains the possibility that many of the legionaries, in addition to the 1500 in the fortress, were permanently outposted to smaller forts which would not be listed in the *Notitia*, especially if the soldiers were all under the command of the prefect of the legion. The evidence is not sufficient to state categorically that the legion was only 1500 strong, nor that it was about 6000 strong and split into detachments, but on balance, the evidence from El Lejjun suggests that Seston was correct.

The survival of the pre-Diocletianic legions in full strength cannot be demonstrated in all cases, except by analogy. On the Danube in the fourth century, men from *Legio III Italica* raised by Marcus Aurelius, were in garrison at Regensburg, Burghofe, Kempten, Fussen and Zirl, and there was also a detachment in the field army (Filtzinger *et al.* 1986, 99; *Not. Dig. Oc.* XXXV 17–19; 21–2). It is no doubt much too simplistic to suggest that each of the 6 detachments of *Legio III Italica* numbered about 1000 men, thereby making a total of approximately 6000 for the whole legion.

Van Berchem (1952, 110–1) points out that the figure of 1000 men for the later legions is convenient because it is most compatible with the slight information which has come down to us. It is significant that according to the *Notitia*, men from *Legio III Diocletiana*, which was presumably one of Diocletian's new creations, were located at five different places. The legion is listed in the *comitatenses* of the *magister militum per Thracia*, at a place called Andro in the command of the *comes limiti Aegypti*, and at three places under the *dux Thebaidos* (*Not. Dig. Or.* VIII 5–37; XXVIII 18; XXXI 31, 33, 38). Williams (1985, 247, n.6) concluded that the Tetrarchic legions were the same size as those of the early Empire, commenting that for the legions listed in different places in the *Notitia* 'the conclusion is hardly avoidable that these were parts of legions, not whole legions', a point which Duncan-Jones has to concede (1978, 552), even though by his calculations he pares down the numbers of men in Diocletian's Egyptian garrisons to very low levels, far below the figures postulated by Jones (1964).

Ultimately, the full complement of men in individual legions, vexillations, *alae* and cohorts, and whether or not they were split up between different forts, is of purely academic interest. The most important factor is how many men there were in the frontier forts and other fortified places at any one time and how they functioned. All very well for a military commander to know that there were four or five thousand men of any particular unit distributed in other locations; this knowledge would scarcely help him, since perceived threat and the numbers of men actually available in the flesh, not on paper, and not on sick lists or AWOL, would be much more important considerations, and this cannot be known at a remove of 1700 years.

Duncan-Jones was able to show that in the fourth century units were very small or divided up into small contingents, and there is an inescapable impression that in this era the Romans were, so to speak, spreading the butter very thinly to make it go further. This need not have been the case at the end of the third century, and it is hard to believe that the Emperor who devoted himself to the 'strengthening in every possible way of the existing system of frontier defence' (Warmington 1953, 173) would then risk the ruination of his objective by reducing the size of units or dividing them up into penny packets, unless there was adequate support from other units or very limited threat to the area concerned. This is exactly the kind of unsubstantiated speculation that is difficult to prove or disprove but easy to deny. The question still remains, was it Diocletian who set the trend for reduced units in the later Empire, or Constantine? Is there any justification for Zosimus' praise of Diocletian's frontier arrangements, or his accusation that Constantine weakened them?

The frontiers under Constantine

Evidence for Constantine's repair of frontier works is not as great as it is for Diocletian's activities, but if the latter had already strengthened the frontiers, it is arguable that Constantine had only to add a few finer details and repair those forts which had fallen into decay or suffered damage since the Tetrarchy. According to Eutropius (3.10), Constantine battled against the Franks and Alamanni in Gaul, and he definitely seems to have taken great care to restore and strengthen the fortifications of the Rhine. He enlarged the bridgehead fort opposite Mainz (Mainz Kastell) and the baths at Wiesbaden were repaired. Tile stamps of *Legio XXII Primigenia C(onstantiniana) V(ictrix)* were found both there and at a site near Florsheim, which may indicate that there was further building of a military nature there (Baatz *et al.* 1982, 217). In the hinterland, road posts between Cologne and Trier were fortified, at Junkerath (*Icorigium*) and Bitburg (*Beda*), as was Neumagen (*Noviomagus*). Both Koblenz and Boppard received walls at this time (Cüppers *et al.* 1990, 131–4).

Opposite Cologne, the important bridgehead fort of Deutz (*Divitia*) (**fig. 4**) was built, protected by a very wide ditch and berm, and walls with foundations 12m (40ft) thick (Horn *et al.* 1987, 89). It could house 900 men, and perhaps in part refutes the accusation of Zosimus that Constantine weakened the frontiers. If he weakened them elsewhere, he certainly did not weaken Deutz. Other bridgehead forts on the Danube may owe their origins or have been strengthened by Constantine, such as *Celamantia* opposite Brigetio. The two forts at Oescus and Sucidava, facing each other across the Danube, may have been rebuilt (Johnson 1983a, 255). On the Danube–Iller–Rhine frontier, Constantine continued the work of his predecessors, and the fort at Isny, east of Lake Constance, was built (Filtzinger *et al.* 1986, 350).

Mocsy (1974, 280) attributed to Constantine most of the building and rebuilding on the *ripa Sarmatica*, the section of the Danube facing the territory of the Sarmatians. He suggested that Diocletian was responsible for the Devil's Dyke earthworks in advance of the frontier, and Constantine reverted to the traditional methods of Danube frontier defence. On the other hand, Soproni (in Lengyel and Radan 1980, 222) argues that it was Constantine who utilized the earthworks, as an accessory to his frontier works on the Danube. By the fourth century, the forts and strong points on this part of the Danube are more dense than they were in the early Empire (**fig. 5**).

The troops of Constantine's frontier army are as imperfectly known as those of Diocletian. Concerning the Danube, van Berchem (1952, 99) avers that Diocletian kept the legions intact at their bases, and placed cavalry units elsewhere at forts along the river line; then Constantine removed these cavalry units for his field army, compensating for the vacuum that this caused by splitting up the legions and spreading them out in detachments among the forts in which they are listed in the *Notitia*. Jones (1964, 99) also sees a major reorganization on the Danube frontier in Constantine's time, most likely after the wars with the Sarmatians towards the end of his reign, during which Diocletian's system was considerably damaged.

Probably as a result of Constantine's reorganization, in Pannonia units called *cunei equitum* either replace the vexillations of cavalry, or operate in conjunction with them, as listed in the *Notitia*. The *alae* disappear, and the cohorts are relegated to the hinterland, replaced on the frontier by units called *auxilia*. Next to nothing is known about the *cunei*. Literally translated, it means 'wedge', and may be related to a method of fighting, using the shock tactics of a charge, but this is only guesswork. The units were in existence by 375, when they were specifically mentioned in a law granting tax exemptions for troops who had served for five years; soldiers of the frontier units are styled *qui in ripa per cuneos auxiliaque fuerint constituti* (*Cod. Th.* 7.13.7). Mommsen thought that the *cunei* derived from the barbarian units, but there is no evidence or support for his theory. They may

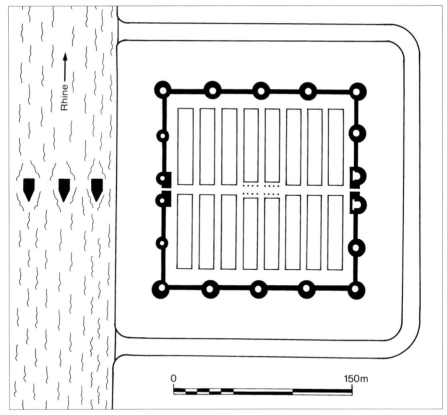

Fig. 4 *The bridgehead fort* Divitia *at Köln-Deutz, opposite the city of Cologne on the Rhine. (Redrawn by G. Stobbs from Petrikovits 1971.)*

simply represent the old cavalry units of *alae* and *cohortes equitatae*, but if so, this change of name was not universal over the whole Empire, and the origins of the *cunei* remain obscure.

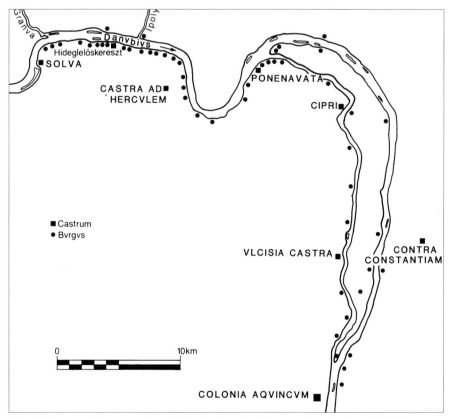

Fig. 5 *Towers and forts on the Danube bend in the reign of Constantine. (Redrawn by G. Stobbs from Soproni, in Lengyel and Radan 1980.)*

Ripenses and *Limitanei*

Van Berchem (1952, 87) concluded that the reorganization of the army and its division into two parts, field army and frontier army, was to be dated in the reign of Constantine, specifically between 311 and 325. The former date derives from an inscribed bronze tablet, found at the Roman fort of Brigetio on the Danube, bearing the Latin text of an Imperial rescript of 9 June 311. The latter date is that of a law of Constantine (*Cod. Th.* 7.20.4) dated 17 June 325. Both documents concern the terms of service and privileges of soldiers and veterans, and can be used to distinguish the differences between certain classes of troops.

The text of the Brigetio Table implies that the soldiers of the legions and the cavalry vexillations belong to the superior class, while the *alae* and *cohortes*, not specifically mentioned, belonged to the inferior. This is the normal division between legions and auxiliary units that had existed from the early Empire. The law of 325 is more detailed, and distinguishes between three classes of troops: first the *comitatenses*, then the *ripenses*, and finally the *alares et cohortales*. The division between the mobile army (*comitatenses*) and the frontier troops (*ripenses, alae, cohortes*) was now complete. Van Berchem (1952 87–8) suggests that the Constantinian reforms took place gradually, beginning in those areas under his direct control, and extending to the other provinces after he had won them from his rivals. The final change can possibly be dated even more closely, to the period between 321 and 325. Crudely inscribed on the top edge of the Brigetio Table are the names of Licinius and Constantine, with their respective titles. Licinius' (*trib. pot.* IIII; *Imp.* III) date to 311, but Constantine's (*trib. pot.* VII: *Imp.* VI) are dated to 321, when he visited the Danube garrisons. Van Berchem's theory is that at that date he confirmed the privileges granted by the law of 311, but as soon as he had removed Licinius in 324, he instituted his reforms in the following year.

The distinction between *comitatenses* and *ripenses* probably dates from some short time before 325. The term *ripenses* is sometimes rendered as *riparienses* (*Cod. Th.* 7.1.18 and 7.4.14). These troops were less privileged than the *comitatenses* in the laws of 325 and 375 (*Cod. Th.* 7.13.7.3 and 7.20.4). *Ripenses* is the title for all higher grade frontier troops, whether they are legions, *equites, cunei equitum*, or *auxilia*. The term *limitanei* had wider connotations, since it embraces all the troops of the frontier armies. Van Berchem (1952, 100–1) discerned two shades of meaning in the way in which the word was used. In the broad sense, *limitanei* refers to the troops along the *limes;* in the narrower sense it denotes the militia legally bound to defend and cultivate their lands. In the sixth century this was how the laws of Justinian defined the *limitanei*, whose duties were to defend the cities of the frontier and cultivate the earth (*terra colere*) (*Cod. Just.* 1.27.2.8). The sixth-century use of the word is not necessarily synonymous with that of the fourth, and may have been applied anachronistically by later writers to the frontier arrangements of former emperors.

The ancient sources credit Severus Alexander with the introduction of *limitanei* to the frontiers (*SHA* Severus Alexander, 58), but the use of the term is anachronistic. The life of this Emperor is almost totally fabricated; some authorities maintain that it is really a portrait of Julian, while others like Jones (1964, 650) suggest that the portrait is of Constantine. Jones also suggests that the author was trying to influence Constantine's frontier policy by hinting that soldiers tied to the land would have a vested interest in defending those lands.

Diocletian is accredited by the Byzantine author John Malalas (*Chron.* 12.308) with establishing *limitanei* in the forts on the eastern frontier. Van Berchem (1952. 21) accepts this theory, concluding that although they were not called *limitanei* at the time, such troops, tied to their lands, already existed under Diocletian. There is little support for this theory. Even if it were true for the east, that would not necessarily imply that the same was true of the rest of the Empire, and as Warmington (1953, 173–4) points out, frontier troops were not yet as static as all that, since some of the *alae* and cohorts still took part in expeditions away from their bases.

The frontier troops of the late Empire are characteristically portrayed as ineffectual, feeble and worthless, having lost their fighting abilities and become little more than an ill-organized rabble. It is certain that the best recruits went into the *comitatenses* and the inferior ones into the frontier troops, as illustrated by a law of 372 (*Cod. Th.* 7.22.8), but this should not suggest that there were no standards at all. The units were still organized and the procedure for recruitment and enrolment was still properly carried out. Jones (1964. 612; 649–51) disagreed with this view of the *limitanei*, and it is worth summarizing his arguments. If these troops were tied to the land with inalienable rights to their allotments, it would seem needlessly extravagant to supply them with payments in kind and cash, but they were indeed paid in this way all through the fourth and fifth centuries. If they owned lands, there should have been no need for the laws granting land to veterans, but this is what was done. As for their effectiveness, some of the frontier troops were on occasion drafted into the field armies, where they were given the title of *pseudo-comitatenses*. Even as late as the reign of the Emperor Honorius this procedure was still adopted, illustrating the fact that the *limitanei* survived until the end of the Empire in the west; they survived even longer in the east. One can perhaps be forgiven for imagining that if the *limitanei* were so perennially useless, then at least one emperor between Constantine and Justinian would have noticed, and applied some thought to the matter.

Conclusions

Parker (1933, 189) concluded that 'the work of Constantine in separating the field army permanently from the frontier army is not an innovation, but the culmination of a natural process in the history of the Roman Imperial army'. In that case, it is not important whether it was Diocletian or Constantine who was responsible for the final break, for it was bound to happen sooner or later. The emphasis on cavalry forces was already apparent in the mid-third century, and the usefulness of maintaining a standing mobile army, additional to the frontier troops, gradually established itself as the constant wars with other Roman armies and with barbarians became endemic on all fronts. From the reign of Gallienus or even earlier, the theory if not the practice was already germinating.

Diocletian established a short period of recovery and restored the frontiers. He may have had a small *comitatus* but if he did he made no special provisions for its veterans in his laws and possibly did not see it as a permanent institution. Once he had repaired the frontiers he may have put most of the troops back into the forts along them. Zosimus says (2.34) that the frontiers housed the whole army; this may not be such an unfounded exaggeration. Constantine made the final choice and it seems that the creation of the *comitatenses* properly belongs to him.

There are those who say that Constantine was much more interested in protecting his throne rather than the frontiers. This shows a lack of imagination, since the two are so closely bound together as to be indivisible. Who could blame him for taking his self-preservation very seriously? He had charge of the whole state, and the example of the last half century had been one of violent assassination. The division of the Empire between four rulers had been excellent in theory, perhaps, but had not worked in practice. Sole rule therefore probably seemed the best alternative. Constantine needed to survive for some time if the state was to be put in order. He could not help the Empire from beyond the grave.

The charge that he weakened the frontiers, dealing them a 'mortal wound' as Gibbon described it, denies his military talents (Warmington 1953, 175). He may have changed some of Diocletian's arrangements for frontier defence, and it is true that the provincials who suffered the first blows under barbarian attacks, before the field army arrived to protect them, could not appreciate the finer points of military strategy. But it is not true to say that Constantine neglected the frontiers. The evidence for his construction work demonstrates that he undertook to keep the buildings in repair, and having repaired them, he probably did not empty them of troops afterwards. If he did remove troops, to a disastrous extent, why did not some of his successors redress the balance? In 443 an interesting law was passed which might have some relevance to the weakened state of the frontiers (*Nov. Th.* 24). The *duces* are exorted in this law to 'restore the soldiers to their ancient number' and to supervise their daily training. Furthermore they should keep the forts in repair, 'according to the ancient regulations'. In other words, the numbers of men in the past had been larger, and provision had been made for their proper training. If in 443 the *limitanei* had declined, and the frontiers were not so well defended, then the successors of Constantine must accept a large proportion of the blame.

III

BARBARIANS AND BUREAUCRATS

THE ARMY FROM CONSTANTINE TO JUSTINIAN

By the beginning of the fourth century the Imperial Roman army had been transformed into that of the late Empire. It did not survive the following centuries without alteration, but after the reign of Constantine a narrative history of the army, documenting all the modifications that were made to it, and all its vicissitudes of success and failure, is impossible. The *comitatenses* are not much in evidence in the archaeological record, nor can archaeology throw much light upon the *limitanei*. Documentary evidence is a little more abundant, but not so abundant as it is for the earlier Empire, because of the comparative lack of epigraphic sources. The literature is vast, but it is incomplete, being both sporadic and selective, and some of it is of dubious value, not least because of the strong pagan or Christian bias which influenced most writers.

One of the main sources, if not *the* main source, for the fourth century army is Ammianus Marcellinus, whose narrative is generally considered to be reliable. He was an officer who had served on the staff of Ursicinus, *magister equitum* from 349 to 359, and *magister peditum* from 359 to 360. Ammianus wrote about events he had witnessed, or at least those which had occurred in his lifetime. His account is detailed and thorough, and very readable, providing a wealth of information about the army. His history ends in 378 with a description of the battle of Adrianople. Less reliable but no less interesting is the *New History* of Zosimus, who wrote in Greek, probably in the early sixth century. He used a variety of sources to compile his history, notably Dexippus, Eunapius and Olympiodorus. Ammianus and Zosimus are the only historians who provide anything like a complete account; the other sources are much more fragmentary.

The Roman army of the fourth century was, on the whole, successful until the two great disasters at Adrianople in 378 and the Frigidus in 394, which respectively destroyed first the eastern and then the western armies. Julian's success at the battle of Strasbourg and his subsequent campaigns against the Franks and the Alamanni (357–9) cannot be attributed solely to a stroke of good fortune or be dismissed as simply literary eulogy passed down to us without a basis of fact. If his Persian campaign was catastrophic, this does not necessarily reflect on the quality of the army. Many other fine armies had met with disaster in Persia. The wonder is that what was left of Julian's army escaped complete annihilation, though this may have been due to Persian vacillation as much as to Roman pertinacity.

Valentinian and Valens

In the fourth century, the age of aggressive, punitive expeditions was not quite extinguished, though all thought of territorial expansion had been abandoned. Valens took the war against the Goths across the Danube, and Valentinian fought beyond the Rhine. The frontiers were restored over much of the Empire, particularly in the north. Yet by the end of the fourth century and the beginning of the fifth, writers such as Vegetius and the unknown author of *De Rebus Bellicis*, appropriately styled the Anonymous, were urging the emperors to make changes to the army to improve its performance. This has led some scholars to seek a detectable turning point at some date in the fourth century, before which all was fully functional and after which all was chaos. Some modern authors have seen this turning point in the battle of Adrianople, or the Frigidus, or a combination of the effects of both battles. The question is bound up with the fall of the west and the survival of the east, and no wholly satisfactory answer has been put forward which explains exactly what happened, nor why. The battle of Adrianople destroyed the eastern army, and yet it was the Western Empire which collapsed, and was split up into the barbarian kingdoms by the mid-fifth century. Explanations which have been advanced for the fall of the west include shortage of manpower, economic decline, administrative corruption, increasing barbarization of the army, debilitating civil wars. Probably all these factors had a part to play without being individually decisive.

When Valentinian was declared emperor on 26 February 364, at Nicaea in Bithynia, the army of Julian's Persian expedition had been badly mauled and had just extricated itself from a precarious position. The frontiers were everywhere threatened 'as if trumpets were sounding the war note throughout the whole Roman world' (Ammianus 26.4.5–6). The Alamanni were devastating Gaul and Raetia, the Sarmatians and Quadi attacking Pannonia, the Goths plundering Thrace. Britain was subjected to raids by Picts, Scots, and Attacotti, and Moorish tribes were harassing the African provinces.

At the request of the army, Valentinian appointed a colleague to share the throne with him; his choice of his brother Valens probably depended less on his ability than on his loyalty. At the end of 364 the brothers divided the Empire and the army between them, Valentinian going to the west, basing himself at Trier, and Valens to the east to begin the campaign against the Goths. Valentinian concentrated on the restoration of peace on the frontiers of the western half of the Empire. He had to delegate the wars in other theatres to subordinates, sending a trio of his officers to Africa (Ammianus 26.5.14) and eventually replacing the unsuccessful generals in Britain with Count (*comes*) Theodosius, the father of the future Emperor Theodosius I. The division of the Empire was not yet intended to be permanent, but it foreshadowed the fifth-century split.

Britain had been devastated by a '*barbarica conspiratio*', a barbarian conspiracy, though there is no real evidence that there had been any collusion between the barbarians. The attacks probably came about through coincidental opportunism. The devastation is not detectable archaeologically, but according to Ammianus, the situation was so bad that Theodosius had to take extra troops with him to Britain (27.8.3), named as *Batavi*, *Heruli*, *Jovii* and *Victores* (27.8.7). Having fought his way into London, Theodosius gradually restored Britain to its former prosperity. The major source for his activities is Ammianus' narrative. His restoration of the frontier works is not definitely attested except at Birdoswald on Hadrian's Wall, where rebuilding inside the fort is dated by a coin of Valentinian I. Elsewhere, any repair work of vaguely late date is attributed to Theodosius without firm evidence. It is possible that he was responsible for the series of fourth century watchtowers along the Yorkshire coast, stretching from Filey to Huntcliff, and possibly further in both directions, though none have yet been found beyond these two points.

Coin evidence suggests that most if not all of the forts north of Hadrian's Wall had already been abandoned when Theodosius arrived in Britain. If any of them were still occupied in 367, it seems that they were definitely given up thereafter. Theodosius may have withdrawn the troops, along with his dismissal of the mysterious *areani* or *arcani* (the reading is obscure). These were scouts or intelligence gatherers, according to Ammianus, whose duties were to travel about over long distances to warn the Romans of likely trouble. It seems that they had also been giving information to the natives and were therefore untrustworthy.

On the Rhine, Valentinian prepared the campaign against the Alamanni with diligence and care, assembling troops of various kinds until he had quite a large army (Ammianus 27.10.5–6). He may have brought frontier units from their forts to join the field armies, giving them the title *pseudo-comitatenses*, which distinguished them from the true *comitatenses*. Zosimus (4.12) says that Valentinian levied a vast army of young men, from barbarians living near the frontier and from Roman provincial farmers, but this levy may have been carried out after the fighting was over, in order to bring the frontier garrisons up to strength. Whatever the composition of his campaign army, by 368, fully recovered from his illness of the previous year, Valentinian was ready to take the war into enemy territory, with the Illyrian and Italian legions under Count Sebastianus (Ammianus 27.10.6–16). After 368, Valentinian took the title 'Alamannicus Maximus' in celebration of his victory (Filtzinger *et al.* 1986, 109).

When the offensive was concluded, Valentinian repaired and refortified the Rhine frontier, with fortresses and towers, and with bridgehead forts on the opposite bank of the river wherever they were necessary (Ammianus 28.2.1). Archaeological evidence corroborates, and also supplements, the details given in the literary sources, revealing that there was an extensive building and rebuilding programme on both the Rhine and Danube in the joint reigns of Valentinian and Valens. It was the last of its kind. After this time, there were only inexpert repairs and minor alterations for as long as the sites remained in use (Petrikovits 1971, 187).

The frontiers were already equipped with forts and towers, and several emperors had been active builders, such as Diocletian and Constantine, so it is difficult to pinpoint the work of Valentinian with any certainty, except where inscriptions leave no doubt that the building or rebuilding is attributable to him (**fig. 6**). In Pannonia, two inscriptions were found in the vicinity of Esztergom in modern Hungary, one from a watchtower and one from a fort (*CIL* III 3653; 10596). In Noricum, the *burgus* at Ybbs (*Ad Iuvense*) was constructed by soldiers from *Lauriacum, milites auxiliares Lauriacenses* (*CIL* III 5670).

Repair work on the Danube–Iller–Rhine *limes* (**fig. 7** and see **fig. 6**) has been attributed to Valentinian (Drack 1980); some of the towers on this frontier, running eastwards from Basel, have yielded Valentinianic pottery (Johnson 1983a, 163). It is probable but not proven that the fort called *Robur* which Ammianus (30.3.1) says that Valentinian built near Basel is to be found in the bridgehead fort opposite the city. The fortresses at

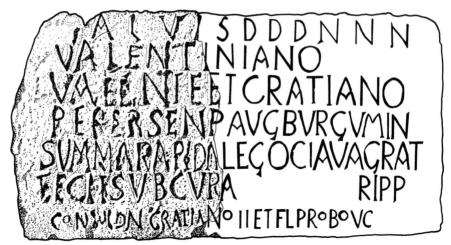

Fig. 6 *Building inscription of 371 from the watchtower at Kleiner Laufen (Switzerland), one of the few Roman military installations whose Latin name is attested on an inscription –* Summa Rapida *can be clearly seen at the beginning of the fifth line. Another watchtower at Rote Waag yielded a similar inscription also dated to 371. (Redrawn by G. Stobbs from Drack and Fellman 1988.) See also* **fig.** *74 for plan of Kleiner Laufen.*

Carnuntum, *Lauriacum* and *Vindobona* were strengthened and the fleet base was moved from Carnuntum to *Vindobona* (Genser 1986, 777–8). Coins of Valentinian from Cuijk on the River Maas, and pottery finds from Engers on the Rhine suggest that these sites were also built or rebuilt as part of Valentinian's reconstruction policy (Johnson 1983a, 146; 153).

As for the rest of the long frontier from the Danube to the North Sea, and for the internal road systems with their fortified posts and towers, only tile and brick stamps can be used for dating purposes, and the value of these has been questioned. As more evidence accumulates, the argument naturally undergoes refinement, so that some of the fourth-century work once unhesitatingly labelled Valentinianic can now be assigned to other emperors. Nevertheless, Petrikovits' statement (1971, 187), that Valentinian was the most active builder on the whole frontier after the emperors of the catastrophic era 260 to 284, has not been convincingly challenged. The system of frontier defence in Valentinian's reign consisted of forts and strong points along the frontier itself, with the roads linking them guarded by watchtowers. The internal roads were guarded in the same way, and fortified granaries ensured the safety of the food supply. River crossings were protected by bridgehead forts, and a series of fortified landing places and harbours preserved river traffic from danger. There is some evidence that Valentinian built fortifications, probably watchtowers, in the territory of the enemy. In barbarian lands across the Rhine, he abandoned his attempt to establish a fortification; in the territory of the Quadi, he ordered a fort to be built (Ammianus 29.6.2). This may not be the whole story: as Johnson points out, watchtowers have been found across the Danube at Wagram am Wagram, Etsdorf and Zielberg (1983, 306 n. 84). Supervision of the enemy in this way was long established Roman practice, and no one can justifiably accuse Valentinian of lack of thoroughness.

The campaigns against the Alamanni and other tribes, and then the reconstruction of the frontiers could not be undertaken without attention to the organization of the army. After Julian's Persian expedition, the available troops were divided up between the two Emperors, who made every effort to increase the size of the army and to maintain it at strength (Jones 1964, 149). One of their first considerations seems to have been for their veterans. A law passed in November 364 (*Cod. Th.* 7.20.8) outlines the privileges to be granted to veterans. Only 11 years earlier, Constantius had passed laws designed to curb the activities of those veterans who had turned to banditry. The new law may have been designed to ease their lot and provide no excuse for resorting to crime. In the same year, a law was passed to protect the provincials from the extortionate practices of the soldiers (*Cod. Th.* 7.4.12). Valentinian tried to root out corruption throughout the Empire, but had little success.

With determination, the Emperors turned to the matter of recruitment. In 365, there were tougher measures to round up deserters and punish those who harboured them (*Cod. Th.* 7.18.1), and then to identify and catch all likely candidates who had hitherto slipped through the net, such as those able-bodied men who were masquerading as

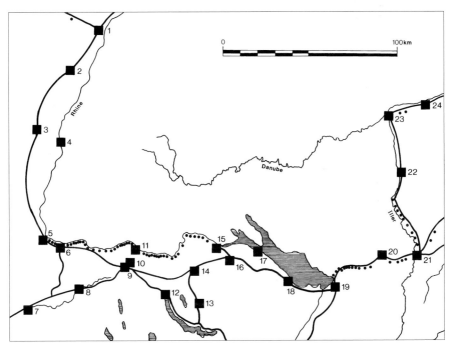

Fig. 7 *The Danube–Iller–Rhine* limes *in the reign of Valentinian I. (Redrawn by G. Stobbs from Drack 1980.)*
Key to numbered sites: 1. Strasburg (Argentorate) 2. Ehl (Helvetum) 3. Horburg (Argentovaria) 4. Breisach (Brisiacum) 5. Basle (Basilia) 6. Kaiseraugst (Castrum Rauracense) 7. Solothurn (Salodurum) 8. Olten 9. Altenburg 10. Windisch (Vindonissa) 11. Zurzach (Tenedo) 12. Zurich (Turicum) 13. Irgenhausen 14. Winterthur (Vitudurum) 15. Burg (Tasgaetium) 16. Pfyn (Ad Fines) 17. Constance 18. Arbon (Arbor Felix) 19. Bregenz (Brigantium) 20. Bettmauer (Vemania) 21. Kempten (Cambodunum) 22. Kellmünz (Caelius Mons) 23. ?Febiana 24. Günzburg (Guntia)

servants and camp-followers when they could have been more usefully employed in the ranks (*Cod. Th.* 7.1.10). Spreading the net wider, the optimum height qualification for recruits was reduced (*Cod. Th.* 7.13.3). The avoidance of military service by the drastic measure of cutting off one's own fingers or thumbs was countered in 367 by forcibly employing such men in some branch of the service regardless of their disability (*Cod. Th.* 7.13.4). By the following year, the Emperors had evidently lost patience: all those who had mutilated themselves to avoid joining the army were to be burnt to death, and where appropriate their masters were also punished for not having prevented the occurrence (*Cod.Th.* 7.13.5). Conscription was annual (Jones 1964, 1098, n. 30), and by 370 even the workers on the Imperial estates were not exempt (*Cod. Th.* 7.13.2).

These laws pertain to the years when Count Theodosius led his expedition to Britain, Valentinian was fighting the Alamanni on the Rhine and Valens was campaigning on the Danube against the Goths. Even though the Roman armies were ultimately successful, the rate of wastage would place a great strain on manpower. Every available recruit would be vital, which state of affairs is reflected in the series of laws enumerated above.

The methods of assembling the campaign armies are only hinted at in the sources. Special recruitment of both permanent soldiers and temporary allies would be necessary, as well as mobilization of troops from other areas. The regional armies would not necessarily suffice for waging either an aggressive or defensive war. The division of the army into mobile units and frontier units did not obviate the need for long-distance and sometimes large-scale troop movements. Ostensibly it was the threat of removal to distant provinces which caused Julian's army to revolt and proclaim him Emperor in Gaul. When he marched eastwards to do battle against Constantius, the troops presumably did not raise the same objections, and units from Gaul probably fought in the Persian war.

Troops brought from other provinces probably did not return to their original locations once the wars in which they had taken part were concluded. It has been suggested that the *Galli* in the army lists for the east (*Not. Dig. Or.* XXVIII 28; XXXVIII 24; XL 46) may represent units originally composed of Franks who came to the east with Julian; they are denoted by the symbol of a throwing axe, a typically Frankish weapon (E. James 1988, 51–2). But it is equally probable that these are old units from the army of the Principate, and in any case, Frankish in origin or not, they probably did not contain any Franks by the time they were listed in the *Notitia*, since they would have been kept up to strength by local recruiting.

When peace was restored on the Rhine and Danube, the army would be distributed among the forts and strong points on the roads and frontiers, and in the cities. Before he began his campaign against the Alamanni, Valentinian put garrisons into the cities in Gaul and Germany (Zosimus 4.3.4). It is unlikely that he would remove all these garrisons once the campaigns were over, though he may have reduced them. The extensive overhaul of the frontiers would be effective only if there were sufficient numbers of soldiers to man the forts and towers, and it would seem particularly incongruous to lavish so much concentrated effort on the actual buildings and none at all on providing the relevant personnel. It is clear that in Britain and on the Rhine frontier Valentinian instituted a thorough and fundamental reorganization (Hoffman 1969, 344–52). Troops from the field armies were redeployed into the frontier armies to man the forts; Hoffman attempts to identify the original campaign units which provided the frontier troops (ibid., 353–7).

From the laws concerning recruitment it can be seen that Valentinian did all he could to keep the army supplied with men, and he also paid attention to a feature that is of equal if not greater importance than merely assembling recruits. According to Zosimus (4.12) he trained them thoroughly, so that 'for fear of their discipline and experience' there were no disturbances on the Rhine for nine years.

The first concern of the Emperor Valens when he parted from his brother in 364 was to settle accounts with the Goths, who had pillaged their way through Pannonia and Thrace; in 365 they lent assistance to the usurper Procopius. From 367 to 369, Valens campaigned across the Danube, in enemy territory. He was not outstandingly successful each year (Ammianus 27.5). In the first year, he could not get to grips with the tribes at all, and in the second year the Danube floods made it almost impossible to operate. But in the end dogged persistence won the day, and the Goths were forced to come to terms because they were short of supplies, and all trade with the Roman Empire had been stopped. Valens was able to conclude peace while definitely in the ascendancy. He limited trade with the Goths to two sites on the Danube which have not been identified with certainty.

Since the Persians were restive, Valens turned his attention to the eastern frontier, departing for Antioch in 370. There were no decisive battles, but quite a lot of ineffective political negotiation, punctuated from time to time by some military skirmishing (Ammianus 27.12).

Like Valentinian in the west, Valens was an active builder and restorer of the frontiers in the east. 'He built new forts and repaired existing ones, furnishing them with what was needed, height where too low, thickness where too weak' (Themistius *Oration* 10; Heather and Matthews 1991, 44). The repair and rebuilding work on the lower Danube frontier was carried out while Valens was campaigning. Although it is beyond doubt from the epigraphic evidence that building and rebuilding work was carried out at many places under Valens, architecturally speaking it is difficult to distinguish his work from that of his successors. After the settlement of the Goths in 376 and especially after the battle of Adrianople, there was a wave of destruction which Theodosius I repaired (Scorpan 1980, 121–2 and n. 48). Overhauling the army, Valens did his best to correct abuses, such as the time-honoured trick of claiming the pay of dead men, and selling off at a profit the supplies intended for the troops.

While Valens was attempting to come to terms with Persia, the seeds of disaster were sown on the Danube frontier by the apparently innocuous and potentially profitable settlement within the Empire of the Goths, who were seeking asylum from the Huns. Many of these Goths were drafted into the army and sent to the eastern frontier, but this did not absorb enough of them to relieve the pressure on the food supply. The resultant famine, coupled with the short-sighted exploitation of the Goths by the Roman officials steadily escalated over the next eighteen months. Finally there was a revolt. The result of that was the defeat of the Romans at Adrianople in 378. Valens was killed in the battle, and the eastern army was almost destroyed. In his analysis of the *Notitia* lists, Hoffman enumerated, as far as it is possible to deduce, the units which had been lost. He concluded that many infantry units had been destroyed and never rebuilt (1969, 452). But this is not the only effect that the battle may have had. Those units still attested by name in the *Notitia* presumably escaped complete destruction, but there may only have remained a small cadre of experienced men around which to reconstitute the units. Efficiency and effectiveness may have been much impaired, and unfortunately this is something that cannot be deduced from dry statistics in the *Notitia Dignitatum*.

Theodosius I

The sole surviving Emperor Gratian, son of Valentinian I who had died in 375, brought the younger Theodosius from Spain to take over the eastern half of the Empire, augmented by the addition of the dioceses of Dacia and Macedonia (Jones 1964, 156). It took three years of fighting before Theodosius brought the Goths to terms in 382, when he allowed them to settle in Thrace. The treaty which he made with them has not always been viewed in a favourable light, either by his contemporaries or by modern scholars, who censure Theodosius for his leniency towards the Goths. They were settled on the very lands they had ravaged, unsupervised by the Romans and permitted to live according to their own laws. This autonomy was what appalled those objectors who recorded their reactions in writing. Synesius hated barbarians on several counts, and took the opportunity to give vent to his feelings in his *De Regno* (14–15). He lamented the degradation of the name of senator, which was once a respectful office, but could now be handed out to barbarians. Class-conscious to a marked degree, he pointed out that those who used to be servants were giving orders in public life, and that the state was protected by barbarians of the same stock as the slaves. More pertinently, he declared that Theodosius had treated the barbarians softly in making them allies, bestowing political rights upon them and giving them lands to farm. Synesius warned that instead of interpreting this generosity as nobility on the part of the Romans, the barbarians only thought of it as weakness.

Other writers viewed the matter in a different light. Pacatus, in his Panegyric to Theodosius, spoke favourably of the barbarians, but such eulogistic writings perhaps do not count as unbiased opinions. Themistius, in *Oration* 16, declared that it was better to fill Thrace with farmers and soldiers than with corpses. In *Oration* 10 he talked of the Romans bestowing peace, not buying it, and in general he advocated a policy of tolerance (Daly 1972, 362–3; Heather and Matthews 1991, 43). Salvian took the view that the barbarians were there to stay, and had to be reckoned with. They had to be either assimilated, or defeated, and since the latter was not possible he advocated a fusion of the two cultures (Dauge 1981, 375). Paulinus of Nola (*Carmen* 17) thought that the essential task was to Romanize the barbarians. Both he and Orosius considered that the barbarians would be acceptable if they were made into good Christians (Dauge 1981, 320).

The wider political and social implications of the treaty have been examined by Heather (1991, 158–65) and Wolfram (1988, 131–8). The military implications are much disputed, and Theodosius has been blamed, perhaps unjustly, for tilting the balance in a situation already well advanced by flooding the army with barbarians.

Barbarization of the Army

The text of Theodosius's treaty (*foedus*) of 382 is unknown, and therefore the terms of military service exacted from the Goths also remain unknown. The exploitation of barbarian manpower was not unusual, but it seems that the terms laid down in the negotiations of 382 departed from normal practice. Before it can be stated how these terms differed, it is necessary to enquire what constituted normal practice. Usually, after the conclusion of a war, a treaty was made stipulating that the enemy should contribute a number of men to the Roman army, either *en masse* and annually thereafter, or by some similar arrangement. It was at one and the same time a means of removing potentially dangerous young men, of increasing the size of the army, and of gradually Romanizing the barbarians. The soldiers raised in this way could be distributed among existing units, thus diluting their barbarian influence, or they could be kept together, organized and trained as a regular unit, and sent to distant provinces to reduce the likelihood of their deserting to the enemy if rebellion should break out. This sort of treaty was made with tribes who remained outside the Empire and was a time-honoured method of raising men for the army.

Wholesale immigration of tribesmen into the Empire was a matter demanding a different response. Sometimes defeated tribesmen (*dediticii*) were settled inside the Empire in fairly large numbers. Other groups of barbarians entered voluntarily. Tribes had clamoured to be allowed to cross the frontiers since the Empire came into being, and had sometimes been admitted and given lands. MacMullen (1990, 49–50) usefully lists examples of these occurrences: under Augustus 50,000 Getae settled in Moesia; Tiberius allowed 40,000 Germans into Gaul and the Rhineland; Marcus Aurelius received 3000 Naristae into the Empire; Probus admitted 100,000 Bastarnae and Constantine settled 300,000 Sarmatians on lands in Thrace, Italy and Macedonia. The numbers are, by MacMullen's own admission, suspect, but they serve to illustrate the magnitude of the problem. In the late Empire the numbers of barbarians seeking admission dramatically increased.

The methods of dealing with both the prisoners of war and the free tribesmen were similar, but not rigidly standardized. A common feature of such settlements was the stipulation that the tribesmen must defend the sections of the frontier where they had been granted lands, or that they must contribute troops for the army. There were probably more types of settlement than our sources reveal (Liebeschuetz 1991, 13), and attempts to classify them into sharply defined groups, using only their names, achieves at best a limited success. Two groups which may be similar are the *laeti* and the *gentiles*, but beyond the fact that both names refer to groups of people who were not citizens and seem to be distinct ethnic entities, it cannot be discerned whether they enjoyed the same status. The two words may not have been interchangeable and perhaps denoted technical differences that would have been obvious to the Romans but are lost to us.

Gentiles

The term *gentiles* probably embraced several slightly different groups of people. It could be used of the free tribes living beyond the frontiers, and those barbarians settled inside the Empire. Units of *gentiles* were to be found in the bodyguard (*schola*) of Diocletian, and at a later period in the *scholae* of the *magister officiorum* in both halves of the Empire (*Not. Dig. Or.* XI. 6; 10; *Oc.* IX. 7). A large number of Sarmatian *gentiles* served in the army in Italy (*Not. Dig. Oc.* XLII. 46–70). In some instances *gentiles* and *laeti* are mentioned together, sometimes commanded by the same officer (*Not. Dig. Oc.* XLII. 34; 35; 42; 44), Grosse (1920. 210) thought that the *gentiles* ranked lower than the *laeti* since they were always mentioned in second place, but this is not proven. Virtually nothing is known for certain about their relative status.

Laeti

The *laeti* are found only in Gaul and Italy, and had existed in Gaul since the days of the Tetrarchy (Jones 1964, 620). Originally the word may have been applied to provincials who had been in captivity in barbarian lands and who had been brought back into the Empire (Liebeschuetz 1991, 12). Grosse traced the term to a Germanic root denoting a class of people who were only half free (1920, 208–9). The *laeti* were settled on lands set aside for them, and were obliged to provide men for the army. The status was hereditary. A law of 399 refers to *terrae laeticae* (*Cod. Th.* 13.11.10), while another law passed thirty years earlier in 369 refers to *praepositi* in charge of the *laeti*. Thus it can be seen that their settlements were supervised, most often by military officials, though on occasion they could be attached to cities and supervised by the appropriate civilian authorities. In the army, *laeti* are referred to by Ammianus in Constantius' army (21.13.6), and the *Notitia* lists a dozen *praefecti laetorum* in Gaul (*Not. Dig. Oc.* XLII 33–44; E. James 1988. 45; Grosse 1920, 208).

The settlement of various tribes as *laeti* was a successful arrangement. It was no deterrent to personal advancement to be born a *laetus*, according to Zosimus (2.54), such was the origin of the Frankish usurper Magnentius. The Franks were settled as *laeti* in the cities of Trier, Amiens and Langres by Constantius Chlorus after he had defeated them in battle (E. James 1988, 39). Julian confirmed what was in reality a *fait accompli*, when he agreed to let the Salian Franks who had surrendered to him remain inside the Empire in Toxandria, around the mouth of the Rhine. They kept the peace for a century. They expanded their territories very quietly while the Romans were preoccupied with the Goths, but since there was no outcry against them, the lands they appropriated were presumably already vacant, or at least they were obtained without evicting anyone (Drew 1991, 4). The Franks who had settled inside Roman territory enjoyed better relations with the provincials than with their own countrymen still outside the Empire (Liebeschuetz 1991, 8). The Franks in Roman service seem to have had no problem with their dual identity. A gravestone (*CIL* XIII 3576) records a man who describes himself as both Frankish citizen and Roman soldier: *Francus ego cives, Romanus miles in armis* (E. James 1988, 42). Burns (1984, 10) explains that the two concepts are not competitive. The man could have a tribal social life and family, which in no way affected his loyalty to Rome. On the northern frontiers, the two cultures were gradually merging in any case, and on purely archaeological grounds it is difficult to recognize Romans and barbarians as distinct entities. The frontier troops used home-made pottery and jewellery, and their burials reveal a mixture of styles attesting to the broad acculturation of Germans and Romans on the Rhine and Danube (MacMullen 1990, 54; Burns 1984, 136–9; 1984, 11–13). Indeed, the terms *miles* and *barbarus* were by now synonymous (Dauge 1981 312).

Foederati

The employment of barbarians from beyond the frontiers, by means of an alliance with a tribal leader or a client king, had always been accepted as a method of increasing the size of the army for campaigns. Such troops fought under their own leaders, attached to the army for the duration of the war, then on the conclusion of peace they would return to their homes. On occasion, they might be recruited into the regular army to fill gaps in the ranks, or sometimes whole bands of them might be transformed into regular units, but most often they remained outside the army. Their chiefs would normally be strongly supported by Rome, sometimes subsidized, and kept in power in order to ensure that the frontiers were protected at least in part by tribes who had every reason to be on friendly terms with the Empire.

The term *foederati* is not an easily definable one, since it covers several different kinds of troops. In the late Empire, it denoted troops raised from barbarians settled within the frontiers as well as those raised from outside. The practice of settling barbarians by treaty arrangement on lands inside the Empire became more common from the end of the third century, when many frontier areas were devastated. Such settlements were widespread and frequent. Leibeschuetz (1991, 11) points out that no one has yet successfully explained why there was so much empty land within the Empire, yet this certainly seems to have been the case, since the barbarians did not displace Roman landowners or free peasants.

It should not be interpreted as a sign of weakness on the part of the Romans that they accepted so many tribesmen into the Empire. Two of the most famous settlements, of the Visigoths in Aquitaine by Constantius in 418, and the Burgundians in eastern Gaul by Aetius in 443, were made 'from a position of strength' (Goffart 1980, 58). Goffart argues that, contrary to popular opinion, displacement of provincials hardly entered into the matter. Of course, neither Constantius nor Aetius envisaged that they were to be instrumental in founding two of the major barbarian kingdoms in Gaul. The settlements were regulated by Roman law, on the basis of co-operation between the tribal leaders and the Romans.

In order to support the barbarians, subsidies were given (*annonae foederaticae*) (Jones 1964, 611), which may have been paid in kind at first, and later commuted into annual payments for the upkeep of the troops which the tribes were to furnish for Rome as part of their treaty obligations (Bury 1958, vol. I, 42). It used to be thought that where the barbarians were billeted on the provincials by the system of *hospitalitas*, the 'guests' were entitled to a share of the property of their Roman hosts, but Goffart's re-examination (1980) of *hospitalitas* reveals that the system was probably based on a redistribution of the tax revenues, which were diverted to support the barbarian military contingents. His theories have not met with universal acceptance. One of the problems, apart from the lack of contemporary documentary proof, is the fact that the procedure may not have been established on a uniform footing throughout the whole Empire, and may have changed from time to time.

Foederati could also describe conglomerations of men, not all of the same ethnic background, who had gathered around a leader. The bands of Goths following Alaric probably contained an ethnic mixture of different tribesmen. There can be no direct link with the original Goths who crossed the frontier in 376. Liebescheutz (1992) raises the question of whether Alaric was leading a nation or something more properly described as an army.

The distinctions between these *foederati* and the *bucellarii* are probably blurred. *Bucellarii* were private armies composed of retainers of a powerful magnate, or sometimes of a general like Stilicho. Liebeschuetz makes the point that the men who joined these private armies perhaps did so because their particular leader could guarantee them long-term employment (1991, 45).

Whatever their origin, the *foederati* attached to the army would be answerable to the Roman high command, but like the earlier *foederati*, their immediate commanders would be their own leaders. They were not part of the regular army.

By the sixth century, the *foederati* in the eastern army were quite different. These were regular troops, paid, trained and disciplined, like the rest of the army. The change presumably came about at some unknown date in the fifth century. These units were recruited exclusively from barbarians at first, then in the sixth century Romans were also admitted. Bury (1958, vol. I, 43; vol. II, 76) describes them as the most important and useful part of the field army. The old-style *foederati* of the fourth and early fifth centuries were now called 'allies' (from the Greek *symmachoi*) in the eastern army. Hence, caution is necessary when using late Roman sources which mention *foederati*, since anachronistic misuse of the term can be misleading.

Barbarian soldiers and officers

Many barbarians served in the regular army, and some of them rose to high rank; an exhaustive list of barbarian officers would fill several pages. The more famous names include Magnentius, originally a *laetus* who became emperor briefly after the murder of Constantius (Zosimus 2.42; 54), and Arbogast, the Frankish *magister militum* under Valentinian. Richomer, *comes domesticorum* under Gratian, and Bauto, consul under Arcadius, were also Franks (Ammianus 31.7.4; Zosimus 4.33; 53; 54; 55). Under Theodosius, the Scythian Modares became *magister militum*, and the great general Stilicho was a Vandal.

In addition to individual recruitment of tribesmen to fill gaps in existing units, enrolment of large groups of barbarians in the army had been common practice since the early Empire. Marcus Aurelius used Germans to fight against Germans (*SHA* Marcus 21). Claudius II enrolled Goths after defeating them (Zosimus 1.46). Constantine's army at the battle of the Milvian Bridge was full of Germans, Gauls and Britons (Zosimus 2.15).

The barbarian soldiers were, with few exceptions, loyal to Rome, and served her well. There was little sense of nationality among the Germanic tribes, and no unity, so that the dichotomy which modern readers might read into the labels German and Roman did not necessarily exist for the men who signed up for 20–25 years' service. Although the numbers of barbarians in the army may have seemed excessive, the cultural and moral superiority of the Romans ensured their subjection. The settlements of tribesmen were supervised by Roman officials, usually called *praepositi*, and the barbarians in the army were under the command of Roman, or thoroughly Romanized, officers. The Germans who attained positions of authority in the army and in civilian office were more Roman than the Romans, attuned to Roman civilization and ways of life.

Theodosius I and the treaty of 382

The process of barbarization of the army was already well under way by the time Theodosius made his treaty with the Goths, and the settlement of groups of tribesmen on Roman soil was nothing new. The crucial factor in the settlement of 382 concerns the status of the Goths, and their obligation to provide soldiers. Whereas other tribes inside the Empire were subject to Roman supervision and to Roman law, the Goths were governed by their own chiefs, and were therefore more or less autonomous. Jones calls this a grave breach with precedent (1964, 157). The contingents which the Goths were obliged to furnish for the army are the subject of much discussion. It is important to distinguish between the Goths serving in the regular army, who had nothing to do with the treaty arrangements, and the troops provided by the agreement of 382 (Heather 1991, 162–3). These would be called for whenever specific campaigns were being prepared by negotiation with the Gothic chiefs. They would not appear in the official lists such as the *Notitia* (Heather 1991, 162), because they were *with* rather than *in* the Roman army (Rémondon 1964, 191). Liebeschuetz (1986, 463) points out that in documentary sources after 378, the eastern army is divided into Romans and barbarians, but this does not mean that the distinction is purely ethnic. The regular units, denoted by the title Romans, contained a high proportion of barbarians, who served for a specified length of time, subject to Roman discipline. The distinction between Romans and barbarians is made in documentary sources because the troops styled barbarians were not part of the regular army.

Jones and others affirm that the Gothic soldiers were commanded by their own officers, but this has been disputed, or at least refined. Heather (1991, 162) explains that although the Gothic princes were left in charge of their own men, these princes were ultimately under the overall command of Roman officers. Wolfram (1988, 133) also states that the Gothic leaders received only subordinate commands. The idea that the Goths had attained a dangerous power is somewhat modified, and though the destruction which they and other barbarians wrought on the Empire is indisputable, it seems unfair to lay all the blame for the collapse of the Roman world on Theodosius I and the Goths, as Zosimus implies (4.26–35). Other ancient authors, no less biased towards the Goths, or towards Theodosius, than Zosimus was against them, point out that the Goths served Rome faithfully (Jordanes *Getica* 28.145; Pacatus 32). Somewhere between the two extremes must lie a germ of truth.

The response to barbarization

Synesius (*De Regno* 14–15) recommended the removal of all barbarians from high office, and talked of purifying the army, which has ominous racial overtones to twentieth-century readers. In the eastern Empire, the Gothic threat was dealt with summarily on more than one occasion. Immediately after the Roman defeat at Adrianople, sealed orders went out to the commanders of the eastern troops to summon the Goths in the army to a pay parade, and then to put them all to death (Ammianus 31.16.8; Zosimus 4.26). Further purges of the army were carried out in 386 when another group of Goths were massacred at Tomi, and there was more slaughter after the revolt of Gainas in Constantinople. Gainas had been instrumental in the assassination of the praetorian prefect Rufinus, but afterwards he led a march on Constantinople for reasons which remain obscure. He was defeated, and fled, only to be killed by the Huns. Thereafter, in an attempt to reduce the proportions of Germanic tribesmen in the army, the eastern army began to recruit from the indigenous population, especially from the hardy tribes of Isaurians. It did not prove possible to maintain the army without recruitment of barbarians, but the numbers were kept small and more easily controlled. As mentioned above, by the sixth century troops with the title *foederati*, raised from barbarian tribes, were part of the regular army, subject to the same discipline as all other troops.

For some time the eastern army was weakened, since by purging it of the Goths, some of the best fighting elements had been removed. Fortunately, the Huns were temporarily defeated, albeit with great difficulty, in 408–9, and Theodosius also managed to resolve the Persian question. There were only two wars on the eastern frontier in 421–2 and 441–2, so that the government was able to concentrate on the defence of the Danube (Jones 1964, 204). Territorially, the east was not so difficult to defend as the west. This gave the eastern emperors an opportunity to build up a dual system of defence, utilizing both the army and clever diplomacy united to subterfuge, which the Byzantines developed into an art.

The western army did not find it so easy to meet the barbarian challenge by purging itself of undesirable elements. When an attempt was made to do so, the timing was faulty. On 13 August 408, the Romans in Honorius' court massacred the Germans among the Emperor's followers, and finally sacrificed Stilicho, to their immediate disadvantage. However dubious his motives may have been, Stilicho was a capable general, and the soldiers would follow him. By removing him and also weakening the army at the wrong time, the western Roman court found itself almost defenceless. The respite granted to the east did not occur in the west, and there were fewer opportunities for indigenous recruitment. When Alaric sacked Rome, the necessity of coming to terms with him meant that the anti-German elements of the court had to be silenced (Rémondon 1964, 213). The western army never ceased to recruit barbarians, and never succeeded in removing them as the east had done. All that could be achieved was to preclude barbarians from the high commands. On the other hand, and perhaps more significantly, although the Western Empire accommodated the barbarians, it failed to assimilate them properly, and with this vacillating state of affairs it sealed its own doom.

Decline of the Army

Barbarization alone does not wholly explain the changes in the army which were detectable to fourth- and fifth-century authors, but the concomitant factors which resulted from the process were harmful. After Adrianople, and then the battle of the Frigidus, there was an urgent need to rebuild the armies of east and west. The two armies did not completely disappear, but when they were eventually reconstructed, it could be said that most of the links with the Roman armies of the past had been severed. It was not necessarily a question of shortage of manpower; it was a shortage of trained manpower, which is vastly different. This is one of the reasons why the apparent recovery after the disastrous battles of the late fourth century was not as effective as, for example, the seemingly effortless recovery after the loss of two expeditionary armies in the Dacian campaigns under Domitian. Military disasters had occurred in the early Empire without leading to collapse, and ravaged lands had been restored, but that was before the decades of exhaustion that the late Empire had experienced without respite.

The sources are deceptive. The poems of Ausonius and the letters of Sidonius attest to a reasonably settled life in late Roman Gaul, given that the circumstances were not ideal. But the recovery of Gaul after the ravages of the Frankish and Alamannic raids was probably far from complete. Similarly neither east nor west fully recovered from the effects of Adrianople and the Frigidus. The army had diminished in public esteem, as indicated by the marked reluctance of most men to serve in it (Dill 1905, 236). This reluctance among Romans meant that the soldiers were mostly barbarians on both sides whenever so-called Roman armies clashed in civil wars, but Roman tradition, discipline, training and fighting methods had not yet been entirely extinguished in the early 370s (Delbrück 1921, 25). At the end of the fourth century this changed, and the process of decline already apparent in the army took a firmer hold, making it impossible to reverse the trends towards complete barbarization (Liebeschuetz 1991, 2).

The law codes bear witness to the measures to which Theodosius was driven to refurbish troops from 378 onwards. Many of the laws were designed to unmask those who sought to avoid military service by one method or another. In 380, there was an effort to enforce the rule that sons of veterans must enlist (*Cod. Th.* 7.22.9). Then there were penalties for those who offered slaves for the army instead of suitable recruits (*Cod. Th.* 7.13.8 and 11), and stronger measures against men who mutilated themselves to avoid service. In order to discourage the practice, it was declared that two mutilated men would be taken in place of one whole one (*Cod. Th.* 7.13.10). By 406, all scruples about the unsuitability of slaves had been abandoned in the west, and the emperors were calling them to arms (*Cod. Th.* 7.13.16).

It may have seemed that the shortages of manpower could be solved instantly by filling the ranks of the army with barbarians and by negotiating with various allied chieftains for temporary contingents of tribesmen to fight in specific wars. But the losses of Adrianople were not to be counted simply in numerical terms of manpower. What had been lost were experienced men, disciplined and trained to Roman standards. If, in the past, it had always proved possible to rebuild the army systematically and methodically, the situation now was too precarious and the danger too widespread to allow for anything other than rapid, piecemeal responses, which differed in each half of the Empire.

The Eastern Empire conducted its successive purges and endangered itself by reducing the size of its army, but it survived by a combination of good fortune and good management, and remained Roman by tradition even if it became Oriental in fact. Its territory was more homogeneous and easier to defend, and even though it was bordered by the Persian Empire, the threat posed by this sophisticated enemy did not cause the disintegration that the barbarians caused in the west.

The Western emperors never appointed a German *magister militum* after the removal of Stilicho. With the exception of Ulfilas and Sigisvult, who were Goths, after 408 all the *magistri* were Romans (Jones 1964, 177). But if the high-ranking officers were no longer barbarians, the troops were still recruited from tribesmen. The West retained an effective army under Aetius, but its lack of Romanization became more and more apparent. The army was constantly in the field for many seasons, and was highly mobile and successful, which implies that the administration and supply system was still functional (Elton 1992, 170). For each campaign more barbarians were employed, from outside as well as from inside the Empire, and their large numbers 'presented formidable problems of control' (Liebeschuetz 1991, 3). Barbarians were not naturally disciplined. Even Pacatus (32), in praising the Goths, has to admit that it was unusual that the barbarians stayed at their posts, did not pillage and loot, and did not cause confusion. Ammianus had no very elevated opinion of barbarians; in scattered references, collected by Dauge (1981, 333–49), he describes them as inhuman and vicious, using all the stock epithets. With more insight from a military point of view, he says they are discouraged by the slightest set-back, disorganized, incapable of following any coherent plan, and unable to foresee a train of events. In other words, they were thoroughly unmilitary from a Roman point of view.

Zosimus (4.31) has another point to add, which may concern only one army at one particular time, but is none the less deeply significant. He says that no record was kept of those enrolled in the army, and the deserters whom Theodosius had reinstated could go home whenever they felt like it, substituting other men in their places. Granted that modern armies are much more highly trained in various special tasks than was the Roman army, chaos would have resulted if, for instance, a tank driver in Normandy in 1944 had decided to go home, substituting the nearest garage mechanic to do his job for a few months. Such a lack of central control and lapse of disciplinary standards was nothing less than disastrous. Combined with the lack of a cadre of trained men to hand down tradition, and the lack of active training to remedy this defect, the downward spiral accelerated alarmingly and could not be stopped. This point is made succinctly in connection with another army at another time, observed closely by an Englishman in 1781: 'The Prussian army, being composed chiefly of strangers of different countries, manners, and religion, are [*sic*] united only by the strong chain of military discipline; this and a most rigid attention to keep up all the forms and discipline established, constitutes a vast and regular machine, which being animated by the vigorous and powerful genius of their leader, may be justly accounted one of the most respectable armies in Europe; but should this spring, however, languish but for an instant only, the machine itself, being composed of such heterogeneous matter, would probably fall to pieces, and leave nothing but the traces of its ancient glory behind' (Britt 1985, 59). It could be said that Roman discipline had 'languished but for an instant only', but the damage was done.

In these circumstances the process of training and of Romanization could not operate. Lack of training would cause irreparable harm in a very short time. Delbrück, while ultimately arguing for German supremacy over the Romans, points out that with the disappearance of discipline and training, Roman combat methods also disappeared as a matter of course (1921, 220). It can be no accident that Vegetius, in the very first chapter after his preface and fulsome dedication, perhaps to Theodosius I, points out that it was discipline and training which enabled the Roman armies to conquer all peoples. He goes on to say that 'a small force, highly trained, is more likely to win battles than a raw and untrained horde'. As Milner explains, in his translation of Vegetius' work, 'small highly trained legionary armies are at the core of Vegetius's recommendations' (1993, 3, n. 4).

Training is eased when there is a cadre of experienced soldiers round which to build up each unit, so that the original ethnic background of the new recruits is hardly of any significance. Romanization of tribesmen in the army is similarly eased when Roman culture is in the ascendancy. Neither of these elements applied after the battles of Adrianople and the Frigidus, and the situation was compounded by other serious factors. Delbrück (1921, 231) says: 'It has been possible time and again to restore discipline … even after the most difficult disruptions, whenever an unrivalled commander stood at the top and the war treasury was regularly able to provide the necessary sums.' But at a time when both dynamic commanders and lots of money were needed, the Roman Empire had neither. If the army could have been Romanized and trained as it had been in the early Empire, the Western Empire may have survived longer. But the procedure for training an army and for Romanization of the barbarians required a commodity which was never granted to the west: time.

The break-up when it came proceeded rapidly, from the first decade of the fifth century. The inability of the western government to defend the Empire arose from lack of centralized administrative control and impoverishment of resources. Civil wars between usurpers accelerated the decline. Constantius II withdrew troops from Britain in 407; three years later Honorius decided against trying to regain the island. The army was withdrawn from Spain in 411 (Collins 1991, 75). The western Empire shrank to a shadow of its former self. Italy was naturally the first priority, the second was Gaul, virtually the only other province that was defended. Even the Rhine frontier was allowed to be overrun. The *magister militum* Aetius, though a Roman, had been a hostage among the Huns, and increasingly used these ties of loyalty to recruit Huns for his army, with which he successfully fought Burgundians and Visigoths in Gaul. Appeals for help from the other provinces were ignored. Aetius directed western policy for several years and has been blamed for the collapse of the west. Collins (1991, 81) suggests that, if someone had murdered Aetius sooner, the west may have had a chance of survival. Collins does not offer any names of candidates who could have filled Aetius' place, and the chances are that just as disaster followed the murder of Stilicho, the earlier removal of Aetius would merely have precipitated an earlier collapse.

The exact date when the western Empire ceased to exist is hard to ascertain. There are successive stages, all equally qualified for the honour, but even after the widely accepted date of 476, Roman forms of law and military institutions were not completely dead, surviving as they did in the barbarian kingdoms. The date at which the western Roman army ceased to exist is no less problematic. There was no formal disbandment centrally directed from Ravenna or Rome. It could be said that even the soldiers serving in the army were not really sure of their demise as an institution. A famous passage from Eugippius' *Vita Sancti Severini* (7.28) best illustrates this. He describes how, while the Romans were in power, soldiers were maintained in many towns at public expense to guard the frontier. But when this custom ceased, several whole units of soldiers disappeared. The men at Batava (modern Passau, at the junction of the rivers Inn and Danube) remained at their posts, and sent a delegation to Italy to find out why they had received no pay. Some days later, their bodies floated down-river and came to rest on the banks, silent testimony to the end of Rome's ability to keep her Empire intact and to defend her frontiers.

Administration and Organization

Administrative and organizational procedure was not standardized throughout the entire history of the late Roman army. Between the fourth and the sixth centuries, there was continual modification and adaptation, most of which is unfortunately not well documented. Ammianus described the army of the fourth century, and Procopius that of the sixth, but as Jones points out (1964, 607) it was in the fifth century when the major changes took place, precisely that period not covered by the sources. During this time the western army disappeared and the eastern army was modified to emerge as the much altered Byzantine army. Thus modern scholars glimpse only the beginning and the end, and are forced to make intelligent guesses as to what happened during the transitional phase.

The overall size of the military establishment is not definitely known. One of the problems is that the size of individual units is not attested, and another difficulty is that the army would not remain at a standard strength at all times. Before and after campaigns, numbers would vary immensely, and in any case paper strengths are of little use for practical purposes. This is illustrated in a letter written by General Berthier to Napoleon, from Dijon in April 1800, at the start of the Marengo campaign. Berthier estimated that he would cross the Alps with about 30,000 men, 'as a general reckons, not as clerks do, a difference you will be able to appreciate more than anyone else' (Yorck von Wartenburg 1902, vol. I, 174).

Ancient sources are not especially valuable in estimating overall army figures, even when they appear to be quite specific. No manpower statistics are given for the units listed in the *Notitia*, so it is not possible to arrive at anything more than an informed speculation by using that source alone. Various figures are available for the size of expeditionary armies. Orosius (7.36.6) gives a total of 5000 men for the campaign against Gildo, and Claudian (*De Bello Gildonico* 418–23) lists the troops which took part in the war. Using the two sources in conjunction, Varady (1961, 367–8) concluded that the strength of a legion was 1200 and that of the units of *auxilia* 500. But an army on campaign is not necessarily representative of a standing army; it is not unknown for unit size to be increased when being placed on a war footing. The Byzantine writer John Lydus (*De Mensibus* 1.27) says that Diocletian's army numbered 389,704 men and the fleets contained 45,562, but unfortunately he gives no dates, and it is quite certain that the army as Diocletian found it in 284 was greatly increased by the time of his abdication twenty years later. Despite these drawbacks, attempts have been made to produce a figure for the strength of the army. Mommsen (1889, 257) concluded that there were 554,500 men in service, which agrees more or less with Jones' much later estimate of 600,000 (1964, 683). It should be remembered that this is at best an academic exercise, and the figures given can be neither absolutely accurate nor constantly applicable from the fourth to the sixth century.

The army was distributed through the provinces and on the frontiers, and divided into different categories of troops, with a graded hierarchy. The most important troops with the highest status were the *scholae* or Imperial Guard. According to the *Notitia* the *scholae* were divided into five units in the west and seven in the east. Each unit may have been approximately 500 strong, but the earliest verifiable figures belong to the reign of Justinian, and may or may not be applicable in retrospect. When the western emperors ceased to command the armies in person, the *scholae* declined in importance, and were finally abolished by Theoderic. In the east, the *scholae* declined in importance as fighting troops, becoming purely bodyguard and ornamental parade-ground units. The Emperor Leo replaced them with a mere 300 *excubitores* (Jones 1964, 613–4; 658).

The *protectores domestici* originated from the first body of *protectores* raised by Gallienus, consisting of men loyal to himself and acknowledged by this distinction. The title denoted neither a rank nor a specific function. The institution became a kind of officer school. Men who were promoted from the ranks became *protectores* before going on to other appointments. In order to gain experience, some of them could be sent to join the staffs of various field commanders, as Ammianus relates (15.5.22). He was one of the ten *protectores domestici* in the entourage of Ursicinus when he was sent to replace Silvanus, not such a peaceful undertaking as it ought to have been in normal circumstances.

The additional title *domestici* dates from some time in the third century, to distinguish those men in the Emperor's immediate circle from the ordinary *protectores*. They were not strictly a bodyguard, but were treated as one unit even though they were split up and widely dispersed for practical purposes (Jones 1964, 636). After some years' service in the ordinary *protectores* soldiers went on to the command of a unit. Flavius Abinnaeus was appointed *praefectus alae* at Dionysias in Egypt after serving as a protector, and so was his successor (*Abinnaeus Archive*, nos 1 and 2).

There were further changes in the fifth century, when the *protectores* became a more static body. In the past, the men passing through the service presumably had no statutory term to complete, but would be promoted according to personal merit and the exigencies of the army. This flexibility disappeared in the fifth century, and men were appointed for almost life-long terms, which meant that the use of the *protectores* as a staff college came to an end.

The hierarchy of the other units of the army can be deduced from the army lists and the law codes. The codes distinguish between *comitatenses* and *limitanei*, indicating the the former troops were superior. The *limitanei* may have declined as time went on but they were still part of the regular army, and not merely a hereditary militia tied to their lands, as has been suggested. If they were so low in status, it would hardly have been appropriate to transfer whole troops of them into the *comitatenses*, as was done on occasion (Jones 1964, 649–54). This simple division into frontier troops and mobile army, however, does not sufficiently refine the argument. In the *Notitia* the units of *palatini* take precedence over all other units. These were originally troops of the field army attached to the Emperor, and they retained their higher status even when transferred to the regional armies. Next in importance came the *comitatenses* consisting of cavalry vexillations and the legions, then the *limitanei*, consisting of the higher grade *ripenses* and the lower grade *alares* and *cohortales*. There was no rigid uniformity throughout the Empire. In Britain, on the upper Danube and on the eastern frontier, there were units styled simply *equites*, meaning vexillations of cavalry, then legions, and the old-style *alae* and cohorts. Further down the Danube the cavalry units were called *cunei equitum* and the infantry units *auxilia*. The variety of terminology, coupled with the transfers of frontier troops into the field armies and vice versa, all serve to complicate the issue.

The high command

Constantine divested the praetorian prefects of their military powers, replacing them with the newly created *magister peditum* and *magister equitum*. The only units which did not come under the command of these officers were the *scholae*, which came under the direct supervision of the Emperor, via the *magister officiorum*, a civilian official, who probably commanded solely in an administrative capacity, and never in the field. Constantine probably intended that the two military *magistri* should be equal in power and influence, to provide a counter balance to each other, as the consuls were intended to do. Collegiality was a long established tradition in the Roman Republic and Empire (O'Flynn 1983, 4). It seems that more than one *magister* could be appointed. There were at least two *magistri equitum* under Valentinian (Ammianus 39.3.7). The senior of these officers who were in the presence of the Emperor added *in praesenti* or *praesentalis* to their titles. Eventually, in the west, *magister peditum praesentalis* gained the ascendancy over all other officers, and the division between cavalry and infantry commanders disappeared, probably after Merobaudes gathered all power to himself in the reign of Gratian and Valentinian II (O'Flynn 1983, 5–6). Certainly Arbogast and Stilicho enjoyed unrivalled power while in this office. In the *Notitia*, the western *magister peditum praesentalis* had command of all the troops, whether they were cavalry or infantry, and of the *laeti* and of the fleet as well, giving him supremacy over the whole western military establishment (*Not. Dig. Oc.* XXVIII 23; XXXVI 7; Grosse 1920, 183–4; O'Flynn 1983, 4).

The titles *magister peditum, equitum, militum* and so on, were inconsistently applied, even to the same commander. In the law codes, during the same year (349) Silvanus is addressed as both *magister equitum et peditum* and *comes et magister militum* (*Cod. Th.* 7.1.2; 8.7.3). Other forms include *magister utriusque militiae* and simply *magister militum*, both of which titles imply by their terminology an all-embracing command.

The men who filled these posts were outranked only by the prefect of the city and the praetorian prefects. High on the social scale, they were superlatively addressed as *Perfectissimi, Clarissimi, Illustrissimi*, and later as *Magnifici* and *Gloriosi*. In the west, the *magister peditum praesentalis* held the title *Patricius* from 416 onwards (*Cod. Th.* 15.14.14), an extremely prestigious rank, which survived into the Middle Ages simply as 'the Patrician'. He was not only in command of all the armed forces, but when the Emperors dwindled in power and importance, he became de facto Regent as well. The Eastern Empire was differently organized. There, the *magistri militum* never attained the preponderance of power and influence that their western colleagues held. Even when the emperors were not military men themselves, they still retained the overall command of the army, and as an added safeguard, the power of the praetorian prefects was always greater than that of the *magistri*. Thus the command was greatly centralized in the west and decentralized in the east (Mommsen 1889, 264–5; Grosse 1920, 186).

There were regional *magistri* such as the *magister equitum per Gallias* (*Not. Dig. Oc.* I. 7; VII. 63.111.166). During the war against Eugenius, Theodosius I temporarily increased the number of *magistri* to five (Zosimus 4.27.1–2). Henceforth there were two *magistri praesentales* at court and three regional ones, styled *magister peditum et equitum per Orientem, per Thracias*, and *per Illyricum* (*Not. Dig. Or.* I. 6–8; VII–IX).

The immediate substructure of the commands of the *magistri* is imperfectly understood owing to lack of evidence. Each would have an *officium* of administrative staff, as the law codes reveal. In 441, there were 300 *officiales* serving the *magister militum* Ariovindus (*Nov. Th.* 7.4). The titles and functions of these officials is unknown, and it is not certain whether the information concerning Ariovindus' offices is standard over the whole Empire. The administrative establishments of each *magister* may have differed, tailor-made perhaps, to suit the needs of each region.

The generals

In the early Empire, the military commanders in the provinces were at one and the same time generals and civil governors. When the civil and military functions were separated, the civil government of the provinces was left in the hands of the *praeses*, and the troops were commanded by the *dux* (pl. *duces*), meaning literally leader, whence we derive the English title Duke and the Italian Il Duce. This change from the old-style provincial government to the new did not take place overnight, and naturally there were exceptions to the rule, whereby the *praeses* commanded troops or the *dux* took over civil functions.

Dux was originally a title given to an officer acting in a temporary capacity above his usual rank. He could be in command of a collection of troops in transit from one point to another, or in temporary command of a complete unit. In the third century the *dux* became a regular officer, often associated with *comes* as attested in the sources where the titles are listed side by side (*Cod. Th.* 6.14.3; 7.1.9).

Comes, literally companion, was an honourable title bestowed on members of the Emperor's entourage. It did not automatically bestow a rank at the same time. Later it denoted a variety of regular functions, in both civilian government and military affairs. Constantine formalized and graded the *comitava*. The *comes sacrarum largitionum*, for instance, was the late Roman equivalent of a finance minister, and the *comes domesticorum* was the commander of the *protectores domestici*. When the command of the *comes* was a military one, he was styled *comes rei militaris*, a suitably vague title with no indication of rank or importance, which could vary from a minor frontier command to the equivalent of a *magister militum*. Since there seems to be no sharp division between *duces* and *comites* in command of frontier troops (Grosse 1920, 156; Varady 1961, 355), it is convenient to discuss them in conjunction.

With the exception of the *comitatenses* and *palatini*, who were under the direct command of the *magistri*, the *duces* commanded the rest of the provincial troops. Their authority could extend over more than one province, where frontier conditions required it. His title if he held command over one province was simply that of the provincial name, such as *dux Africae* or *dux Aegypti*; when it extended over a frontier area comprising more than one province he might be styled *dux limitis* (*Cod. Th.* 7.22.5; *Not. Dig. Oc.* I. 38; 39), but these titles were not rigidly standardized, for instance the *dux limitis Scythiae* (*CIL* III 764=*ILS* 4103) was in charge of the frontier of one province, combining both forms of title. The law codes also attest the use of the title *comes limitis* (*Cod. Th.* 8.5.52)

The *duces* were responsible to the *magistri militum*, but also had the right to correspond directly with the Emperor (Grosse 1920, 158). The duties of the *dux* are outlined in the law codes (*Cod. Th.* 7.1.9; *Nov. Th.* 24.1). He was primarily responsible for the military protection of the sector of the frontier or other area assigned to him, and as part of this task he was to ensure that fortifications were built where necessary and the existing ones were kept in good repair. Valentinian I was particularly interested in this last instruction, threatening the Frankish Teutomeres, *dux Daciae ripensis*, that if he neglected his duties in this respect, he would be brought back to the frontier and compelled to erect at his own expense the fortifications which he should have erected with the aid of the soldiers and at public expense (*Cod. Th.* 15.1.13).

The *dux* also had charge of recruiting and assigning men to units. Constantine insisted that the *duces* should inspect all recruits who had already been approved, and weed out those who were unsuitable (*Cod. Th.* 7.22.5). The *dux* supervised the collection and distribution of provisions for the troops, and since the administration of the food supply was the responsibility of the praetorian prefects, the staff of the ducal *officium* had to send quarterly returns to them (*Cod. Th.* 11.25). In addition to these military and administrative skills, the *dux* fulfilled a judicial function, since soldiers who committed crimes could be tried only in the military courts, by 'the person to whom the direction of military affairs has been entrusted' (*Cod. Th.* 2.1.2), a phrase which neatly circumvents the need to distinguish between *comes* and *dux*.

Until the reign of Valentinian I, the *dux* was usually a man of equestrian rank. Consistently showing favour to military men, Valentinian elevated the *duces* to senatorial rank (*Cod. Th.* 6.23.1; 6.24.11). The various *duces* who are attested in the sources must not be regarded as permanent fixtures. Command structure was altered as time passed and defence requirements changed. The *dux Aegypti* was appointed from the reign of Constantine until about 384, when he was replaced by a *comes rei militaris per Aegyptum* (*Not. Dig. Or.* XXVIII 13). The *dux Africae*, a *vir perfectissimus*, appeared at the beginning of the fourth century and was replaced very early, about 330, by a higher ranking officer who was a senator and *vir clarissimus*. The *dux Arabiae* is listed in the *Notitia* as both *dux* and *praeses* with two distinct sets of staff (Grosse 1920, 163). In Britain, there were two commands, the *dux Britanniarum* in the north (*Not. Dig. Oc.* XL) and the *comes litoris Saxonicis* (*Not. Dig. Oc.* XXVIII), who had charge of the south-eastern parts of the island and also once had command of the northern coast of Gaul, sensibly uniting the two areas affected by Saxon raids. These commands are confusing, because the *Notitia* seems to reflect a situation in Britain that predates the late fourth century (Grosse 1920, 166; 173).

Duces in Gaul were the *dux tractus Armoricani et Nervicani*, and *dux Belgicae secundae* (*Not. Dig. Oc.* I 45; 46; XXXVII: XXXVIII). No other source attests them. The command of the first extended over five small provinces, which contained one cohort and several troops called *milites*; the second *dux* commanded the fleet on the Sambre, and one unit of cavalry and one of infantry.

On the Danube, there were four *duces*, of Dacia ripensis (*Not. Dig. Or.* I 55), Moesia prima (*Or.* I 56), Moesia secunda (*Or.* I 52), and Scythia (*Or.* I 53). The Moesian and Scythian commands were later temporarily united (*Cod. Th.* 7.17.1).

This list is by no means complete, but serves to illustrate the sometimes transitory nature of ducal commands, the interchangeability of *duces* and *comites*, and the varied extent of their authority. This suggests that there was a certain flexibility in the appointments, all supervised by the Emperor according to the suitability of the candidates and the needs of Imperial defence.

Officers and men

Army officers were usually styled *praepositi*, *tribuni* or *praefecti*. *Praepositus* was at first not a rank, but was a title used where none other existed (Smith 1972b, 264) to indicate an officer temporarily in charge of a troop, most often vexillations while in transit to and from a war zone. Later it was applied to men in charge of standing units, such as the *numeri* of the early Empire. The men in such posts were not all of the same status; they could be prefects or tribunes, or in the case of the *numeri*, legionary centurions. *Praepositus* was a widely used title in the late Empire, and like *comes* it embraced a wide variety of commands, differing in importance. There were *praepositi* in the *scholae* (*Cod. Th.*

6.13.1), and *praepositi legionis* (*Cod. Th.* 7.20.10; *CIL* III 3653), as well as *praepositi cohortis*. Rather less specific are the *praepositi militum, equitum* and *auxilii* (*CIL* III 5670a=*ILS* 774; *CIL* III 3370=*ILS* 2787; *ILS* 2786). A *praepositus* was placed in charge of the settlements of the *laeti* (*Cod. Th.* 7.20.10). The title was sometimes used in place of prefect, as demonstrated in the case of Flavius Abinnaeus, who was in reality prefect of an *ala*, but was addressed in correspondence as *praepositus*.

The African frontier was divided into sectors each commanded by a *praepositus limitis* (*Not. Dig. Oc.* XXV 21–36; XXX 12–19; XXI 18–28; 31). These officers were subordinate to the *duces* of each of the three provinces of Africa, Mauretania and Tripolitania.

The title of tribune was also a widely used term denoting men of different rank. The highest ranking were tribunes of the *scholae*, answerable to the *magister officiorum*. Besides these there were the tribunes of the cavalry vexillations, *auxilia* and legions of the field army, and of the cohorts of the *limitanei*. Some tribunes performed special tasks, such as the *tribuni civitatis* in Egypt, who combined military, administrative and judicial functions, as if he were a governor.

The *Notitia* regularly lists prefects of legions in the Eastern and Western Empires. *Praefecti alae* are found only in the west (*Not. Dig. Oc.* XXVI 13; XXXV 23; 26; 33; XL 35; 37; 38; 45; 55). Flavius Abinnaeus was appointed *praefectus alae* at Dionysias, and although he was often addressed as *praepositus*, he was sometimes styled *praefectus castrorum Dionisiados* (*Abinnaeus Archive*, 14–15). If there was any strict value to be placed upon such titles, it clearly had not impressed itself upon the populace at large nor the bureaucrats who corresponded with Abinnaeus.

In the new army units of the late third and the fourth centuries, the internal command structure was altered and the junior officers given different titles. In the old-style units the usual officers, such as decurions and centurions, were retained, and these presumably carried out their various duties as they had always done. Despite the impression given by the administrative sources that old and new units operated together, this is not certain; all that we have in many cases are the names, which in themselves mean next to nothing. Far too little is known about the new units of the late Roman army to be certain whether there were vast changes in administrative organization, though at a guess, tightened bureaucratic control would necessitate alternative divisions of labour. During the high Empire, from the late Republic to roughly the end of the third century, it is possible to divide the known officers into those with mainly administrative functions and those who commanded in the field. This is unfortunately not so clear in the late Roman army. The problem is compounded by an almost complete lack of definite dates pinpointing the moment when officers' titles came into and went out of use, and uncertainty as to whether some titles represented merely regional or short-lived fashions, with no direct relevance to other sectors of the Empire, or to different epochs.

The highest ranking junior officer of the late Roman army was the *primicerius*, found in the service of the *duces* of Africa and Sardinia (*Cod. Just.* 1.27.2), and among the *protectores domestici* (*Cod. Th.* 6.24.7; 8; 9) and the *scholae* (*Cod. Just.* 12.29.2).

Next in rank came the *senator*, an officer about whom very little is known, except that he was to be found in the *scholae* and some infantry units (*CIL* V 8760; VIII 17414; *Nov. Th.* 21). He was senior to the *ducenarius*, about whom there is more specific information, since according to Vegetius (2.8) he commanded 200 men. This officer served in the *scholae*, and in cavalry and infantry units. It is not certain whether the rank still existed in the fifth century (Grosse 1920, 119).

The *centenarius*, by analogy with the above named officer, ought to have commanded 100 men, like the centurions who had all but disappeared in the fourth century, except in the old-style units. Lydus mentions *centenarii* (*De Mag.* 1.48; 3.2.7.21), and they were found in the *scholae*, the ducal *officia* as well as in infantry (*CIL* V 8740) and cavalry units (*CIL* III 14406a, *cataphractarii*; V 8758, *sagittarii*). *Centenarii* also served as *agentes in rebus* and the title was used in the Visigothic laws to describe a commander of 100 men (Jones 1964, 258; 587).

Two of the lower-grade officers were the *biarchus* and *circitor*, whose duties are not known, but may have been concerned with the food supply. The earliest attested *biarchus* is *ILS* 2805 dating to 327, and attesting one Flavius Iovianus who was *bearchus* [*sic*] *draconarius*, or standard bearer with the rank of *biarchus*. The *draconarius* carried the dragon standard; the old-style *signiferi* were still in existence, possibly equated with the less well attested *semafori* (*CIL* V 8752).

The unavoidable conclusion is that there are huge gaps in our knowledge, not only about the functions of those officers whose titles have come down to us, but also about an indeterminate number of officers who have completely disappeared from the record.

Administration

Any army, whether permanent or temporary, demands a vast administration if it is to function properly. A standing army not only needs to supply itself with the necessaries of life, and to document all its activities from day to day, but also inevitably finds itself embroiled in matters of arbitration and lawsuits with other military establishments and with the civilian population. The administration of the buildings and the land in military ownership would have been staggering in isolation, without the abundant details of personnel and finance, all of which kept many officials in permanent employment.

Administration was carried on at three levels: Empire wide, provincial, and locally for each unit. All three were inextricably linked. The praetorian prefects were ultimately responsible for Imperial administration of the armed forces, principally for supplies and recruitment. Rations and recruitment are discussed in another chapter; here a brief description of the supply system is given.

The supply of food to the army was part of the taxation system, and reflects the work of Diocletian at the time when he took over a bankrupt Empire on the verge of collapse. Collection of food for the soldiers (*annona*) and for horses (*capitus*) was undertaken three times per year, and transported to state granaries (*horrea*) which were fortified and guarded by the army, but the officials who supervised the apportionment and distribution of food were civilians (Jones 1964, 626). Contributions were differently assessed in different parts of the Empire according to farming methods and needs of the army.

Transport could be a problem. The majority of army units were clustered together on the frontiers, and though most forts had quite large territories in which to grow their own food, and in addition efforts were made to supply them from their own regions, sometimes supplies had to be brought from distant provinces to the frontier storehouses. The wastage rate from decay, and no doubt from theft, was presumably quite high. The mobile army had no permanent forts, and so caused different problems of supply. It is not improbable that the field army could eat its way through the surrounding countryside in a matter of days, and it is only imperfectly known how the military authorities overcame this problem. Armies on campaign would require strenuous service from their supply systems. In 358, Constantius decreed that on campaign, soldiers should receive normal rations two days out of three, and bread and wine every third day (*Cod. Th.* 7.4.4). In the following year, he authorized soldiers to take twenty days' rations from the storehouses to sustain them on campaign (*Cod. Th.* 7.4.5).

Distribution of rations was controlled as tightly as possible, and much ink was expended on the writing of warrants to authorize troops to draw rations, without which the official in charge was not supposed to issue supplies. A potential squabble is documented in the law of 357 issued by Constantius and Julian to the praetorian prefect (*Cod. Th.* 7.4.3). The *comes rei militaris* in Africa had appropriated supplies from the storehouses on his own authority, and the law states that he is to be firmly reminded that he must go through the proper channels, first informing the *vicarius* (the deputy of the praetorian prefect), in writing, of the number of subsistence allowances to be drawn and to whom they must be issued. One can imagine the frustration of the *comes* in question on receipt of this piece of circuitous bureaucracy, sent to him on Imperial authority via the offices of the praetorian prefect. How the Romans would have loved telephones.

There was naturally still room for corruption, and the law codes are largely concerned with prevention of fraudulent practices. One method of preventing any unit from drawing more than it was entitled to was to check on actual unit strength as opposed to paper strength. The offices of the praetorian prefect received reports on these and all other matters via the staff of the *duces* and *comites*. If the allowances from storehouses were checked, there remained the exploitation of the provincials by the soldiers, who were ever alert for an opportunity to extort food and whatever they could get, wherever and whenever they could get it.

Gradually, the delivery of supplies in kind, which was at best a cumbersome procedure, was commuted into money payments. Under Valentinian I the *limitanei* received supplies for nine months and money payments for the remaining three (*Cod. Th.* 7.4.14). During the fifth century, commutation into money payments proceded faster in the west than in the east, and was simplified by the substitution of a standard rate of payment, whereas in the east there was a varied rate of conversion, based on the local market prices and other considerations (Jones 1964, 460–1).

The transition from payments in kind to payments in gold is highlighted in a law of 409 (*Cod. Th.* 7.4.30), in which it is stated that once the commutation figures have been agreed, then the requisitioning of supplies in kind should cease. But the staff of the *officium* of the *dux* in Palestine had been attempting to extract supplies, and in consequence the *dux* was threatened with a hefty fine.

As Jones points out (1964, 461), the tax payments in cash enabled the praetorian prefects to build up a surplus in gold, which could be used to finance wars. In addition the wastage rate inherent in the old system could be avoided, and transport difficulties considerably lessened.

Of the officials who worked in the offices of the provincial commanders, very little is known. There are lists of these minor officials in the *Notitia* and in the *Codex Justinianus* (1.27.2), but unfortunately there is only a partial correspondence between the titles of the various staff. Some of the men working for the army would be civilians, as is common in most army administrations. Records of the men in service, daily returns of the whereabouts of each man, details of their pay, and of unit finances would be kept at each headquarters. There would also be judicial matters to attend to, and the administrative sections of all but the smallest units were probably divided into subsections.

Records kept by the units would probably be duplicated in the *officia* of the regional commanders. The head of the administrative bureaux, whether of the *magister militum*, the *dux* or *comes*, was the *princeps*. These men wielded great power, simply by dint of their assimilation of knowledge. There may have been a *princeps*, of much lower rank, in charge of unit administration. Financial matters were dealt with by the *numerarii*, usually two to a unit. Their reputation was presumably quite low, if the number of laws concerning them is any guide (Grosse 1920, 130). The other clerical assistants were perhaps called by various names at different times, and in different provinces, which may explain why there are a few officials who appear to have been short-lived, or only attested in one region. For instance, the *a libellis*, *subscribendarius* and *regerendarius* are probably three names for the same functionary, none of them attested before the fourth century. Their duties were probably concerned with supplies (Grosse 1920, 135).

The picture presented here is one of a well-organized army, tightly administered and controlled, and indeed, potentially, the late Roman army could have been just as bureaucratically efficient as its predecessor of the first three centuries AD. But it is probably only partially true. It has already been pointed out that the fifth century, the least well-documented era, is the one where most far-reaching changes occur in the army, and in the opinion of some scholars it is the century when everything begins to fall apart. Among contemporary writers of the late Empire, there was a definite backward-looking trend. Vegetius, the Anonymous and Zosimus all lament the lack of organization and the decline of administrative skills which had made the army great in the 'good old days'.

The sixth-century army

The terminology used in the sixth century was either purely Greek, or Latin transliterated into Greek, which became the official eastern language in 439 (Rémondon 1964, 212). The law codes, however, continued to be produced in Latin, despite the fact that sentences were pronounced in court in Greek.

The basic fourth-century army is still recognizable in the sixth century, with *limitanei* on the frontiers and *comitatenses* (though they were not called by this name) in the field army. The *scholae* and *protectores* still existed, and so did the *foederati*, but it has been pointed out elsewhere that though the same terms were employed to describe various units of the army, their tactical function had undergone some changes. The *scholae* and *protectores* had become show-case troops, and the *foederati* were now regular troops.

The changes were mostly the result of prolonged evolution, culminating in the work of Justinian. First of all he created more *magistri militum*, dividing the command of the *magister militum per Orientem* by splitting off some of his territory under a *magister militum per Armeniam*. The *magister militum per Africam* had jurisdiction over Sardinia and Corsica as well. He was eventually replaced by a new official, the exarch, a much more powerful individual, who embodied both civil and military functions, with the civil subordinated to the military. Thus Justinian reversed the process of separation of the two branches of the Imperial government, though the first exarch is not attested until 591 (Grosse 1920, 297). In origin, the title did not connote any specific rank; in late sixth-century practice, the exarchs of Italy and Africa were the equivalent of kings, attending to civil, military, judicial and religious matters alike, and answerable to no one except the Emperor.

Justinian carried out repairs to the frontier works, and built new ones. He hoped to create a system of defence whereby the *limitanei* could repel attacks without assistance from the field armies. He accordingly increased the number of *duces* in command of the *limitanei*, with the preponderance on the eastern frontier facing Persia. After the reconquest of Africa and Italy, he reintroduced *duces* on those frontiers as well, though the evidence for Africa is greater than that for the north Italian frontier.

Recruitment to the units of the frontier and field armies seems to have been local and also voluntary. Jones discerned that all references to conscription had been edited out of the law codes, and yet Justinian was able to keep his army, admittedly smaller than its predecessors, up to strength, presumably by using volunteers. The proportion of Romans to barbarians in the regular army was higher than it had been in the past. The absence of the apathy that was so marked in the fourth and fifth centuries may be explained by the fact that local recruitment soothed men's worries about being torn from their homes to serve in distant provinces. Instead they would be able to serve near their homes, which they would have a vested interest in defending (Jones 1964, 668–71). On the other hand, this cannot be the only explanation of Justinian's success in keeping his armies up to strength. If men were happiest serving near their homes, some explanation must be found for the fact that Justinian was able to send armies to fight wars abroad. One important factor which may have played a part was the relatively stable situation compared to the disruptions of the past; perhaps the soldiers were much more enthusiastic about taking part in wars of aggression, with all their potential for adventure and lucrative gain, than they were about fighting desperate wars of defence, where the only perk was survival. As for the quality of the soldiers' daily lives, either at home or abroad, there had been no radical improvement. Pay was often in arrears, leading to mutinies now and then.

The employment of barbarians had not ceased, even though the percentage of barbarians to Romans was lower. Procopius describes the erstwhile *foederati* as troops serving under the obligations of a treaty like the Goths of the fourth century (*History of the Wars* 3.11.2–5). Since his readers would know what he meant by *foederati* in his own day, he does not bother to explain the differences. The units, now regular, and commanded by Roman officers, still contained many Goths, and also Heruls (Jones 1964, 664). At the same time these barbarians were also recruited as 'allies' (*symmachoi*), who were like the old-style federates, serving under their own chiefs for the duration of a campaign. Procopius writes of the Huns, who contributed 600 mounted bowmen, and of another 200 Huns and 300 Moors as allies (*History of the Wars* 3.11.11; 5.5.4).

Finally, the *bucellarii* had not been suppressed, probably because the private armies of some of the generals provided a lucrative source of trained men who could fight in wars. They formed a large part of the expeditionary armies, and were bound to the Emperor as well as their general by the swearing of an oath of allegiance (Grosse 1920, 289).

Justinian's conquests were accomplished by means of strict financial stringency and determination. They were not long lasting, however, and he failed in his efforts to re-establish the Roman Empire. The army with which he set out to achieve them would have been only partially recognizable to Diocletian or Constantine, and the army which he handed on to his successors had changed even more, meriting the label Byzantine rather more than Roman.

IV

RECRUITMENT

The Fourth and Fifth Centuries

The regular army

CITIZENS

As the *Theodosian Code* outlines, certain groups of people were debarred from military service (7.13.8). Slaves were only enlisted in times of emergency, such as occurred in 357 with the rebellion of Gildo, when Roman senators were urged to send some of their slaves into service (Jones 1964, 614). Freedom and two *solidi* were used as incentives for slaves to join up in 406, and those who had gained military experience by having soldiers as masters were particularly sought after (Jones 1964, 614). In general, however, those who were involved in degraded professions, such as cooks, bakers and innkeepers, were excluded from military service, as were freedmen. Citizens who held respectable positions, for example provincial officials and *curiales*, were also exempt.

Although some men undoubtedly joined the army voluntarily, the majority entered under the label of conscripts. A rule in existence in 313, probably created by Diocletian, decreed that veterans and the sons of soldiers were obliged to sign up if they were physically capable (*Cod. Th.* 7.23.1). This law was altered by Constantine in 326, when he offered the sons of veterans the choice of enrolling in their local *curia* or serving in the army. This change did not exist long, before the law reverted to that outlined in 313.

An annual conscription appears to have been initiated under Diocletian in which, as Ammianus records (31.4.4), a tax (*aurem tironicum*) was sometimes substituted instead of levying men from a province. The levy of recruits relied on the same assessment system as prevailed for the land tax, resulting in this particular tax falling squarely on the shoulders of the rural population. A recruit was obviously an expensive commodity, and only the largest landowners were individually liable to provide one or more men. Consortia (*temones* or *capitula*) were formed from smaller landowners who, although being collectively responsible, would take it in turns to provide one recruit.

Abuse of this system was inevitable, with governors making fortunes by charging landowners enormous commutation rates, and then, as suggested by Jones (1964, 616), securing recruits by offering bounties at lower rates to casual volunteers. In 375 Valens, in an attempt to make the tax fairer, and thus less prone to corruption, ruled that a recruit was worth 30 *solidi*, plus a further 6 which he required for kit and expenses. This 36 *solidi* would then be divided, according to assessment, amongst the consortium, who in turn would reimburse the member who was actually supplying the recruit (*Cod. Th.* 7.13.7). Furthermore, he ruled that the landowner supply the recruit from registered tenants or their sons, it being strictly forbidden to substitute vagrants.

From the fourth century onwards, the Roman army suffered from a lack of recruits. The devastation of frontier zones, particularly along the Danube and the Rhine, during the third century, resulting in the reduced ability of these regions to supply recruits, has been held as a primary reason for the manpower shortage which affected the Empire during the late period (Boak 1955, 157–62). Depopulation from plague is also felt to have contributed to the problem (Gilliam 1961). As Liebeschuetz stated, however, these factors can only form part of the answer (1991, 11).

There is abundant evidence to show that military service had become unpopular amongst the citizens. A series of laws were created to deal with the problem of self-mutilation, in which men resorted to cutting off their thumbs in order to avoid enlistment: Ammianus states that this practice was alien to the Gauls, but prevalent in Italy (15.12.3). In 313, Constantine declared that veterans' sons who mutilated themselves in this way, were to be ordered to serve in the city councils (*Cod. Th.* 7.22.1). Severe action was taken by an enraged Valentinian in 368 when he ordered those who committed this crime to be burnt alive (*Cod. Th.* 7.13.5). Theodosius in 381, three years after the disastrous battle of Adrianople, realizing that a man with no thumbs was better than no man at all, decreed that they should still be forced to serve, adding that if mutilated men were offered by the taxpayer, two were required in the place of one 'whole' recruit (*Cod. Th.* 7.13.10).

Although there was obviously a recognized problem which required some legislative solution, it is probably unwise to believe that such a practice is indicative of an extreme loathing or fear of military service. During all periods, a percentage of men have endeavoured to avoid enlistment, or at least evade active service once enrolled. There are numerous reported cases of the latter from both World Wars, particularly the First (*Burgoyne Diaries* 1985, 44–5). More recently, at the start of the Gulf War, staggering figures were quoted concerning the number of American troops who were sent home on sick leave due to gun-shot wounds to the feet before the enemy were engaged. Whilst it is possible that some of these injuries were legitimate accidents, the very number involved suggests that many were deliberately self-inflicted.

Another problem with which the state was faced was recruits escaping in transit to their allotted units. A circular letter to all city police officers from the Thebaid to Antioch from a *comes Orientis* under Valens states that: 'Having received the recruits being sent from the diocese of Egypt from the recruitment officers you will convey them to Antioch at your peril, knowing that if any of them escapes, the person through whose negligence he is proved to have run away will not get off without punishment' (Jones 1964, 618; *Chr. I.* 469). To reduce the risk of escape, recruits were sometimes incarcerated each night in the city prison where they broke their journey (*V. Pach.* 4).

Despite rigorous precautions, desertions were commonplace, particularly, it seems, amongst those recently enlisted: 'We have learned that before they [the recruits] have become associated with Our victorious eagles, many recruits depart, either to the places from which they were inducted or wherever they please, and that other men, moreover, desert who have been entered on the lists as beginners in military service, although they may not yet be said to have served under Our standards.' (*Cod. Th.* 7.18.9.1). Three further laws in the *Theodosian Code* specifically refer to this problem, 7.18.4; 6; 14.1, dating respectively from 380, 382, 403, whilst the example quoted above dates to 396.

Men had always dodged enlistment, but no doubt their absence proved less of a problem to earlier emperors, for whom there was no acute shortage of recruits, be it conscripts or volunteers. The fact that later emperors found it necessary to enlist even mutilated men suggests desperation, and not purely moral indignation at their cowardly behaviour.

Ostensibly, joining the army was still quite an attractive prospect. Privileges were awarded to those who enrolled. On taking the oath, a soldier who joined the cohorts or the *alae* became exempt from paying the poll tax (*capitatio*). A constitution of 311 records that those who served in the legions or vexillations, however, received *capitatio* exemption for four people (Jones 1964, 617). *Comitatenses* and *ripenses* were granted immunity for themselves, their parents, and their wives by Constantine in 325: if any or all of these relatives were lacking, then the amount which would have been paid on their account would be deducted from the tax due on their property (*Cod. Th.* 7.20.4). These generous grants were later curtailed, and in 370 Valens reduced the exemption to include only the soldier and his wife (*Cod. Th.* 7.13.6). Five years later this law still applied to the *ripenses*, but *comitatenses* were also granted immunity for their parents after five years in service (*Cod. Th.* 7.13.7.3).

What caused such apathy towards military service amongst the citizens, particularly when the Empire was so seriously threatened? As Liebeschuetz rightly notes, many citizens would not have been aware of the gravity of the situation (1991, 20). Those that were, were primarily concerned with defending their home and village, rather than enlisting in the army and being posted to foreign lands. Furthermore, the prospect of distant postings was worrisome for those with responsibilities at home, as can be see from the following letter to the *praepositus* Abinnaeus (19): 'I am writing to you about my wife Naomi's brother. He is a soldier's son, and he has been enrolled to go for a soldier. If you can release him again it is a fine thing you do ... since his mother is a widow and has none but him. But if he must serve, please safeguard him from going abroad with the draft for the field army ...' Indeed, there appears to have been a considerable lack of patriotism amongst the citizens, who, disillusioned with their own corrupt government and the extortionate taxes it imposed on them, together with the often outrageous behaviour of the military, actually sided with the invaders, by whom it was felt they would be better treated. Furthermore, landowners were loath to see their tenants go into military service, even during times of obvious need: when the food supply to Rome was being cut off by Gildo, the commander in North Africa, senators in Rome managed to thwart attempts to have their tenants conscripted into the army (Symm. *Ep.* 6.58, 62, 64). The reason for this reluctance is not clear, but Liebeschuetz suggested that the landowners may have hoped to reach a mutually beneficial arrangement with the enemy (1991, 21). A more fundamental and understandable reason may simply have been a desire not to continually have your best workforce taken from you by the army: landowners could only guarantee their financial security if they had fit, competent tenants to work the land.

This apathetic approach by the citizen population towards enlistment resulted in the government having to look elsewhere for recruits, namely amongst the barbarians.

BARBARIANS

Although military service was not popular with the citizens, it held many more attractions for the barbarians, who were enticed into enlistment by the prospect of a higher standard of living. There was also the potential for lucrative advancement within the army: barbarians who held the rank of *magister militum* during the late fourth–early fifth century included Stilicho (Vandal), Fravitta (Goth), and Arbogastes and Bauto (both Franks) (for a full list of barbarian officers and tribunes serving during the fourth century see Mac-Mullen 1988, Appendix A).

One aspect of military life was as unpopular with the barbarians as it had been with the citizens: postings away from home. A serious situation was caused by Constantius, who ordered the Gallic legions under Julian to be transferred to the Orient, ignoring the fact that they had voluntarily enlisted under the promise that they should never have to serve beyond the Alps (Ammianus 20.4.1–5). On hearing the order the soldiers revolted, and hailed Julian Augustus. Julian refused this offer, but permitted the men to stay, saying 'And since it is the charm of your native land that holds you back and you dread strange places with which you are unacquainted, return at once to your homes; you shall see nothing beyond the Alps, since that is displeasing to you' (20.4.16).

By far the greatest number of barbarians who served in the army were Germans, although many other races contributed their share, including Persians, Sarmatians, Armenians and Iberians.

Although it seems probable that most barbarians who joined the army did so on a voluntary basis, there were several other methods by which they could be acquired. It was common practice for emperors to demand recruits from a defeated enemy as a condition of peace (Ammianus 28.5.4; 30.6.1; 31.10.17; Zosimus 2.15.1). Prisoners of war were also drafted into the army, and Zosimus records several instances where recruits were obtained in this way, including an incident under Probus, in which he defeated the Burgundians and the Vandals, and had 'all the captives ... sent across to Britain where they proved very useful to the Emperor in subsequent revolts' (1.68.3).

A large-scale method of supply was by the system of *laeti*, which was apparently confined to Italy and Gaul, and appears to have been in existence in the latter province since the time of the Tetrarchy (Jones 1964, 620). It operated by the government setting aside particular areas of land (*terrae laeticiae*) on which barbarians who sought refuge within the Empire were settled. In return for this right to settle, they were under a hereditary obligation to provide recruits for the army. *Laeti* were usually supervised by military officials: a law of 369 refers to *praepositi* being in charge (*Cod. Th.* 13.11.10), although they were occasionally supervised by civilian authorities when attached to cities. The *Notitia* records twelve *praefecti laetorum* in Gaul (*Oc.* XLII).

A group which may have been similar to the *laeti* is the *gentiles*. The term apparently could denote either barbarians living within the Empire or free tribes living beyond the frontiers. The *Notitia* mentions *gentiles* and *laeti* together, apparently on occasion being commanded by the same officer (Oc. XLII.34; 35; 42; 44).

Gentiles are mentioned several times by Ammianus (14.7.9; 20.8.13; 27.10.12), and the *Notitia* mentions them as serving in the *scholae* of the *magister officiorum* in both the Eastern and Western Empire (*Or.* XI.6; 10; *Oc.* IX.7). The status these troops were accorded is not known, but, because they were always mentioned after *laeti*, Grosse believed that they were inferior to them in rank (1920, 210). Proving such a theory would, however, be difficult without corroborative evidence.

Numerous units within the army were named after barbarian tribes, recruits being initially enlisted from the people from whom the unit title was derived. It is unlikely, however, that local recruitment would have been maintained, and most units, despite their title, probably contained a mixture of both barbarians and Romans, with both groups being commanded by officers (be they Germans or Romans) appointed by the Roman government, and receiving their equipment, pay and rations from Roman officials.

The recruitment of large numbers of Germans into the Roman army should not be viewed as the disastrous policy it has often been branded. Firstly, in the light of the shortage of 'home-grown' recruits, the government was forced to fill the ranks by other means, and no known Roman writer has ever stated that the majority of Germans were anything other than courageous fighters. Secondly, it is difficult in this age of nationalism to comprehend that when Germans on the Roman side were fighting against Germans on the opposing side, there was not a tendency for the two groups of Germans to rally. In reality, however, tribal wars were commonplace, and the only danger for the Romans would arise when Germans belonging to the same tribe were ordered to fight each other. A good illustration of this lack of nationalistic feeling comes from Ammianus, who records an incident where the Frankish officer Silvanus, accused of aspiring to the purple, contemplates returning to his own people, but is warned against this course of action by Laniogaisus, who states that his fellow-countrymen would kill him or would accept a bribe to hand him over to the Emperor (15.5.16). He therefore decides to stay and take his chances amongst the Romans. Ammianus does, however, record several cases where German elements within the army were believed to be responsible for the leakage of information to the enemy (14.10.8; 16.12.2; 31.10.3; 29.4.7). The number of such incidences is not great, and they were a small price to pay for the otherwise exemplary service the Germans gave to the Roman army.

Irregular Troops: Federates (*Foederati*)

Throughout her history, Rome had endeavoured to make mutually beneficial treaties with client kings or the leaders of tribes along her frontiers. In times of need, they would be called upon to supply troops, serving under their native leaders, usually for local campaigns, but occasionally further afield. On completion of a particular campaign, the troops would return to their homes. Occasionally, however, some would be enlisted into the regular army to bring units up to strength, or they might sometimes be formed into regular units. Ammianus records several instances where the Roman army was supplemented in this way, receiving help from Saracens (23.5.1), and Armenians (23.2.2), amongst others. Julian was apparently not wholly in favour of this policy, however, declaring that the Roman Empire should not rely on foreign troops for her defence (Ammianus 32.2.1–2).

By the late Empire, the term *foederati* came to mean barbarian troops from outside *or* inside of the Empire. The upkeep of these troops was subsidized by the Roman government. This *annona foederatica* was apparently initially paid in kind, but was later commuted into yearly payments (Bury 1958, vol. I, 42).

Units of *foederati* were not necessarily composed of men from the same ethnic background. They could be collections of men who had attached themselves to a particular leader.

The disastrous defeat of the eastern Roman army at the battle of Adrianople in 378, however, significantly changed the nature and importance of federate troops. Due to the depletion that the eastern army suffered, Theodosius I was unable to activate sufficient military strength to deal with the resultant Gothic threat. He decided, therefore, in 382 to sign a treaty with the Goths in which the latter were to provide troops in return for being granted permission to settle within the Empire. This time, however, the troops were to be led by their own chiefs, breaking away from the tradition of federates being subject to Roman authority (for a full discussion see Chapter 3).

Bucellarii

Bucellarii, as already mentioned, were soldiers privately employed by civilian or military magnates, such as Stilicho, Rufinus and Aetius. The term literally meant 'biscuit eater', a *bucella* being a military biscuit. Bands of *bucellarii* could contain both Romans and barbarians. The establishment of these groups of retainers lies in the late fourth century.

By the sixth century, *bucellarii* were held in such significant numbers by various military individuals that they often formed substantial additions to the expeditionary armies their employers commanded.

Men who served in the *bucellarii* could often rise to high positions within the army, an example being Sittas, who became *magister militum* of Armenia under Justinian.

The Sixth Century

The *Codex Justinianus* contains no references to conscription, or to the hereditary obligation of the sons of soldiers to serve in the army, implying that under Justinian, recruitment was voluntary. Literary evidence would suggest that when men were needed for expeditionary forces, recruiting drives would be undertaken in areas such as eastern Asia Minor and the Balkans. According to Procopius, Belisarius travelled around the whole of Thrace, and by offering money was able to gather volunteers for enlistment (7.10.1–2). Similarly, in 549 Germanius 'by expending great sums of money, part of which was furnished by the emperor, but most of which he furnished unstintingly from his own resources ... easily succeeded ... in raising a great army of very warlike men in a short space of time... ', from Byzantium, Thrace and Illyricum (Procopius 7.39.16–17).

Evidence for recruitment in the sixth century is scarce, and the few surviving documents all relate to conditions in Egypt. Units of *comitatenses* appear to have recruited men from the local population. A document dating to 508 records that two brothers from Arsinoe, serving as *clibanarii*, were stationed in their home city (*SPP* 20.131).

Based on the evidence of two letters, it appears that only descendants of soldiers were allowed to serve in the *limitanei*, although they were under no obligation to do so (Jones 1964, 669; *Chr.* I, 470; *P. Ryl.* 609).

Although *foederati* as defined above were still employed by Justinian in the sixth century (now known as 'allies'), the term had apparently changed its meaning at some point during the fifth century. Procopius commented on this change, but unfortunately did not fully explain what the term meant at his time of writing, only stating that anyone could be enlisted as *foederati* (1.11.3–4), implying that Romans as well as barbarians could be recruited into such units. Furthermore, certain laws in the *Codex Justinianus* suggests that the *foederati* were now classified as belonging to the regular army (Jones 1964, 664).

The reasons behind the abolition of conscription and hereditary obligation are unclear, since, as Jones remarks, service in the army in the sixth century was as unattractive as it had been in the fourth and fifth centuries (1964, 669–70). Jones believed that the answer may have lain in the worsening economic situation, which resulted in more men being unemployed, and thus turning to the army to earn a living (1964, 670). Localized recruitment into the static units of both the field army and the frontier troops may also have proved an incentive for enlistment, since foreign postings had always been a deterent to recruitment (Jones 1964, 670). Certainly, citizens seemed to have formed a large proportion of the troops serving in the army under Justinian. The situation regarding the ethnic structure of the army fluctuated throughout Justinian's reign, with a gradual increase in the use of barbarian manpower, although this never reached the proportions prevalent during the fourth and early fifth centuries. Teall (1965, 319) believed one of the reasons for this may have been the plague of 542, and its subsequent recurrences, which may have wiped out a third of the population in the east. War weariness, and the associated drain on human resources, particularly during the prolonged Gothic war, probably also forced the Roman government to recruit or hire more barbarian troops to fill the ranks. It was during the Gothic war that Procopius recorded the Gothic leader Totila as expressing the following view on the Roman army, although it was more likely the disgruntled sentiments of the writer (8.30.17–20): 'But the vast number of the enemy [the Romans] is worthy only to be despised, seeing that they present a collection of men from the greatest possible number of nations … . And do not think that the Huns and Lombards and Eruli, hired by them with I know not how much money, will ever endanger themselves for them to the point of death.' The full implications of such a disparate army are discussed in Chapter 9.

The Recruitment Procedure

A period of examination, the *probatio*, had to be undergone before a recruit was entered in the records of a unit. Vegetius states how important it was that this examination was thorough: 'An army never makes fast progress if the selection procedure in approving recruits has been awry. And as we know from practice and experience, it is from this cause that so many defeats have been inflicted on us everywhere by our enemies …' (1.7). He goes on to complain that the recruits levied from landowners (see above) were those that their masters found no use for, and were therefore unfit for service. The job of selecting soldiers was one that should, according to Vegetius, be reserved for great men. The number of available great men was limited, however, and men unsuited to military life did, naturally, slip through the net.

Various physical requirements had to be met by the prospective soldier. A law dating to 326 concerning the sons of veterans, stated that those between the ages of 20 and 25 were eligible (*Cod. Th.* 7.22.2). The age limits were gradually relaxed, however, being firstly lowered to 18 (*Cod. Th.* 7.13.1), and then, with regard to veterans' sons who had managed to dodge their call-up, increased to an upper limit of 35 (Jones 1964, 616). A document dating to 505 concerning the enlistment of *limitanei*, records that the tribune at Hermopolis was ordered by the *dux* of Thebaid (Egypt) to check that the potential recruit Heracleon was, amongst other requirements, 18 years of age before he was entered on the books of the unit (*P. Ryl.* 609). Exactly how strictly these limits were adhered to is questionable, particularly during periods of crisis, such as the fourth century, when recruits were not enlisting in large enough numbers for the army to be choosy.

There were also restrictions regarding height (see below). Vegetius records the qualification for the *alae* and first cohort of the legions as being a minimum Roman measurement of 5ft 10ins (about 1.77m, 5ft 9ins) (1.5). He makes the point, however, that these height requirements were probably reasonable in the golden age of the Empire when demand was easily met by supply, but unrealistic in his time when military service had become an unpopular burden (1.5). That there was truth in this observation may be demonstrated by the fact that in 367 the minimum height qualification was lowered to 5ft 7ins (Roman measurement; 1.70m) (*Cod. Th.* 7.13.3).

According to Vegetius, there were certain physical qualities which the recruiting officer should look for in the candidate (1.6): alert eyes, straight neck, broad chest, muscular shoulders, strong arms, long fingers, small stomach, slender in the buttocks, muscular calves and feet. None of these attributes (except possibly long fingers) would be out of place as requirements for a modern military medical, since a primary concern is that a recruit should show as little tendency as possible to heavy weight gain.

The profession and background of the recruit were also considered important. Vegetius writes that candidates should be rejected if they were fishermen, fowlers, pastry cooks, weavers, or anyone engaged in the textile-mills (1.7). On the other hand, masons, blacksmiths, wainwrights, butchers and hunters were deemed suitable military material. With regard to the background of the recruit, those from the country were considered better suited to arms than those from the city, since the former are more accustomed to hard work, whilst the latter are enured to luxury (1.3). Vegetius states that if necessity demands city-dwellers be enlisted, their lack of suitability can be overcome by subjecting them to drill, enduring heat and dust, carrying heavy loads, feeding them a moderate, rural diet, and camping in tents.

Once the recruit had passed this stage of the selection process, his physical ability was then tested for a minimum of four months (Vegetius 1.8). As has been noted by Milner in his translation of Vegetius (1993, 8–9, n. 4), this period of training is not attested in any other sources, implying that it was either an invention by the author, or that it may have been used by those units who filled vacancies by choosing recruits from a large pool of soldiers.

According to Vegetius, at the end of this four-month period, the recruit was 'tattooed with the pin pricks of the official mark' on his skin, was entered on the records and took the military oath (1.8; 2.5). There is no known evidence for recruits receiving tattoos during the principate, but a document from 295, recording the minutes of a court hearing, implies that soldiers were given some form of identity disc (Davies 1969, 218):

On 12 March 295 in the forum at Theveste, Fabius Victor, together with Maximilianus, was brought before the court, and the prosecutor Pompeianus addressed the court: 'Fabius Victor [defendant's father] has been appointed recruiting officer with Valesianus Quintianus, the *praepositus* of Caesariensis. Maximilianus, the son of Victor, is a good recruit, and since he has the qualities to be approved, I submit that he be measured.' Dio the proconsul said, 'What is your name?' Maximilianus replied, 'What reason have you for wanting to know my name? I cannot serve as a soldier, because I am a Christian.' Dio replied, 'Get him ready.' When he was being got ready, Maximilianus replied, 'I cannot serve as a soldier. I cannot do evil. I am a Christian.' Dio the proconsul replied, 'Let him be measured.' When he had been measured, his height was read out by an equerry: 'He is five feet, ten inches [1.77m].' Dio said to the equerry, 'Give him the *signaculum*.' Maximilianus resisted and replied, 'I do not do so. I cannot serve as a soldier. I am a Christian. I do not accept the *signaculum* of the secular world, and if you give me the *signaculum*, I will break it, because it has no validity. I cannot carry a piece of lead around my neck after the sign of my Lord.' Dio said, 'Remove his name.'

It must therefore be assumed that by Vegetius' time the wearing of a lead disc had been replaced by a tattoo (Jones 1987, 149). A quote from the doctor Aetius implies that by the sixth century, tattooing soldiers was a common practice (8.12): 'They call "tattoos" that which is inscribed on the face or some other part of the body, for example on the hands of soldiers, and they use the following ink. [The recipe follows.] Apply by pricking the places with needles, wiping away the blood, and rubbing in first juice of leek, and then the preparation.'

Having received his tattoo/identity disc, the recruit would then take the military oath (*sacramentum*). According to Watson (1981, 44), the process utilized under the Republic was probably still employed during the Empire. It involved two stages: firstly, one recruit would be chosen to recite the entire oath, a process called the *praeiuratio*, after which the other men would take it in turn to say '*idem in me*' ('The same in my case'), and thus take the oath. Vegetius records the form the oath would take (2.5): 'They swear by God, Christ and the Holy Spirit, and by the Majesty of the Emperor which second to God is to be loved and worshipped by the human race. For since the Emperor has received the name of the "August", faithful devotion should be given, unceasing homage paid him as if to a present and corporeal deity. For it is God whom a private citizen or a soldier serves, when he faithfully loves him who reigns by God's authority. The soldiers swear that they will strenuously do all that the Emperor may command, will never desert the service, nor refuse to die for the Roman State.' Ammianus records the nature that the oath of allegiance to Julian took: '… aiming their swords at their throats, they swore in set terms under pain of dire execrations, that they would endure all hazards for him, to the extent of pouring out their life-blood, if necessity required; their officers and all the emperor's closest advisers followed their example, and pledged loyalty with like ceremony' (21.5.10).

The final task was for the recruit to be entered into the records of the unit he was assigned to (*in numeros referre*). This was legally essential, as it was this act which confirmed the recruit's status as a soldier, as a law in the *Digest* demonstrates (39.1.42): 'An individual starts to have the right to make a will from the time when he has been entered on the records; before that time he does not have the right. Accordingly, men who are not yet on the records, even although they are selected recruits and travel at public expense, they are not yet soldiers. To be classified as soldiers, they must be entered on the records.'

CONDITIONS
OF SERVICE

Pay

The men

THE ISSUE OF EQUIPMENT

By the late period soldiers were primarily paid in kind. Most goods were produced in state factories (see chapter 6), but items were still regularly obtained by levies. Ammianus records the preparations which Constantius made for civil and foreign wars (21.6.6): 'Nevertheless, equipment ... continued to be made ... every order and profession was burdened, supplying clothing, arms, and hurling-engines, nay even gold and silver, and an abundance of provisions of all kinds.'

The standard uniform with which each man was provided comprised a shirt (*sticharium*), tunic (*chlamys*), cloak (*pallium*) and presumably boots (Jones 1964, 624). Unfortunately, there is no evidence to tell us how long these garments were supposed to last before replacements were issued. Gradually the issue of clothing was commuted into gold, and in 423 it was declared that five-sixths of the revenue from the clothing tax should be allocated to the soldiers as a cash payment for clothing, with the remainder going to the factories for the production of uniforms for recruits and common soldiers (*Cod. Th.* 7.6.5).

The men were also issued with arms, although there is no record of how this was done, or how often they were renewed. Similarly, horses were supplied to those who required them.

A statement from Procopius implies that by the sixth century the issue of equipment had been completely replaced by a cash payment, since he records Belisarius telling his men before battle (5.28.14): 'And let no one of you spare horse or bow or any weapon. For I will immediately provide you with others in place of all that are destroyed in the battle.' Precisely how efficient this system was is doubtful, since men might scrimp on the cost of their equipment in order to save some of the money for their own private use.

The supply of military equipment during campaigns was understandably a major problem for the state. Not only did equipment need to be supplied at the beginning of a campaign, but replacements for those lost, or irreparably damaged in battle, had also to be furnished. Lack of treasury funds during the reign of Justinian caused repeated delays in the dispatching of aid to campaigning generals: Procopius records one instance where the commander John had been sent with a begging letter from Belisarius to Justinian (7.12.1–10): 'We have arrived in Italy, most mighty Emperor, without men, horses, arms, or money, and no man, I think, without a plentiful supply of these things, would ever be able to carry on a war.' Horses were apparently in such short supply during the siege of

Naples that a consul was 'obliged to remain, altogether against his will', until one could be found (Procopius 7.26.13–4).

It was sometimes possible, however, to utilize the equipment of a defeated enemy: Zosimus states that on the capture of the city of Bersabora 'those arms which were suitable for Roman warfare were given to the soldiers, but those suitable only for Persian use were either burned or thrown into the river' (3.18.6). An example regarding the seizing of enemy horses comes from Procopius, who records that the commander John, on capturing an enemy scout, forced him to show the Romans where the Gothic horses were grazing (7.18.14–15): 'And first, upon finding the enemy's horses pasturing, all the men who happened to be on foot leaped upon their backs; and there was a large number of such men comprising some of the best troops.'

Further headaches regarding the supply of equipment concerned those men who had been recruited during the course of the campaign. Zosimus recounts one instance where Julian, having found some old arms in a town, refitted and distributed them to those men who had recently enlisted (3.3.1–2).

THE *STIPENDIUM ET DONATIVUM*

In addition to the above, the soldier did receive some regular money. A document dating to 299 and 300 records that an annual *stipendium* was still being paid, as it had been during the Principate, in three instalments (cited in full by Jones 1964, 1257 no. 31). From this record it can be calculated that legionaries and *equites* of an *ala* received 600 *denarii* per year, whilst infantrymen in the cohorts were paid about 400 *denarii* annually (Jones 1964, 623). The auxiliaries were also entitled to a ration allowance (*pretium annonae*) of 200 *denarii* each year. From these figures it appears that wages had remained virtually unchanged since Severan times, making them almost nominal sums by this period due to the high inflation. Annual donatives, paid out on the birthdays and accession days (the latter at five-yearly intervals) of imperial personages, together with their consulates, probably provided the main source of income for troops: legionaries and other high-ranking soldiers were given 1250 *denarii* for each celebration of an Augustus, receiving half that amount for Caesars. Jones (1964, 623) estimates that these men would therefore have regularly acquired 7500 *denarii* per year. It appears that auxiliaries, however, only received 250 *denarii* for an Augustus, totalling 1250 annually (Jones 1964, 623).

Annual payments were evidently still in existence in 360, since Ammianus records that Julian, writing to Constantius II, complained that the soldiers had, amongst other grievances, not received their *annuum stipendium* (20.8.7–8). Precisely when the *stipendium* was phased out is uncertain, although as Jones suggests, it probably lasted until the reign of Theodosius I, under whom Ammianus was writing, since he might otherwise have noted its disappearance (1964, 624). As stated above, however, by this time the donatives were the most important payments the soldier received. Ammianus tells us that on Julian's accession to the purple in 360, the donative amounted to five *solidi* (gold coins) and one pound of silver (giving a sum total of nine *solidi*) (20.4.8). This figure appears to have become the standard issue throughout the period, as does the quinquennial donative of five *solidi*, which is first recorded under Anastasius and Justinian (Zach. Myt. *Chron.* 7.8). According to Procopius, however, Justinian had never paid the accession donative since he had come to power 32 years ago (*Anecdota* 24.27–9). If such a situation had occurred Jones feels sure that other contemporary writers would have commented on the fact (1964, 670). He therefore suggests that Justinian had rationalized the system by converting the quinquennial donative into a payment of one gold piece a year, amalgamating it with the *annonae*, which had by this time been commuted into cash.

A soldier's income was often irregularly supplemented by various means. To encourage acts of bravery, or at least discourage acts of cowardice, monetary incentives were sometimes offered to the troops: Julian, in order to persuade his men to act bravely against the Persians, promised them a donative of 100 pieces of silver each (Ammianus 24.3.3). The troops on this occasion, however, argued that this was insufficient, but were told in no uncertain terms by Julian that the Empire was financially on its knees. Civil wars could often prove beneficial to the soldiers, since they were frequently offered bribes to desert to the other side (Zosimus 4.6.3–4). Large amounts of booty might also be recovered by the men on the completion of a successful battle or siege. Procopius records one instance where, on the capture of the city of Petra from the Persians, 'such an abundance of weapons [was found] that when the Romans took possession of them as plunder, five men's equipment fell to each soldier' (8.12.17–18). Rather amusingly, some of the infantrymen under Belisarius who had managed to acquire horses as booty from the enemy, told their general that since they had now become quite practised in horsemanship, they no longer wished to fight on foot (Procopius 5.28.21–2).

A study of the sources makes one realize how important these extra sources of income were for the troops of expeditionary forces, particularly in the sixth century, since it appears that all too often the men did not receive their regular pay (including donatives) from the state. Procopius cites numerous examples of the soldiers pay being several years in arrears (4.15.55; 4.16.17; 4.18.9–10; 4.26.10–15). Such a situation produced serious morale problems amongst the troops: during the Persian war, Roman troops who had been owed pay for a long time deserted to the enemy (Procopius 2.7.37), and in 549 some of the besieged Isaurian soldiers guarding one of the gates of Rome went over to the Gothic side, because 'for many years nothing had been paid them by the Emperor' (Procopius 7.36.25–6). Furthermore, as stated by Belisarius, the lack of money was resulting in insubordinate behaviour by the men: 'Consequently, since we have fallen behind in regard to the payment of the soldiers, we find ourselves quite unable to impose our orders upon them; for the debt has taken away our right to command. And this also thou must know well, my master, that the majority of those serving in thy armies have deserted to the enemy' (Procopius 7.12.7–9).

Precisely how badly off soldiers were in the late Empire is difficult to say, since conditions varied greatly from unit to unit. Theoretically, they received adequate pay and rations (see below), the latter being probably of a higher frequency and standard than might have been available to the civilian population. Furthermore, it was common practice for soldiers to have slaves who served them as batmen. Although such a situation was obviously more prevalent amongst the higher ranking units like the *scholae*, there is evidence to suggest that soldiers in ordinary regiments may also have owned slaves. In 349, a soldier's family was defined as comprising his wife, children and slaves bought from their salary (*Cod. Th.* 7.1.3). Belisarius, during the siege of Rome, commanded that the attendants of the soldiers be sent out of the city in order to conserve supplies for the combatants (Procopius 5.25.1–4). The keeping of slaves by soldiers of all ranks would tend to suggest that they received sufficient money to enable them to save some for purposes other than purely the maintenance of themselves, their wife and children.

The officers

A document dating to 300 records that the *praepositus* and *equites promoti* of *Legio II Traiana*, received a *stipendium* of 18,000 *denarii*: this would total an annual salary of 54,000 *denarii* (Jones 1964, 644). A slightly later document gives a figure of 36,000 *denarii* for the *stipendium*, and although it is almost double the previous amount, inflation would have meant that in reality, this did not constitute a rise in salary (*P. Oxy.* 1047; Jones 1964, 644).

Owing to inflation these cash payments became nominal, and eventually the 'pay' consisted mainly of multiple allowances of *capitus* and *annonae* (see below).

Rations

The men

The rations (*annonae*) which the soldiers received for themselves and their horses were distributed to them in various ways. The *limitanei* appear to have collected their rations and fodder (*capitus*) from storehouses (*horrea*) within or adjacent to their forts (Jones 1964, 626). During peacetime the *comitatenses*, having no permanent bases, generally received their supplies by more flexible methods, possibly drawing their rations from the revenues of the province in which they were temporarily stationed. Special arrangements, however, were required to provision the field army on campaign. If an emperor was personally commanding the expeditionary force, as often occurred during the fourth century, either an attendant praetorian prefect, or the prefect in charge of the particular area, organized the procurement of supplies. By the fifth century, however, when emperors were generally not personally involved, a deputy praetorian prefect was appointed to undertake the collection of provisions (Jones 1964, 628).

Evidence suggests that the diet of the Roman army was reasonably nutritious and well-balanced. The basic peacetime ration issued to the troops consisted of bread (generally made from corn), fresh and cured meat (usually pork), wine and oil.

The production of commodities such as bread, wine and oil for the army fell on the civilian population. Bread was usually supplied by the bakers' guilds and country landowners. The *Codex Theodosianus* refers to a complaint received from the city council of Epiphania, who stated that it had become too expensive to supply the troops with aged wine. It was therefore agreed that from November 398 the soldiers should be provided with new wine drawn from the latest batch (7.4.25). The latter regulation still applied during the reign of Justinian (*Cod. Just.* 12.37.10).

These basic items could obviously be supplemented by a large range of goods, including cheese, pulses, fruit, nuts, seafood (particularly oysters), fish, poultry, eggs and vegetables (Dixon and Southern 1992, 91–3; Davies 1971). A wide range of wines were available, ranging from sour to sweet, together with beer (*cervesa*) made from malted grain (probably wheat) which was particularly popular in the north European provinces

(Dixon and Southern 1992, 93). The only evidence regarding the amounts of rations received per day by the men comes from some sixth-century Egyptian papyri (*P. Oxy.* 2046; 1920 – the former of these is used here): 1.4kg (3lb) of bread, 1kg (2lb) of meat, 1.1l (2 pints) of wine and 0.07 l (¹/₈ of a pint) of oil. As Jones notes these amounts seem enormous, and he suggests that they may have been obtained 'by some financial juggling', possibly by using the fodder allowance to obtain more food for the men (1964, 629).

The diet of the army when on campaign was necessarily different, some items being substituted for those which did not go stale or rot as quickly. A law dating to 360 states that expeditionary troops received hardtack (*bucellatum*), bread, ordinary wine (*vinum*), sour wine (*acetum*), salt pork and mutton, which were supplied as follows: 'hardtack for two days out of three, bread on the third day; *vinum* one day, *acetum* on the other; salt pork for one day out of three, mutton on the other two days' (*Cod. Th.* 7.4.11). The soldiers had to collect twenty days' rations from the state storehouses, and then carry these items themselves whilst on campaign (*Cod. Th.* 7.4.5).

Yet again, the basic campaign diet could be supplemented. There are numerous references in the ancient sources whereby the troops procured various extra items either by living off the land or capturing enemy supplies: fruit (Ammianus 24.3.14; Procopius 3.17.10), cured meat from Persians (Procopius 8.12.18–20), fresh meat including veal (Ammianus 24.1.5; 24.5.2), beans (Procopius 8.12.18–20), gourds (Procopius 2.18.18).

The task of baking both *bucellatum* and bread for expeditionary forces fell on the civilian population, with all privileges and exemptions being suspended (*Cod. Th.* 7.5.2; 11.16.15). The corn which was used to make both the bread and hardtack was also sometimes made into porridge, although the following comment from Ammianus would lead us to believe that it was not a particularly popular food: 'And the Emperor [Julian], who had no dainties awaiting him, after the manner of princes, but a scant portion of porridge ... a meal which would have been scorned even by one who served as a common soldier ...' (25.2.1–2).

The diet of the army under siege is fully discussed in Chapter 9.

The fodder (*capitus*) ration mainly consisted of barley, supplemented by chaff and hay. According to a law of 363, the men had to collect the hay and chaff themselves if the stores were within 32km (20 miles) of their base. If, however, it was stored further afield, the state would make the necessary arrangements for its delivery (*Cod. Th.* 7.4.9). In 362 a ruling was made to the praetorian prefect of the East that fodder would not be issued until August 1 (*Cod. Th.* 7.4.8). This implies that the horses were put out to pasture during the spring and summer, only receiving rations when the grass had dried up (Jones 1964, 629). Although units of *limitanei* sometimes had permanent pastures attached to their forts, the field army relied on using public pastures, a situation which became extremely unpopular with the civilians. In 398 Arcadius ruled that the army was forbidden to use the public pastures belonging to the city of Apamea, together with those owned by the citizens of Antioch, adding, however, that provision for the grazing of military animals should be made by the city councils (*Cod. Th.* 7.7.3). In 415 instructions were issued to the praetorian prefect of the East and the *magister militum* that the 'ruinous practice by which the meadows of Our provincials are being molested and harassed by the soldiers' should cease to be allowed (*Cod. Th.* 7.7.5).

Various laws dating to the last half of the fourth century imply that attempts were being made to have the rations for men and horses commuted into large amounts of money by the following scam: provisions were not collected at the proper time when there were abundant supplies, but were left in the storehouses until there was a scarcity when even more money could be demanded for the same rations (*Cod. Th.* 8.4.6, dating to 358). Until the early fifth century, different rules regarding this abuse were imposed in different parts of the Empire, with the frontier troops in the west having this abuse legalized long before the *limitanei* of eastern army.

The *comitatenses* appear to have always, to some extent, received their rations in kind, although commutation into money by the actuary was allowed under certain conditions (*Cod. Just.* 12.37.19; Jones 1964, 672). The reason for this may lie in the fact that, when on campaign, it was presumably more convenient and efficient for their supplies to be organized centrally. During the reign of Justinian officials entitled *delegatores* accompanied the army whilst in transit, with supplies being organized in advance by the governors of provinces along the journey (Jones 1964, 673).

Officers

By the early fourth century the cash salary was mainly, if not entirely, made up of multiple issues of *annonae* and *capitus*. Such payments must have caused considerable inconvenience, since presumably the officer, even if he had a large household, could not consume the large amounts of rations to which he was entitled to receive on a daily basis (Jones 1964, 645). Inevitably therefore, attempts were made to commute some of these rations into money: in 325 it was ruled that *praepositi* and tribunes had to collect their supplies daily, rather than leaving them to accumulate whereupon they would demand money instead; Constantine stated that as a consequence of this practice, the superintendents of the storehouses were demanding money rather than payment in kind from the provincials, and the stocks of rations were decaying, necessitating either a second levy on the provincials, or the troops being issued with rotten food supplies (*Cod. Th.* 7.4.1). By the beginning of the fifth century, however, the government realized they were fighting a losing battle, and the commutation of rations into money was made legal (Jones 1964, 645–6).

By the early fifth century it was apparently standard legal practice for officers to appropriate some of the rations consigned to their men. A law dating to 406 regulates this abuse (*stellatura*), ruling that tribunes were entitled to appropriate rations for seven days (according to Jones) from their men per annum, which they could then commute into money (*Cod. Th.* 7.4.28). The frontier troops apparently suffered greater abuse, since a law of 443 records that the *limitanei* lost one-twelfth of their *annonae* (one month's rations), which was distributed between the *dux,* the *princeps* on his staff, and the *praepositi* of the forts (Jones 1964, 644).

According to several late Roman authors, a common practice amongst the officers was to keep drawing the rations for dead and missing men (Libanius *Or.* 47.31). This custom resulted in units remaining in reality under strength, even though on paper they had a full complement of men (Themistius *Or.* 10. 136b). Synesius records that the *dux* Cerialis pocketed the pay of his men by granting them prolonged leave from their units (*Epistulae* 129). Procopius accuses Justinian of having exploited this practice during the sixth century for the benefit of the state finances (*Anecdota* 24.5–6): 'But the *logothetes* [agents of the imperial treasury] ... would not allow the names of the deceased to be removed from the rolls, even when great numbers died at one time from other causes, and especially, as was the case with the most, in the course of the numerous wars. Furthermore, they would no longer [enlist new recruits] and that for a long period. And the result of this practice has proved unfortunate for all concerned – first, for the State in that the number of soldiers in active service is always deficient; secondly, for the surviving soldiers, in that they are elbowed out by those who have died long before and so find themselves left in a position inferior to what they deserve, and that they receive a pay which is lower than if they had the rank to which they were entitled ...' Although Justinian may have kept some high ranking posts unfilled in order to limit the damage caused by this heavy expense, it seems more likely that some sort of mutually beneficial understanding was being reached between officers and auditors regarding this practice (Jones 1964, 676).

The extent to which some officers exploited their men is alarming. Libanius in 381 paints a lamentable picture of the state in which the troops were kept (*Or.* 2.37–9): 'They starve and shiver, and haven't a penny to their name – all through the probity of their colonels and generals who feather their nests and make the lives of their men a misery. The cavalrymen's horses starve too, and such starving means gold for the officers, above and beyond the pay from the Emperor which passes through the soldiers' hands into their own ... Even the ground is hard to their feet for lack of footwear ...' Although this account was probably exaggerated for political reasons, other authors comment on the exploitative behaviour of the officers (Ammianus 28.6.12–9; Procopius 7.19.13–4; 7.20.1). Procopius (3.13.12–20) records an incident where the praetorian prefect John, in order to cut down production costs and thus make a profit, only baked the bread for the army once, instead of the customary twice. This caused the bread to deteriorate faster, being already rotten when it was issued to the troops. As a consequence many became seriously ill or died. Finally, on a slightly more humorous note, and one which typifies the profiteering mentality of military officers, comes from Synesius, commenting on his *bête noire* Cerialis, stated: 'I have with me the soldiers of the regiment of the Balagritae. Before Cerialis became commander they used to be mounted archers, but when he took command their horses were sold and they became just archers' (*Epistulae* 131).

Promotion

Promotion was, to a large extent, attained automatically by length of service, although merit and hard work also contributed to some degree.

After a man had finished his probationary period as a recruit (*tiro*), he became a cavalryman (*eques*) or an infantryman (*pedes*). From this point on, the man attained the status of non-commissioned officer, and such promotions signified the awarding of multiple *annonae* in infantry units, and *capitus* in cavalry units. Thus, the next on the scale of promotion was the *semissalis*, who received one-and-a-half *annonae* (one *capitus*), followed by the *circitor* or *biarchus* (two *annonae* or one *capitus*), *centenarius* (two-and-a-half *annonae* or one *capitus*), *ducenarius* (three-and-a-half *annonae* or one-and-a-half *capitus*). A senator proabably received four *annonae* or two *capitus*, whilst the *primicerius* of a unit was granted five of the former, or two of the latter (Jones 1964, 634).

All the above stages of promotion could be accomplished within the unit. Transfers from one unit to another were discouraged: a constitution dating to 400, and addressed to Stilicho, *comites* and *duces*, stated that they were not permitted to transfer men from one unit of the field army or *palatini* to another unit, or similarly from the *pseudocomitatenses* or the *riparienses*, such moves requiring imperial authority (*Cod. Th.* 7.1.18).

The next step on the promotionary ladder, that of *protector*, elevated the soldier to the rank of a cadet officer, enabling him to sever his connection with the unit into which he was recruited. Although obviously only a small proportion of men who joined the army would reach this grade, it appears that it was reasonably common for deserving veterans to be rewarded on discharge with the honorary title of *protector* (Jones 1964, 634).

Various complaints were levelled at the system of promotion within the army by contemporary writers, although, to be fair, those referred to by Procopius were more to do with the corruption of the officers than the inefficiency of the system itself (*Anecdota* 24.3–6; see above under the rations of officers). The Anonymous commented on the fact that bottlenecks regarding promotion were commonplace, since men at the top of the ladder were staying in the army, rather than retiring, in order to continue earning the large sums of money to which they were entitled (3.3–8). Such a situation, he declared, was discouraging men from joining due to lack of opportunities for advancement. He offered two solutions to this problem: firstly, all those in receipt of five *annonae* or more should be retired, and secondly, if blockages should still occur, those awaiting promotion should be transferred to another unit which was short of men.

Accommodation

The temporary billeting of troops in cities had been a long-standing tradition, but the practice became more prevalent during the Dominate (MacMullen 1988, Appendix C). Although the *limitanei* were still stationed in forts or permanent camps, the *comitatenses* and *palatini* were generally billeted in cities when not campaigning (Jones 1964, 630). Zosimus, a critic of Constantine, blames him for destroying the security of the frontiers by removing large numbers of troops to the cities (2.34.2). Such a move was probably the most prudent course of action to take in the circumstances, since it was no longer possible to maintain the defence of the frontiers against the numerous, often concurrent, attacks. A strategy was therefore devised in which the frontier zones would be provided with a screen of garrisons based in fortified towns, strongpoints and supply-bases along the lines of communication (Tomlin 1987, 119–20). MacMullen (1988, 176) believed that economic factors may also have influenced this move, since it was easier to supply the army if they were stationed in or near centres of production and exchange, a theory which finds some support in Ammianus (16.4.1). As will be seen, this move did not prove totally successful either for the army or for civilians, but it is difficult to see what other solution would have proved more effective in these circumstances.

The *Codex Theodosianus* contains numerous laws dealing with compulsory quartering. Certain establishments and people were granted exemption, including armourers (7.8.8), painters (13.4.4), the clergy (16.2.8), doctors and teachers (13.3.3; 10; 16; 18), synagogues (7.8.2) and workshops, although the latter were sometimes required to provide stabling facilities for one man (7.8.5).

The onerous burden of quartering was therefore borne by private householders and innkeepers. Citizens were ordered to hand over one-third of their homes to the lodger (*hospes*), the owner, in principle at least, being allowed to choose the best third for himself, and the lodger the second best: the remaining third belonged to the owner (*Cod. Th.* 7.8.5). According to law, citizens were not required to furnish their *hospes* with anything other than a bare room, but in reality much more was often exacted from the 'hosts'. In 340, Constans rather pathetically ruled that no items such as oil, wood and food should be seized by lodgers, but that 'if any person should of his own accord wish to assist a person whom he has received into his home by supplying him with necessary articles ... he should know that this privilege is granted to him' (*Cod. Th.* 7.9.1). A few months later, however, Constantius II outlawed the giving of items to lodgers (*salgamum*), a ruling which was again implemented in 393 by Theodosius I, and by Theodosius II in 416 (respectively, *Cod. Th.* 7.9.2; 3; 4). Another practice which was abolished was that of *cenaticum*, which apparently entailed the hosts being forced to pay for the *hospes'* supper (*Cod. Th.* 7.4.12). In 406, the demanding of baths by tribunes and *comites* was prohibited, only masters of the soldiers being entitled to seek this privilege (*Cod. Th.* 7.11.1). Despite this ruling, however, it was discovered that between 414 and 417, the *dux* of Euphratensis had been exacting a *tremis* a day from his hosts for wood and baths. It was therefore decreed that 'the *duces* of the aforesaid frontier, since they have evidently taken such money illegally for the past three years, shall restore it twofold, and in the future such licence for extortion shall be checked by fear of the same penalty' (*Cod. Th.* 7.11.2).

The billeting of troops in cities was extremely unpopular with the civilians. Zosimus, in his attack on Constantine, declared that he had subjected the cities 'to the outrages of the soldiers' (2.34.2). He further states that the soldiers themselves often caused as much damage to the cities as the barbarian invaders (4.16.5). Disturbing accounts of ill-treatment at the hands of the military are given by several authors. Ammianus comments on the soldiers billeted in Antioch being carried back to their lodgings on the shoulders of passers-by (22.12.6). According to Joshua of Stylites, due to the large numbers of troops stationed in Edessa during 503–5, men had to be quartered, against regulations, by the clergy and shopkeepers. The citizens were beaten up, thrown out their beds, robbed of their supplies and clothes, forced to provide *salgamum*, and wait on the soldiers every demand (86.93–6). Finally, in 505 it was agreed that the burden of housing the soldiers should also be borne by the rich landowners. The *dux* Romanus was then approached by the landowners, who asked him to outline exactly what the troops were allowed to demand from them. He ruled that they were entitled to 91kg (200lbs) of wood, a fixed quantity of oil, and one bed between two men, including the bedding. Romanus' decision implies that the law abolishing *salgamum* was either not rigorously enforced during this period, or was no longer a prohibited abuse.

Further suffering was often caused by the profiteering of military officials, such as the *dux* Cerialis, who exploited Libya by continually moving his troops from one city to another, accepting gold from the cities in exchange for removing the burdensome soldiers (Synesius *Epistulae* 129).

A different type of suffering was inflicted on a widow in Edessa in 396 (Jones 1964, 632). This lady so liked the soldier who was billeted in her house that she allowed him to wed her daughter Euphemia. When they returned to his regular station, however, Euphemia found out that he already had a wife. She was forced to become the slave of this woman, and was subjected to ill-treatment by her. Euphemia somehow managed to escape home, and when the soldier was next drafted to Edessa, his crime was reported by the bishop to the *magister militum*, whereupon he was charged with kidnapping and sentenced to death.

This increasing move towards billeting troops in cities did not only have a disturbing effect on the civilian population, it was also extremely detrimental to the discipline and morale of the soldiers themselves. As MacMullen notes, the majority of men appear to have been lodged in the suburbs of cities, having no physical boundaries to mark off the military sector (1988, 145). By spreading troops around in this manner, the élitist, corporate spirit of the units are damaged, resulting in a collapse of that essential feeling, the *esprit de corps*. Men do not, and probably never have, fought for king and country – they may say that they do, but in the end men fight and die for the glory of their unit and the safety of their comrades. Without this feeling of belonging, therefore, men lose the reason and will to fight (for a full discussion see Chapter 9).

Marriage and the Family

Some believe that the law which prohibited soldiers below the rank of centurion from marrying whilst in service was removed by Severus (Campbell 1978). Evidence to substantiate this view comes from the legal texts of Severan and post-Severan jurists (cited in Campbell 1978), together with the following statement by Herodian (3.8.4–5):

> To the soldiers he [Severus] gave a very large sum of money and many other privileges that they had not had before; for he was the first to increase their pay and he also gave them permission to wear gold rings and to live in wedlock with their wives [?]. All these things are normally considered alien to military discipline and an efficient readiness for war.

This passage has been variously interpreted as meaning that Severus gave soldiers the right to marry or merely that he allowed them to cohabit with women. If, as Garnsey believes, the situation regarding marriage remained the same under Severus, it is difficult to explain why Herodian would have bothered citing a practice, which had been commonplace since the early Principate, as being a specific reason why efficiency and discipline had slackened under Severus. The fact that this ban was extremely unpopular with the soldiers for numerous legal reasons (Campbell 1978), and that Severus owed his position to the military, would make such a move both prudent and understandable, since it would help to further ensure the loyalty and support of the men.

From the early third century onwards then, it appears that soldiers were permitted to marry, and have their families stationed with them. This obviously caused problems regarding who should be responsible for feeding the families, and the *Codex Theodosianus* contains several decrees which relate to this issue.

In 372 Valentinian I ordered that sons of serving soldiers had to be supported by their parents until they were able to bear arms (*Cod. Th.* 7.1.11); prior to this, they had been placed on the regimental roll, and had received rations. It appears, however, that soldiers' families were still obtaining rations in the east in 377 (*Cod. Th.* 7.14.17). A passage in Libanius, however, implies that by 381 Theodosius I must have enforced the rule pertaining in the west (*Orations* 2.39):

> for they [the soldiers] are obliged, of course, to spend their money on the wife and children – for every one of them has both. Nothing stops them getting married and they don't concern themselves with what the mothers and the children will have to live on. So when soldiers' rations are so sub-divided, where can the man get his fill?.

In 406, the government reversed its policy in the east, and Arcadius decreed that both the troops and their families (if present) should receive rations in kind (*Cod. Th.* 7.4.28).

Leave

Theoretically the granting of leave was the responsibility of the provincial *dux, magister militum* or *comes rei militaris*, but in reality a widespread practice had developed whereby lower ranking officers were earning money by selling such grants to their men. The fourth century saw the enactment of harsh laws in order to curb this problem. In 323 Constantine decreed that no tribune, decurion or *praepositus* could grant leave to any soldier (*Cod. Th.* 7.12.1). If any officer disobeyed and granted leave to a soldier, he would suffer deportation and confiscation of property if no hostilities occurred during the man's absence, but if hostilities had occurred, he would face the death penalty. This law was presumably found to cause an undesirable wastage of trained officers who were a very valuable commodity, so in 352 Constantius II declared that if a soldier was granted leave, or left without permission, the tribune and *praepositus* would each be fined 2.3kg (5lbs) of gold (*Cod. Th.* 7.1.2).

Evidence for the requesting of leave comes from the archive of the *praepositus* Abinnaeus, who served during the reign of Constantius II (letter nos 19, 33 and 34). Three letters exist in which Abinnaeus is asked to sanction leave to serving soldiers on compassionate grounds, including the following example from a mother (no. 34):

> To my master and patron the *praepositus*, the mother of Moses. You sent for Heron, my lord patron. So he went to the army. After god we have none to help us but you. So I have sent Athioesis to you, my lord; I implore you by your feet, my lord patron, since you also know that 'five days are a whole year', I implore and beg of you, Sir, to grant him the few days; if you give any order, Sir, tell Athioesis. I pray for your health, my lord patron.

Unfortunately, no copies of Abinnaeus' replies to these requests exist.

By the sixth century the granting of leave had become much more accommodating. Under Anastasius, a tribune was allowed to grant leave to a maximum of 30 men at any one time, but severe penalties were enforced if the number exceeded this level (*Cod. Just.*

12.37.16.2–4). It may be that the earlier legislation which allowed only higher ranking officials the right to sanction leave had proved impracticable, tribunes being capable of dealing with such requests more immediately, and thus more efficiently.

Retirement

Length of service

The length of service required for honourable discharge (*honesta missio*) from the army during the late period varied occasionally, being also dependent upon the status of the unit from which the man wished to retire. Evidence for the early fourth century comes from the Brigetio Table, a bronze tablet dating from 311 which contains a letter from the Emperors Constantine and Licinius to the commander in Illyricum (*FIRA* I, no. 93; Lewis and Reinhold 1955, 528–30). The letter, detailing improvements in tax privileges and discharge procedures, states that men serving in the vexillations and legions qualified for *honesta missio* after 20 years, although they were not entitled to full veterans' privileges (*emerita missio*) until they completed 24 years' service. Initially, Constantine applied the above rules solely to the *comitatenses*, soldiers in the legions and vexillations of the *riparienses* having to serve 24 years to attain honourable discharge. In 325, however, he granted the *riparienses* the same privileges as the *comitatenses* (*Cod. Th.* 7.20.4).

The above periods were the minimum a man needed to serve to receive *honesta missio*. He could, however, serve more years in the army if he desired: inscriptions record men serving in the army for up to 42 years before retiring (*ILS* 2788; 2789; 2796; 9213). According to the Anonymous much money could have been saved by the state if men had been given an honourable discharge when they became senior non-commissioned officers, earning five *annonae*, since most tended to stay as long as possible, receiving donatives year after year and causing a bottle-neck regarding promotion for those below (*De Rebus Bellicis* 5.3–4).

Soldiers rendered unfit for service from wounds, illness or age might receive a *causaria missio*. A Constantinian law dating to 325 states that *comitatenses* were entitled to *emerita missio* if they became disabled for any reason during their service, but *ripenses*, after serving 16 years, only qualified for *honesta missio* if the disability was caused by wounds received in action (*Cod. Th.* 7.20.4).

By the sixth century there was no age limit for service. The regulations which Anastasius issued for the troops stationed in Pentapolis imply that *priores* (NCOs) of all units, both in the *limitanei* and the *comitatenses*, 'were guaranteed against discharge as infirm or unfit for service' (Jones 1964, 675). This privilege only extended to 5 per cent of the strength of each unit.

Discharge certificates

Before the beginning of the fourth century, discharge certificates were extremely rare outside of Egypt, particularly during the Principate (Mann and Roxan 1988, 346). After Diocletian, however, documents attesting *honesta missio* were regularly given to veterans on their discharge in order that they might be better equipped to claim their privileges (Mann 1953, 496–500). Although the exact date of this regularization is uncertain, the Brigetio Table (see above) demonstrates that it was in force by 311.

According to the sources, these documents received a variety of names: in 325, 365 and 400, the *Codex Theodosianus* respectively refers to them as *epistolae, testimonia* and *testimoniales* (7.20.4; 7.1.7; 7.20.12). The latter term is also employed by Vegetius (2.3).

Privileges

All veterans were entitled to immunity from poll tax (*capitatio*). According to the Brigetio Table, soldiers who had completed 20 years' service in the legions and vexillations, or had obtained *causaria missio*, also acquired exemption for their wives. After a man had served his full 24 years, he received poll-tax immunity for four people (*FIRA* I, no. 93; Lewis and Reinhold 1955, 529). These concessions were reduced by Constantine in 325, however, when he ruled that men who had served in the *comitatenses* and *ripenses* for 24 years, or had been invalided out from the former branch, could receive immunity for themselves and their wives only (*Cod. Th.* 7.20.4)

Further exemptions included immunity from curial duties and various taxes, including market taxes, transportation taxes and tariffs (*Cod. Th.* 7.20.2).

The veteran also received a choice of either setting up in business, whereby a cash grant was given, or they could be allocated a plot of land, whereby they would be supplied with two oxen, cash and 100 measures (*modii*) of assorted grain (*Cod. Th.* 7.20.3). By the reign of Valentinian I the grant of money had been abolished, *protectores* (Imperial bodyguards) now receiving double the number of oxen, and 100 measures (*modii*) of each type of grain. Veterans below this rank received one pair of oxen and 50 *modii* of each grain type (*Cod. Th.* 7.20.8). Although the plots of land allocated to the veterans would have been fairly substantial, they were likely to be on waste land, and thus the condition of the soil was probably quite poor (Jones 1964, 636).

Grants of land appear to have disappeared by the sixth century. It may be that because no age limit existed for military service, men could now support themselves quite well on the salary they received from the army (see section on pay above; Jones 1964, 675).

VI

EQUIPMENT

Owing to the heterogeneous nature of the late Roman army, it would be impossible within the confines of this chapter to provide a comprehensive description of the equipment employed. From the late fourth century onwards, barbarian troops were drafted into the army in increasingly large numbers, and the distinctions between barbarians and Romans had blurred considerably, most pieces of armament representing an amalgamation of influences and styles. Although the state arms factories would have imposed some level of uniformity on the appearance of the regular army, the irregular troops would generally have used their native equipment. Many different nations served within the ranks of the Roman army, including Huns, Goths, Saracens and Franks, but to describe the equipment of these peoples would require a whole book in itself. This chapter, therefore, will primarily discuss those items of armament which have been found in 'Roman' archaeological contexts, or are represented on 'Roman' works of art. Please note that 'Roman' denotes all those peoples who resided within the Empire, not all of whom were citizens by this time.

Limitations on space have necessitated the omission of equine equipment from the present study, but much of the evidence has been comprehensively discussed in several recent publications.

State Factories

During the Principate the army acquired its equipment by two methods: its own production and civilian craftsmen. By the fourth century at least, however, the bulk was supplied by state arms factories (*fabricae*).

The primary source of evidence for *fabricae* is the *Notitia Dignitatum*, which lists their location together with the type of goods produced (*Or.* 11 and *Oc.* 9). A perusal of these lists implies that although these factories were probably a Tetrarchic innovation, most, if not all, were established where there were pre-existing centres of production (S. James 1988, 263–71). For numerous reasons major urban centres were an obvious choice, particularly if native industries were already established there, since they would provide accommodation for the work-force, access to all the services required by both the staff and the factory, security against the arms falling into the wrong hands, and very importantly, good communication and transportation facilities. If this location theory is correct, it could be postulated that where no native industry existed, factories would of necessity be located where a military establishment was located, such as in Pannonia, where three *fabricae* were sited at the old legionary bases of Lauriacum, Aquincum and Carnuntum (ibid., 1988, 269).

If centres of production already existed, why was it considered necessary for the state to interfere? The most convincing answer to this question is given by James (ibid., 270) who states that the military disruptions which occurred during the third century would have resulted in large-scale 'dislocation of the established military infrastructure as legions were moved and split up, auxiliary regiments dispersed or destroyed, and many forts, with their production and storage facilities ... abandoned, at least temporarily'. Such a situation would have forced the army to rely less on self-sufficiency, and more on civilian production.

The *Notitia* records the presence of 20 *fabricae* in the western half of the Empire, and 15 in the eastern half. It is evident that the factories were generally situated where the majority of the army was, i.e. throughout the provinces of the Eastern frontier, and the zone behind the Danube and the Rhine. As Simon James points out, for each major sector of the frontier, there are two centres producing body armour (1988, 263). This pattern is so regular it strongly implies that this situation was the result of deliberate planning.

The most commonly occurring type of factory were those producing shields and armour (*scutaria et armorum*) which were evenly distributed throughout the frontier zones of the east and west. Those *fabricae* which produced specialist equipment were fewer in number and were irregularly distributed. Factories producing arrows (*sagittaria*) and bows (*arcuaria*) were confined to the west, a surprising situation when it is remembered that to a large degree archery had always been specifically associated with the east, and that archers were widely employed in both halves of the Empire. James suggested that the reason for their absence in the east may lie in the fact that state centres of production were unnecessary or impracticable here, probably because many of those who had traditionally produced archery equipment were tribesmen, or did not practise their craft in the city centres (ibid., 264). The west, however, did not have an archery tradition, and therefore organized centres of production were required. The distribution of *fabricae* specializing in the equipment of *clibanarii* and *cataphractarii* are necessarily heavily biased towards the eastern half of the Empire, since according to the *Notitia* at least 14 units of this type were situated in the east, whilst only three are recorded for the west (ibid., 1988, 261). Thus, there were three factories solely producing heavy armour in the east, whilst only part of one factory was devoted to the production of such equipment in the west.

The production of clothing for the army was undertaken by state-controlled workshops, again believed to be a Diocletianic innovation. Those producing wool garments were called *gynaecea*, whilst linen tunics were made in *linyfia* (Wild 1976, 51). The dyes used for the above fabrics were produced in *bafia*. Wild believes that no special premises would have been built for the production of clothing, suggesting that existing buildings might have been requisitioned and converted (1967, 658). Their principal function was to provide the soldiers and the Imperial court with clothing, particularly tunics, cloaks and blankets.

Although the *Notitia* provides good evidence for the presence of these establishments in the west (*Oc.* 11), the corresponding entries for the eastern half give no detailed information regarding their location (*Or.* 13). Wild, utilizing the western listings, has recognized three main factors which appear to have determined the distribution of these establishments (1976, 53): firstly, the location of the *comitatenses* in the frontier provinces; secondly, the geographical situation of the main centres of administration; and thirdly, the economic geography of sheep farming.

The huge problems of adequately supplying the army with all the necessary items appear to have been energetically tackled by Diocletian. The distribution of the factories was primarily governed by the location of the troops, although several other factors had to be taken into consideration. Basically, however, they were sited where they were most needed.

Protective Equipment

The helmet

Both archaeological and pictorial evidence for the third century demonstrate that infantry helmets of this period had a bowl with an angled neck guard, a peak, placed either horizontally across the front of the bowl, or pointed in an upward position, and crossed reinforcing bars. The cheek pieces were usually large, sometimes leaving only the eyes, nose and mouth visible: an example of this style of helmet comes from Heddernheim, Germany (**fig. 8**). Representations of this style can be seen on several tombstones, including that of Iulius Aufidius.

Although helmets fitted with masks were undoubtedly used for cavalry displays (*hippika gymnasia*), those which are fitted with cheek-pieces were probably intended for use in battle despite their lavish decoration (Bishop and Coulston 1993, 148). Examples of this

Fig 8 *Third-century iron helmet from Heddernheim, Germany. This style of helmet affords protection to all but the wearer's central facial features. (Drawn by K.R. Dixon.)*

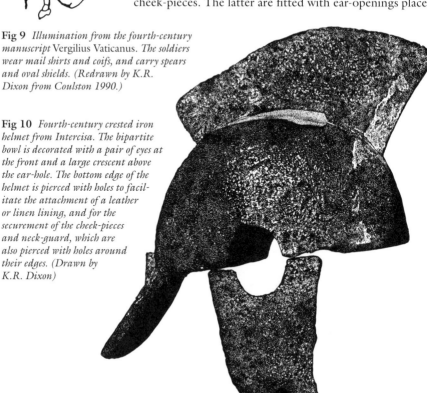

type come from Worthing, England (Dixon and Southern 1992, Pl. 27), Chalon, France (Garbsch 1978, 73–4, pl. 60, fig. 31. 3–4) and Guisborough, England (Garbsch 1978, 73. 59, fig. 31.1–2).

The soldiers depicted on the 'Battle of Ebenezer' fresco from Dura wear some form of scale or mail coifs on their heads (Kraeling 1956, pl. 5). Further evidence for the wearing of coifs comes from the illuminations of the fourth-century manuscript *Vergilius Vaticanus* (**fig. 9**; *Cod. Vat. Lat.* 3225; Coulston 1990, 145).

The beginning of the fourth century heralded a dramatic change in the construction and design of helmets. Helmet bowls were now composite in their construction, the sections of the bowl being attached to a ridged strip which ran from the front to the back of the helmet. The simplest form of these so-called 'ridged helmets' consists of a bipartite bowl, with separate neck-guard and cheek-pieces. The latter are fitted with ear-openings placed

Fig 9 *Illumination from the fourth-century manuscript* Vergilius Vaticanus. *The soldiers wear mail shirts and coifs, and carry spears and oval shields. (Redrawn by K.R. Dixon from Coulston 1990.)*

Fig 10 *Fourth-century crested iron helmet from Intercisa. The bipartite bowl is decorated with a pair of eyes at the front and a large crescent above the ear-hole. The bottom edge of the helmet is pierced with holes to facilitate the attachment of a leather or linen lining, and for the securement of the cheek-pieces and neck-guard, which are also pierced with holes around their edges. (Drawn by K.R. Dixon)*

centrally on their upper edge, corresponding with similar ones on the lower edge of the helmet bowl. The lower edge of the bowl, the neck-guard and cheek-pieces are pierced with holes in order to facilitate the attachment of a leather or linen lining, and to enable the various pieces to be secured to each other. Fifteen to twenty iron helmets of this style were found at Intercisa, Hungary (Klumbach 1973, 103–9, figs 45–57). The bowls were decorated with pairs of eyes, either chiselled or embossed into the metal, and one example was fitted with a crest (**fig. 10**). Traces of silver around the rivets implies that the iron bowls may originally have been covered with a thin silver sheathing. Further examples of this style of helmet are known from Trier (possibly with a chain-mail camail), Augst (the ridge of which had three slots, probably for the attachment of a crest) and Worms (**Pls 1, 2**; Klumbach 1973, 111–17, figs 58–64).

Although the majority of the extant 'Intercisa-style' helmets are extremely plain in their recovered state, two examples from Augsburg-Pfersee (**pl. 3**) demonstrate what the other ones may have looked like when covered with decorative silver sheathing (Klumbach 1973, 95–101, figs 38–44).

There is some representational evidence for the wearing of Intercisa-style helmets, including a gravestone from Gamzigrad dating to the Tetrarchy (**fig. 11**; Srejovic *et al.* 1983, fig. 42).

A more complex helmet construction is represented by two finds from Berkasova, former Yugoslavia (**pls 4–9**; Klumbach 1973, 15–38, figs 1–11). In both cases all that remains is the silver sheathing which originally covered the iron bowls. Helmet 2 has a bipartite bowl, whilst the bowl of helmet 1 comprises four sections. Both helmets are fitted with a band riveted to the inside rim of the bowl, which arches over each eye and has a 'T'-shaped nasal guard attached to it. The shape of the cheek-pieces differs substantially from those seen on the Intercisa-style helmet, covering virtually the entire sides and neck of the head rather than just the cheeks. Although the cheek-pieces on both helmets still

Fig 11 *Gravestone from Gamzigrad dating to the Tetrarchy. The rider wears the fez-style hat synonymous with this period, and carries an axe (not a* francisca*). The infantrymen carries a large oval shield, and wears an Intercisa-style helmet. (Redrawn by K.R. Dixon from Srejovic* et al. *1983.)*

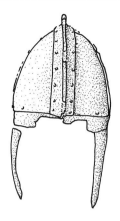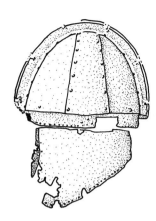

Fig 12 *Ridged helmet of four-piece-bowl construction from Concesti, Romania. Each half of the bowl consists of two non-touching sections which are riveted to a tapering band, giving the appearance that the bowl actually comprises six sections. The brow band and the bowl sections are decorated with lines of punched crosses and discs. (Drawn by K.R. Dixon.)*

appear to have been secured to the bowl in a similar manner to the Intercisa helmets, the neck-guards were attached by means of straps and buckles. The surfaces of both helmets are decorated with embossed patterns, but Berkasova 1 is much more highly adorned than 2, having glass-paste settings on the bowl, cheek-pieces and crest, the latter being held above the ridge by long shafted rivets (**pl. 4**). A similarly decorated helmet with bipartite bowl comes from Budapest, Hungary (Klumbach 1973, 39–50, figs 12–8).

A crested ridge helmet, similar to Berkasova 1, is portrayed on a coin of Constantius I, and Ammianus refers to Valentinian losing his helmet, which was adorned with gold and precious stones, when his chamberlain who was carrying it sank into a bog (27.10.11).

Burgh Castle and Concesti both produced four-piece bowls of similar construction, in that each bowl half comprised two non-touching sections riveted to a tapering band (fig. 12; Johnson 1980, 303–12; 1983b, 70–3; Klumbach 1973, 91–4, figs 32–7). The gilded helmet sheathing from Deurne, although only having four sections to its bowl, had such a wide joining band it gives the impression of having a six-sectioned bowl (**pl. 10**; Klumbach 1973, 51–83, figs 19–21).

All the ridge helmets described above are believed to date from the fourth or early fifth century. A securely dated third-century example, however, was discovered at Dura-Europos (**fig. 13**; James 1986). It consists of a bipartite bowl, with each half being riveted to a central ridge, a 'T'-shaped nasal guard, some form of chain-mail camail and a cylindrical knob projecting from the apex of the helmet, presumably for the attachment of a plume.

The similarity of the Dura helmet to those of the late Roman period is evident, and James has claimed that the example from Dura, which apparently belonged to a Sassanid Persian, substantiates the belief that the late Roman ridge helmets were Partho-Sassanian in origin (1986, 128).

James has put forward the most convincing explanation for the dramatic change which occurred in helmet design towards the end of the third/beginning of the fourth century. He suggests that at a time of crisis in armament procurement, resulting in the establishment of state arms factories under the Tetrarchy, ridge helmets, with their simple design and easier construction, fitted the pressured requirements of the state, who were more interested in the quantity produced rather than the decorative quality (ibid., 131–3).

Klumbach (1973, 9) suggested that the 'Intercisa' style helmets were worn by the infantry, whilst those of the 'Berkasova' type would have belonged to cavalrymen or officers. Evidence to support the latter designated group comes from an inscription on the Deurne helmet, stating that the owner was a member of the *equites Stablesiani*.

A separate tradition, which appears to have run parallel with the production of ridge helmets, is the *Spangenhelm*. This style of helmet, which consists of a multi-piece segmented bowl, can be seen on Trajan's Column being worn by Syrian archers, and by Roman cavalry on the Arch of Galerius (297–311).

Two undated iron helmets, similar in design to those seen on the latter monuments, were found in Egypt. The example from Dèr-el-Medineh (**pl. 11**) comprised six plates riveted to six bands, surmounted by a circular disc riveted to the apex of the bowl (Dittman 1940). A ring was secured to the disc, possibly for the attachment of decorative ribbons, or to facilitate carriage. A brow band was riveted around the rim, arching over the eyes, where a 'T'-shaped nasal guard was attached. The 'Berkasova-style' cheek-pieces and the neck-guard were secured to the bowl by hinges. The second helmet, now housed in the Rijksmuseum van Oudheden, Leiden, consists of four plates riveted to four broad bands, surmounted by a disc. The narrow cheek-pieces are hinged to the bowl (**fig. 14**).

A separate group known as the 'Baldenheim-type' (**pl. 12**), are similar in construction to the Egyptian finds, but have several distinct differences. These helmets are made from iron and bronze/copper alloy, and are formed by shaping four nontouching iron plates into a bowl, slightly overlapping the iron brow band (covered in thin gilded copper) at their lower edge. Four inverted 'T'-shaped gilded copper plates called 'spangens' are then riveted on

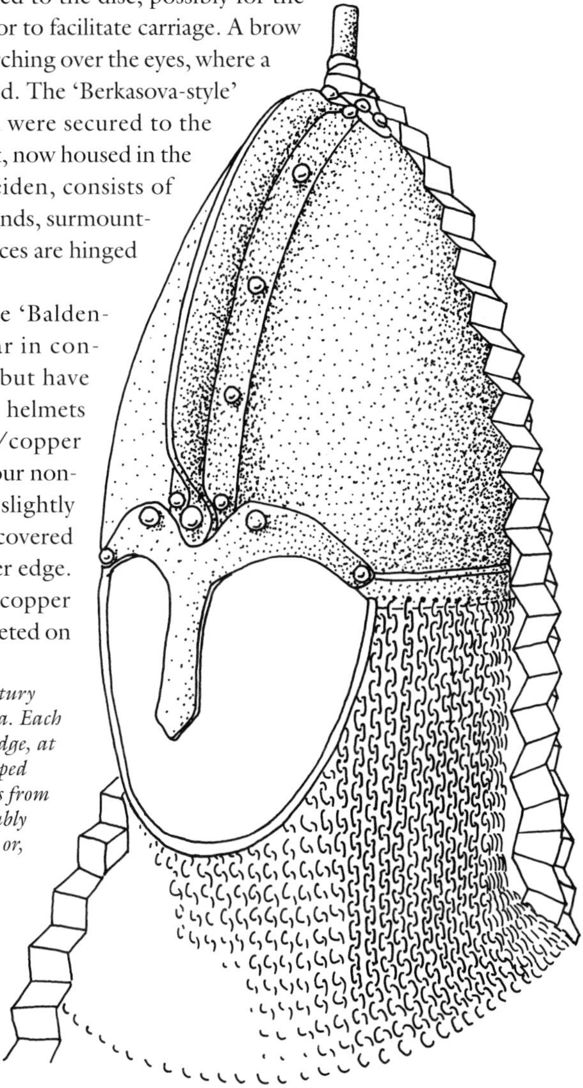

Fig 13 *Reconstruction of the third-century ridged helmet from Dura-Europos, Syria. Each half of the bowl is riveted to a central ridge, at the front end of which is riveted a T-shaped nasal guard. A cylindrical knob projects from the apex of the helmet, and was presumably intended for the attachment of a plume or, as depicted here, a ribbon (based on the near-contemporary Firuzabad reliefs). A mass of rusted mail was found adhering to the right forehead area of the helmet, and James has reconstructed this as a camail covering all but the central features of the face. (Redrawn by K.R. Dixon from James 1986.)*

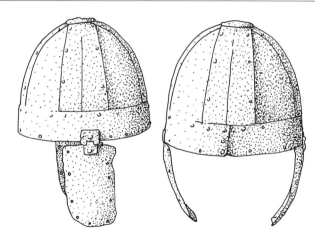

Fig 14 *Helmet of* Spangenhelm *type from Egypt, now housed in the Rijksmuseum van Oudheden, Leiden, consisting of four plates riveted to four broad bands, riveted to a brow band at their lower edge. Narrow cheek-pieces, punched with holes for the attachment of a lining (as is the edge of the brow band), are hinged to the bowl. A disc surmounts the apex of the helmet. (Redrawn by K.R. Dixon from James 1986.)*

to the iron plates, bridging the gaps between the latter. The bottom edge of the brow band and the entire perimeter of the gilded copper cheek-pieces are provided with holes to facilitate the attachment of a lining and the securing of the cheek-pieces to the helmet bowl. The helmet is surmounted by a disc with a fungiform button protruding from its centre, presumably for the attachment of a plume. The gilded copper elements are decorated with various classical and Germanic patterns executed in punched work. The iron plates are silvered on several examples.

All the Baldenheim-style helmets are strikingly similar in design, implying centralized production. James suggested that these helmets were made by Roman craftsmen for Ostrogothic masters (1986, 134).

Body armour

A find of *lorica segmentata* from a temple at Eining, constructed *c.* 226–9, and abandoned by *c.* 260, implies that this type of body armour was possibly still in use until the middle of the third century (Fischer and Spindler 1984, 58–62; Coulston 1990, 147).

Lorica hamata (mail armour) was constructed from copper alloy or iron rings, with each ring passing through the two rings directly above and below. The most common method of assembly was alternate vertical rows of solid rings, and rings with their flattened ends riveted together (**fig. 15**; Engelhardt 1863, pl. 6).

Complete, partial or small fragments of mail shirts have been recovered from a number of sites in third-century contexts. A complete *lorica hamata* was found during the excavation of the siege mines at Dura-Europos (Rostovtzeff *et al.* 1936, 192–7, 204, figs 16–18). It finished just below the waist, with elbow-length sleeves. Another complete mail shirt was included in the Roman equipment thrown

Fig 15 *Section of chain-mail from the Thorsbjerg bog deposit. It is constructed of alternate vertical rows of solid rings, and rings with their flattened ends riveted together. This type of construction appears to have been the most commonly used method. (Redrawn by K.R. Dixon from Englehardt 1863.)*

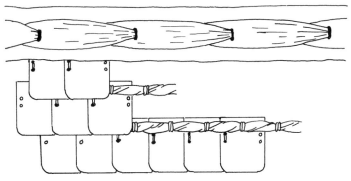

Fig 16 *A well-preserved section of scale armour from Carpow, Scotland. The scales are attached to linen, and some of the leather edging round the neck still remains. Each scale was pierced with holes, enabling them to be secured both to a horizontal cord and the linen backing. (Redrawn by K.R. Dixon from Wild 1981.)*

into the ritual bog at Vimose (Engelhardt 1869, fig. 17). This was knee-length, with sleeves that finished at the elbows. Further examples have been found at Caerleon (Nash-Williams 1932, fig. 16), Rainau-Buch (Planck 1983, fig. 26) and Künzing (Schönberger and Herrmann 1967–8, fig. 25).

Lorica squamata was made from iron or copper-alloy scales, mounted on linen or leather. Each scale was provided with a number of holes, usually grouped in pairs: those at the top were used to attach the rows to the backing fabric, whilst those on either side, linked the scales to each other in overlapping horizontal rows. An extremely well-preserved example of scale armour was found at Carpow, Scotland, in which the linen and some of the leather edging around the neck had survived (**fig. 16**; Wild 1981, 305–8).

A number of sites have yielded ornately embossed copper alloy breastplates. These plates have rivet holes down the long, outer edge, and a curved upper edge which fitted round the front of the wearer's neck. They have been found in association with both scale and mail, an example of the latter coming from Bertoldsheim, Germany, where a rolled-up *lorica hamata* had a chest plate attached to it (Garbsch 1984, figs 1–3). A pair from Manching, Germany, still retain the square-headed pins which would have fastened the two plates together. It seems likely, as Coulston argued, that these plates were not specifically designed for 'parade' or for the *hippika gymnasia*, since they would have functioned equally well as a means of protection in battle (1990, 147).

Representational evidence for both mail and scale shirts during the third century is meagre, owing to the trend of showing deceased soldiers in a state of 'undress' (Coulston 1987). There are some exceptions, however, such as the tombstone of Severius Acceptus of *legio VIII Augusta*, which shows the deceased surrounded by his equipment, which includes a strange style of cuirass shown in bands of vertical strips, and fitted with *pteruges* on the shoulders (Coulston 1990, 142, fig. 2).

Longer length cuirasses became fashionable from the late second/early third century onwards. A beautifully executed mail shirt can be seen on the Great Ludovisi Sarcophagus (Bivar 1972, pl. 9).

Further pictorial evidence for body armour comes from the Synagogue frescos from Dura-Europos (Kraeling 1956). The 'Battle of Ebenezer' fresco depicts soldiers wearing knee-length *loricae*, with sleeves reaching to their wrists. The numerous warriors shown in the 'Exodus' frieze yet again wear knee-length *loricae*.

Artefactual evidence for the fourth century onwards is extremely limited, although mail was recovered from a late fourth-/early fifth-century context at Independenta (Zahariade 1991, 315).

The paucity of sculpture depicting soldiers wearing body armour led many to believe that there was a decreased use of such equipment during the late Empire. This argument was strengthened by a statement from Vegetius, who wrote that heavy armour and helmets had rarely been worn by the infantry since the reign of Gratian (1.20). Coulston argues that this statement by Vegetius probably concerned the condition of the eastern *comitatenses* after the disastrous battle of Adrianople in 378 (1990, 149). Large-scale defeats such as this would have resulted in the loss of huge amounts of valuable equipment. To apply Vegetius' assertion Empire-wide and for the entire late period is unjustified, particularly in the light of representational and documentary evidence from authors such as Ammianus and Procopius.

Pictorial evidence for the fourth century onwards comes from various media. A manuscript illustration for the western *fabricae* in the *Notitia Dignitatum* depicts some form of metallic body armour (**fig. 17**; *Oc. 9*). A fragmentary relief, possibly from the Arch of Diocletian, depicts two soldiers wearing belted, long-sleeved cuirasses of mail and scale

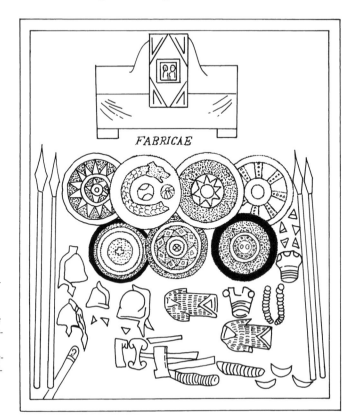

Fig 17 *Illustration from the* Notitia Dignitatum, *denoting the western* fabricae *(Oc. 9). Amongst the items depicted are circular shields, spears, crested helmets, assorted styles of axe, metallic body armour and greaves. (Drawn by K.R. Dixon.)*

Fig 18 *Late third–early-fourth century section of relief, possibly from the Arch of Diocletian, housed in the Vatican Museo Chiaramonti. It depicts two soldiers, both carrying large round shields, and wearing conical helmets. The man on the left wears a knee-length mail shirt, whilst the figure on the right wears a scale shirt. Both* loricae *are depicted with wrist-length sleeves. (Redrawn by K.R. Dixon from Coulston 1990.)*

(**fig. 18**; Coulston 1990, 143). A fourth-century fresco from the Via Latina Catacomb, Rome, depicts a soldier wearing a knee-length, long-sleeved *lorica hamata* (Coulston 1990, 145, **fig. 8**), and the sixth-century ivory throne of Maximian from Ravenna includes four panels which depict soldiers clad in scale or mail cuirasses.

Shields

The most common shield shape in use during the late Roman period was oval. This knowledge is not only based on pictorial evidence, such as the Dura Synagogue soldier paintings (Coulston 1990), and the tombstone of Julius Aufidius from Veria, but more importantly on the stunning finds from Dura-Europos. This site yielded at least 24 complete or fragmentary shield boards, 6 reinforcing bars and 21 bosses (Rostovtzeff *et al.* 1939).

The five most intact boards from this site were oval and slightly concave in form, measuring between 1.07–1.18m (3½–4ft) high, and 0.92–0.97m (about 3ft) wide (Rostovtzeff *et al.* 1939, 326–69, figs 83–4, pls 41–6). They were constructed from 12–15 planks of poplar wood, 8–12mm (⅓–½in) thick, glued lengthwise together. Two holes were cut in

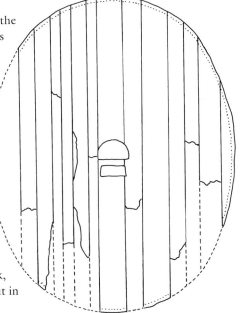

Fig 19 *Oval shield from Dura-Europos, Syria. It consists of wooden planks glued together longitudinally. A rawhide strip was stitched around the edge of the shield which is pierced with holes. The shield was held via the two holes cut in the centre of the board, with the semi-circular hole accommodating the knuckles of the carrier. The dividing strip between the two holes (the grip) would probably have been bound with leather to give greater comfort, and a metal boss (umbo) would have been riveted over the two holes in order to provide protection for the bearer's hand. (Redrawn by K.R. Dixon from Rostovtzeff et al. 1939.)*

the centre of each board, one trapezoidal and the other semicircular in shape (**fig. 19**) in order to accommodate the user's fingers and thumb. Although lacking on these boards, an *umbo* of bronze or iron would have been riveted over the hole in order to provide protection for the bearer's hand (**fig. 20**). Numerous domed, circular examples, ranging from 0.185 to 0.22m (7¼–8½in) in diameter, were found elsewhere on the site, most being

Fig 20 *Third-century bronze shield boss from Mainz. It was attached to the shield board by four rivets. (Redrawn by K.R. Dixon from Thomas 1971.)*

internally fitted with iron handgrips. One of the shields possessed four additional rivets, which may have been used to secure a carrying strap (Bishop and Coulston 1993, 149).

Before a boss or strap, etc., was added, however, the shield was sometimes covered on both sides with hide or linen, or both. This could then be painted, as was the case with most of the Dura examples, three of which were elaborately decorated, depicting scenes from the Trojan War (Rostovtzeff *et al.* 1939, 331–49, pls 41–2), Amazons fighting Greeks (ibid., 349–63, pls 44–5), and a warrior god (ibid., 363–7, pl. 46, 1–2). The reverse of the Amazon shield was painted blue and adorned with radiating lines of red hearts bordered with white, and rosettes (Bishop and Coulston 1993, 149, pl. 4c). Previously it was suggested that because of the ornate nature of these shields, they may have been intended for use as 'sports equipment', but since they are identical in construction to those found on the same site in a definite combat situation, there is no need to accept this theory (Bishop and Coulston 1993, 149).

Unlike earlier shields which were edged with metal strips, the Dura examples were edged with rawhide, which was stitched on through holes pierced along the rim (see fig. 19). Rawhide may have replaced metal in this role because it was cheaper and easier to repair, probably enabling the soldiers themselves to undertake any necessary maintenance.

Fragments of at least three rectangular semicylindrical shields were also recovered from Dura, together with one almost complete example. This was constructed using a different method to the oval shields, consisting of three layers of strips of wood which were glued together, giving an overall thickness of 5cm (2in) (see fig. 19; Rostovtzeff *et al.* 1936, 456–66, pl. 25 and 25A). Both sides of the shield were covered with hide and linen, the obverse being painted red and decorated with various motifs, including a lion (which may have denoted the legion to which the owner belonged), and two Victories flanking an eagle. This example, and the fragments of similar ones, prove that this type of shield, contrary to popular belief, was still in use in the middle of the third century.

Archaeological evidence from the fourth century onwards regarding shields is meagre, and most of our knowledge comes from literary and pictorial sources.

Although there are various depictions of round shields, oval shields still appear to have been the prevalent form. A fourth-century glass beaker from Cologne, Germany, is adorned with four soldiers, each carrying decorated oval shields (**pl. 13** and **fig. 21**), and a silver donative dish from Geneva depicts Valentinian I (or II) flanked by his guards who carry broad oval shields (**pl. 14**). Some of the designs on the latter shields, particularly the

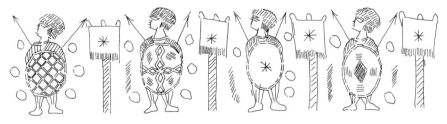

Fig. 21 *Detail of a fourth-century glass beaker from Cologne, Germany. The four soldiers carry decorated oval shields and two spears. The men appear to be clothed in trousers, tunics and cloaks. A* vexillum *stands between each of the men. (Redrawn by K.R. Dixon.)*

Fig. 22 *Detail of a mosaic of the Emperor Justinian flanked by his guards and generals from the church of San Vitale, Ravenna, Italy. The two figures on the right (identified as generals) wear ankle-length cloaks of undyed cloth, fastened at the right shoulder by a crossbow brooch, and decorated with a single rhomboid-shaped patch, or possibly stripe of brown crossing the body from right to left. Underneath the cloak they wear a tunic of undyed cloth, decorated with squares of geometric patterns executed in dark brown. The guards to the left of the generals carry large oval shields, the foremost of which is decorated with a* chi-rho *monogram amongst other designs. Each guard also holds a spear, the shafts of which are decorated with bands of colour. (Drawn by K.R. Dixon.)*

opposed animal heads (first on the left of the photograph), closely resemble the shield emblems recorded in the *Notitia Dignitatum*.

Later evidence comes from two ivory diptychs, one of Honorius, dated to 406, and the other of Stilicho from *c.* 400 (**pl. 15**), which both depict the men resting one of their hands on large oval shields.

The sixth-century mosaics from the church of San Vitale, Ravenna, show Justinian flanked by his generals and guards, the latter of whom carry brightly coloured and ornately decorated oval shields (**fig. 22**).

As has been mentioned above, most of the evidence indicates that shields were decorated. Vegetius states that in order to help soldiers recognize their unit during battle, different signs were painted on the shields, together with the name of the soldier and the cohort or century he was from (2.18). Ammianus records an incident where the Alamanni, fearing the Romans, suddenly noticed the emblems on their opponents' shields, and realizing that they had in fact defeated these troops on a previous occasion, thus regained their courage (16.12.6). Substantial evidence for this practice can be found in the *Notitia Dignitatum*, which records an emblem for each regiment. Although some of these designs can be paralleled with other fourth-century depictions, Grigg (1983, 132–42) concluded that a later copyist, despite basing some emblems on authentic designs and reasonable suppositions deduced from unit titles, also included some which he had simply invented. These emblems must therefore be viewed with caution unless they are corroborated by additional evidence.

Weapons

Long swords (*Spathae*)

The long sword (*spatha*) was the dominant form employed by the Roman army from the late second/early third century onwards. Ring suspension had been replaced by the scabbard runner, and the sword was now carried on a baldric and worn on the left side, rather than the right.

The blades could be decorated in various ways. Pattern-welding was a process which involved forged strands of iron and steel being twisted and welded together, the alternation of the two metals forming many variations in pattern (Anstee and Biek 1961, 71–93). The cutting edges were then welded on to the core, and the whole blade was filed down. Another form of decoration was inlay. Figures, including eagles, gods and military standards, were inlaid into the blade using contrasting metals, particularly *orichalcum*, a golden-coloured copper (**fig. 23**; Dabrowski and Kolendo 1972).

The hilt of the sword comprised several separate components: the grip, guard and pommel. The grips, made of bone,

Fig. 23 *Detail of the third-century sword blade from South Shields, England, inlaid with a figure of Mars on one side and an eagle flanked by military standards on the other. (Redrawn by K.R. Dixon from Rosenquist 1967–8.)*

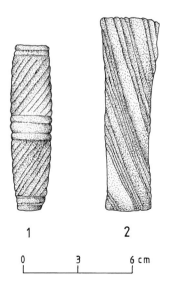

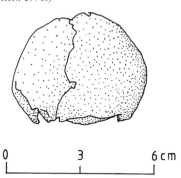

Fig. 24 *Third-century sword grips: 1: Buch (bone); 2: Zugmantel (bone). (Redrawn by K.R. Dixon from Oldenstein 1976.)*

Fig. 25 *Third-century bone pommel from Zugmantel. (Redrawn by K.R. Dixon from Oldenstein 1976.)*

ivory or wood, could be plain, or decorated with spiral twists, a basket-weave design or ribbed (**fig. 24**). The most common pommel shape was elliptical (**fig. 25**), although eagle-headed pommels are depicted on tombstones, sarcophagi and Imperial statues. The guards could be made from iron, copper-alloy, wood or bone. They were rectangular or semi-oval in shape. Some of the swords from the Danish bog finds still retained complete grips; Engelhardt 1869; 1863, pl. 9).

Actual wooden scabbards rarely survive, although fragments were apparently found at Dura-Europos (Bishop and Coulston 1993, 130). Those from the Danish bogs were constructed of wood and covered with leather (Engelhardt 1863, 41, pl. 10. 31).

The metal fittings that were attached to the scabbard are common finds on Roman sites. In order to strengthen the tip of the scabbard, a metal chape was fitted. Heart and peltate-shaped forms were still prevalent during the third century, as was the 'box' chape (**fig. 26**). The most commonly represented form during the third century was the circular chape. They are depicted on numerous tombstones, including that of Aprilius Spicatus (**fig. 27**; Coulston 1987, 142, pl. 2). They were constructed from copper-alloy, bone, ivory and iron, and could be highly decorated with niello (on the iron examples) or engraving (**fig. 28**; Hundt 1953).

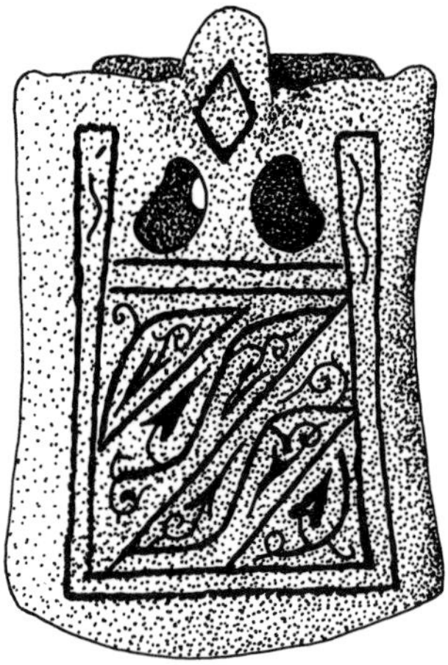

Scabbard slides, through which the baldric was attached to the scabbard, are extremely well represented in the archaeological record. They could be cast in copper-alloy or made from iron, ivory or bone

Fig. 26 *Third-century iron 'box' chape with niello decoration from the Vimose bog find. (Redrawn by K.R. Dixon from Engelhardt 1869.)*

(**figs 29–30**). The runner was fixed to the scabbard by two, or possibly three, studs which protruded from the underside. These were then pushed through corresponding holes in the sheath, and were probably secured by glue, with additional binding being wrapped around both the slide and the scabbard. The most spectacular runners are those cast in the shape of a dolphins (Dixon 1990).

There is good representational and artefactual evidence for the baldric in the third century. Most tombstones depict a wide baldric, worn over the right shoulder, bringing the sword to rest on the left hip (see **fig. 27**; Coulston 1987, figs 1, 2). The finds

Fig. 27 *Detail of the third-century tombstone of Aprilius Spicatus, Istanbul Archaeological Museum. Aprilius carries a small shield and a spear. The scabbard of his sword terminates in a round chape, and is suspended from a wide baldric. He wears a cloak* (sagum), *a tunic and a waist belt fastened with a ring-buckle. (Drawn by K.R. Dixon.)*

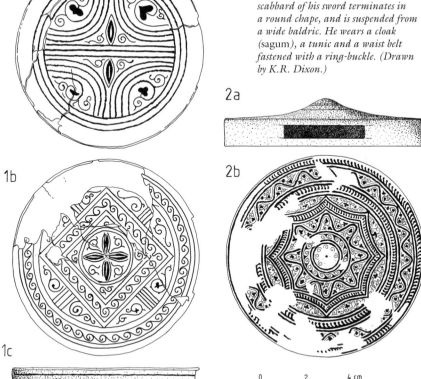

Fig. 28 *Circular iron chapes decorated with niello from Nydam (1a–c), and Reichersdorf (2a–b). (Redrawn by K.R. Dixon from Hundt 1953.)*

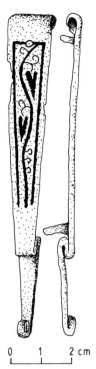

0   1   2 cm

Fig. 29 *Iron scabbard runner with niello decoration from Vimose. (Redrawn by K.R. Dixon from Hundt 1959/60.)*

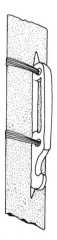

Fig. 30 *Drawing demonstrating the attachment of the bone scabbard slide from London to the scabbard. (Redrawn by K.R. Dixon from Chapman 1976.)*

from the Danish bog deposits (see below) have provided valuable information on how the baldric was fastened. From the extant examples it is known that one end of the baldric was broad and finished in a straight edge, the other tapered to a narrow strip. A *phalera* (circular metal discs), fitted with an eye was attached about 30cm (12in) from the broad end, the eye piercing the leather. The narrow end was firstly brought through the scabbard runner, probably being wrapped round the scabbard twice, and then it was tied to the eye of the *phalerae*. Exactly how the baldric was attached to the scabbard is uncertain. Reconstructions, however, have shown that the best method involves wrapping the strap around the scabbard twice, starting and finishing at the front (see Bishop and Coulston 1993, fig. 91.9); unlike the back start and finish method suggested by Oldenstein (1976, 228–30, figs 11–12), which holds the sword away from the body, causing the end of the scabbard to point inwards towards the legs, this method holds the sword against the body in a more balanced position, causing less discomfort to the wearer.

Four leather baldrics were recovered from the Vimose and Thorsbjerg bog deposits, each site yielding two (**fig. 31**; Engelhardt 1863; 1869; Stjernquist 1954). The more complete example from the former site measured at least 118.5cm (4ft) long, and 8cm (3in) wide, tapering at one end to a width of 1.2cm (½in). A plain, copper-alloy *phalera* with an eye on the back pierced the baldric 28.6cm (11in) from the broad end. One *phalera* on each of the baldrics from this site had a piece of leather from the narrow end of the baldric tied to the eye. The leather was decorated with various motifs, including a dolphin. One of the baldrics from Thorsbjerg was wider, measuring 9.1cm (3½in), and had marks cut into the broad end, implying that a heart-shaped terminal had been attached (Engelhardt 1863, pl. 11, 48).

Numerous baldric fittings have been recovered from sites Empire-wide. There are many styles of *phalerae*, including several from Vimose which had an embossed eagle flanked by military standards in the middle. Openwork examples are fairly common, and range from decorative patterns to extremely elaborate depictions of eagles with thunderbolts under their

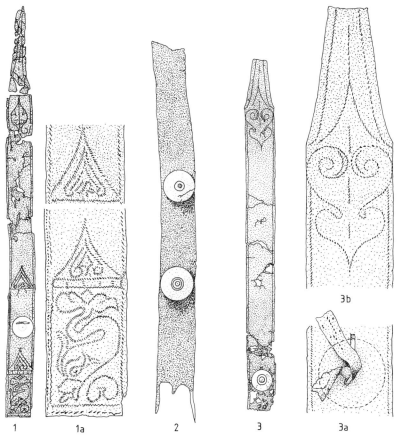

Fig. 31 *Leather baldrics from the Danish bog deposits: 1, 1a and 3, 3a and 3b: Vimose, both retaining* phalerae, *the baldrics themselves being decorated with various designs including a dolphin; 2: Thorsbjerg, retaining two* phalerae. *Scale: 1 and 3 are ⅙ natural size, 2 is ¼ natural size, and 1a, 3a and 3b are ½ natural size. (Redrawn by K.R. Dixon from Stjernquist 1954.)*

Fig. 32 *Openwork phalera from Carlisle, depicting an eagle holding a thunderbolt in its talons. This type of mount was worn in conjunction with a further two open-work plates, one rectangular and the other triangular, on a baldric. An inscription was divided amongst the three mounts, which when viewed together read the following: circular:* OPTIME MAXIME CON(SERVA); *rectangular:* NUMERUM OMNIUM; *triangular:* MILITANTIUM; *which translated means 'Best [and] greatest [referring to Jupiter] protect [us] a troop of fighting men all'. (Redrawn by K.R. Dixon from Allason-Jones 1985.)*

107

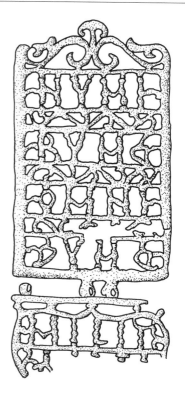

Fig. 33 *Unusual openwork baldric* phalerae *from Egypt depicting Romulus and Remus being suckled by the wolf, surrounded by the inscription* LEG(IONIS) VI FERR(ATAE) F(IDELIS) C(ONSTANTIS) FEL(ICIS). *(Drawn by K.R. Dixon.)*

talons, surrounded by the inscription OPTIME MAXIME CON(SERVA) (**fig. 32**). Examples of the latter type, all very similar in design, have been recovered from Germany, Britain (Allason-Jones 1985; 1986) and North Africa (Ruhlmann 1935). An extremely unusual example depicting Romulus and Remus being suckled by the wolf, surrounded by the inscription LEG(IONIS) VI FERR(ATAE) F(IDELIS) C(ONSTANTIS) FEL(ICIS), was found in Egypt (**fig. 33**; Domaszewski 1910).

The broad end of the baldric was sometimes fitted with an ornamental openwork terminal, hinged along the straight, top edge. A range of plates come from Zugmantel, including rectangular plates, from which the terminal plate was hung (**fig. 34**; Oldenstein 1976, fig. 83). The above plates often carried openwork inscriptions, and when they were worn in conjunction with an eagle *phalera*, they would read: OPTIME MAXIME CON(SERVA)) (*phalera*)

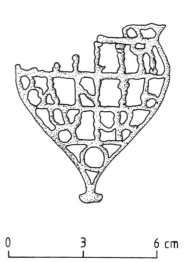

```
0          3        6 cm
L_____|_____J
```

Fig. 34 *Openwork baldric plates from Zugmantel, Germany. These plates would be worn in conjunction with a circular openwork plate (see fig. 40). (Redrawn by K.R. Dixon from Oldenstein 1976.)*

NUMERUM OMNIUM (rectangular plate) MILITANTIUM (terminal).

Recognizably Roman evidence for the late period is limited. A superb example of a fourth-century *spatha* was found in a burial at Köln (Cologne), Germany. The blade was 72cm (28in) long, and 5.2cm (2in) wide. The ivory hilt assemblage was remarkably well preserved, as was the circular chape, which had been gilded with silver and beautifully decorated with niello inlay (*Jahresberichte aus Augst und Kaiseraugst* 1986, 154–7, no. 5).

A new form of chape, introduced during the fourth century, consisted of an elliptical copper-alloy plate, sometimes pierced with holes for rivets and usually fitted with three studs (**fig. 35**; Werner 1966). Several examples of this chape have been found, including one from Liebenau, which was still fitted to the bottom of the wooden scabbard (**see fig. 38**). This style of fitting is also depicted on the Tetrarchy statue from Venice (**pl. 16**).

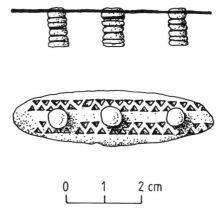

0   1   2 cm

Fig. 35 *Fourth-century scabbard chape from Gundremmingen. (Redrawn by K.R. Dixon from Werner 1966.)*

Three beautifully decorated silver plates which fitted beneath the guard of the hilt were found at Vrasselt (**fig. 36**; Stoll 1938). They are believed to date to the late fourth century (ibid., 250).

The diptych of Stilicho (**pl. 15**) clearly depicts a sword of Germanic origin. Both the hilt and the scabbard slide find parallel in Germanic, not Roman, finds (Behmer 1939, pl. 17.5; Davidson 1962, fig. 1112). The 'waisted' scabbard runners depicted on the Venice Tetrarchy statue, are very similar in form to the bone slides recovered from Nydam (Engelhardt 1865, pl. 8.33), Worms and Niederbieber (**fig. 37**; Oldenstein 1976, fig. 14. 64–5).

Evidence for scabbards comes from Liebenau, where a wooden scabbard, was found with chape and runner still attached (**fig. 38**; Stoll 1938, 138, fig. 3). A fragmentary leather covering for a scabbard, approximately 6cm (2½in) wide, was found associated with a helmet at Deurne (Klumbach 1973, 73, pl. 26.2).

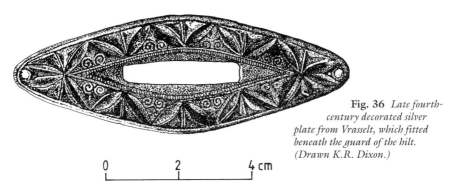

Fig. 36 *Late fourth-century decorated silver plate from Vrasselt, which fitted beneath the guard of the hilt. (Drawn K.R. Dixon.)*

0   2   4 cm

109

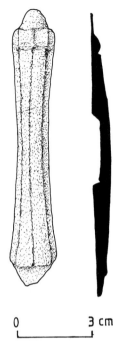

There is no evidence for the continued use of the wide baldric in the fourth century. The diptych of Stilicho shows his sword being suspended on a narrow waist belt (**pl. 15**). Although there are some representations of narrow baldrics from the fourth century onwards, such as can be seen on the diptych of Honorius, dated to 406, narrow waist belts were the common form: soldiers on the sixth-century throne of Maximian suspend their swords from waist belts.

Fig. 37 *Bone scabbard slide from Worms, Germany, extremely similar to those depicted on the St Mark's Tetrarchy statue from Venice. (Redrawn by K.R. Dixon from Oldenstein 1976.)*

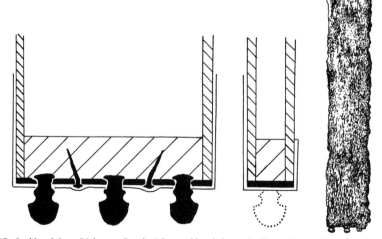

Fig. 38 *Scabbard from Liebenau fitted with a scabbard chape similar to the one from Gundrem-mingen. The detail illustrates how the chape was secured to the scabbard. (Redrawn by K.R. Dixon from Werner 1966.)*

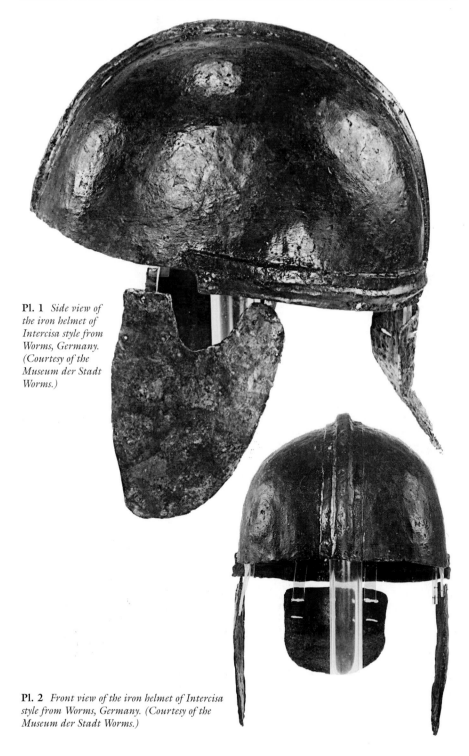

Pl. 1 *Side view of the iron helmet of Intercisa style from Worms, Germany. (Courtesy of the Museum der Stadt Worms.)*

Pl. 2 *Front view of the iron helmet of Intercisa style from Worms, Germany. (Courtesy of the Museum der Stadt Worms.)*

Pl. 3 *Helmet of Intercisa type from Augsburg-Pfersee, Germany. This example retains the decorated silver sheathing which other helmets of this style may originally have had. (Courtesy of the Germanisches National Museum, Nuremberg.)*

Pl. 4 *Helmet from Berkasova (referred to as helmet 1 in text). Only the silver sheathing which would originally have covered an iron bowl remains. The surfaces of the bowl, cheek-pieces and crest are adorned with glass-paste settings and embossed decoration. (Courtesy of the Vojvodjanski Museum, Novi Sad.)*

Pl. 5 *Side view of Berkasova helmet 1. (Courtesy of the Vojvodjanski Museum, Novi Sad.)*

Pl. 6 *Back view of Berkasova helmet 1, showing the attachment of the neck-guard by two small buckles. (Courtesy of the Vojvodjanski Museum, Novi Sad.)*

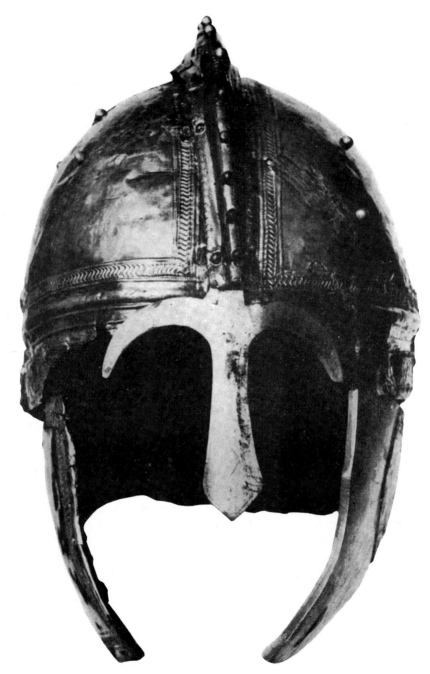

Pl. 7 *Front view of the helmet from Berkasova (referred to as helmet 2 in the text). As with helmet 1, only the silver sheathing which would originally have covered the iron bowl remains. Unlike Berkasova 1, this helmet has a limited amount of surface decoration. (Courtesy of the Vojvodjanski Museum, Novi Sad.)*

Pl. 8 *Side view of helmet 2 from Berkasova. (Courtesy of the Vojvodjanski Museum, Novi Sad.)*

Pl. 9 *Side view of helmet 2 from Berkasova, showing the attachment of the neck-guard by two small buckles. (Courtesy of the Vojvodjanski Museum, Novi Sad.)*

Pl. 10 *Helmet from Deurne, the Netherlands. Only the highly decorated gilded sheathing remains. (Courtesy of the Rijksmuseum van Oudheden, Leiden.)*

Pl. 11 *Reconstruction of the helmet from Dèr-el-Medineh. Made by Richard Underwood and worn by Philip Clark. (Photograph by Richard Underwood.)*

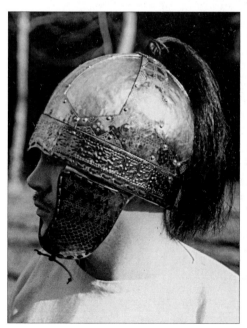

Pl. 12 *Reconstruction of the* Spangenhelm *from Batajnica. Made and worn by Richard Underwood. (Photograph by K.R. Dixon.)*

Pl. 13 *Fourth-century glass beaker from Cologne, Germany. It is decorated with the figures of four soldiers, each of whom carries a patterned shield and two spears. They appear to be wearing trousers, tunics and cloaks. A* vexillum *is positioned between each of the men. (Courtesy of Römisch Germanisches Museum, Cologne.)*

Pl. 14 *Silver donative dish from Geneva, depicting Valentian I (or II) flanked by his guards. Some of the designs on the oval shields carried by the guards closely resemble the shield emblems recorded in the* Notitia Dignitatum. *(Courtesy of the Musée d'Art et d'Histoire, Geneva.)*

Pl. 15 *Ivory diptych dating to* c. *400 of Stilicho, his wife and child. Stilicho wears a long tunic, and a cloak fastened on the right shoulder by a cross-bow brooch. The grip on his sword and the runner on his scabbard are Germanic in style. (Courtesy of the Parrocchia di S. Giovanni Battista Museo del Duomo, Monza, Italy.)*

Pl. 16 *Detail of the Tetrarchy statue from St Mark's Square, Venice, showing the distinctive style of scabbard slide and chape, actual examples of which have been recovered from various sites. (Photograph by K.R. Dixon.)*

Pl. 17 *Military belt fitments dating from approximately 375–50. Although the fitments were cast, this style of decoration is know as 'chip-carving'. (Courtesy of the Rijksmuseum van Oudheden, Leiden.)*

Pl. 18 *Detail from the Great Hunt mosaic from the Piazza Armerina, Sicily, showing two men wearing the fez-type of hat* (pilleus) *which became particularly popular during the Tetrarchy. (Photograph courtesy of R.J.A. Wilson.)*

Pl. 19 *Third-century dragon head from a standard found near the fort of Niederbieber, Germany. The silvered-bronze open-mouthed head is hollow, and originally a pole would have been pushed through the hole in the lower jaw. A long tube of material was fixed to the collar of the head, and once in motion this tube would have streamed out, giving the appearance of a living creature. (Courtesy of Koblenz Museum, Germany.)*

Short swords

Short swords appear to have continued in use during the later period. Evidence for the third century comes from the Künzing hoard, which produced 14 pattern-welded short swords of varying proportions (**fig. 39**; Herrmann 1969; 1972).

Vegetius, writing in the fourth century, states that both *spathae* and smaller swords called *semispathae* were employed (2.15), although no examples of the latter have been found.

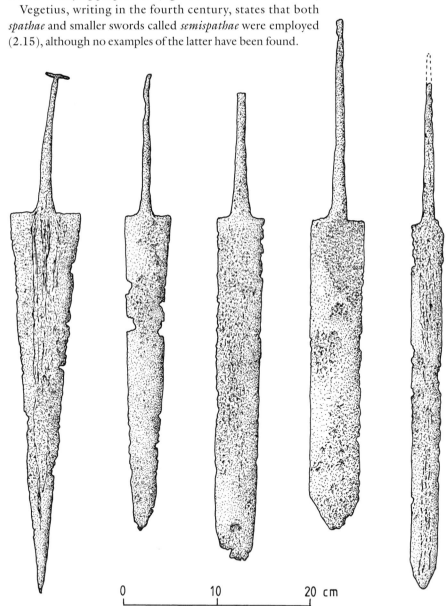

Fig. 39 *Selection of short swords from the third-century Künzing hoard of ironwork. (Redrawn by K.R. Dixon from Herrmann 1969.)*

Daggers

The dagger (*pugio*) continued to be used during the third century, as the remarkable iron hoard from Künzing demonstrates, producing 51 blades, some of which were pattern-welded, and 29 scabbards (Herrmann 1969; 1972). Most of the blades had a distinct waist and a medial rib with a groove running on either side (**fig. 40**; Herrmann 1972, 11). Some of the daggers were tanged, having had entirely organic grips, whilst others had inverted 'T'-shaped grips, terminating in crescentic pommels.

No evidence exists for the use of these double-edged daggers during the fourth century. A common grave find from this period onwards is the single-edged knife: several were found associated with belts from the Lankhills cemetery (Clarke 1979).

Shafted weapons

Evidence for the continued use of *pila* by legionaries during the third century comes from several praetorian gravestones. Most, such as that of Lucianus (Oldenstein 1976, fig. 13. 2), depict a large, bulbous weight placed between the shaft (which usually appears to be bound, probably with leather) and the long iron shank.

Fig. 40 *Iron dagger from the third-century Künzing hoard. (Drawn by K.R. Dixon.)*

Pila heads probably dating to this period have been recognized from several British sites, notably Caerleon, where approximately 55 heads were recovered (Nash-Williams 1932, figs 20–1) Richborough (**fig. 41**; Bushe-Fox 1949, pl. 43. 281–2).

There is abundant artefactual evidence for the types of spearheads employed during the third century. Three main types can be recognized: those with long, thin heads (**fig. 42**),those which are widest at the base (**fig. 43**), and those which are narrow at the base and broadest in the middle of the blade (**fig. 44**). Bishop and Coulston suggested that the narrower bladed type may have been primarily designed for throwing, whilst the broader headed variety may have been better suited to thrusting (1993, 126). Sculptural evidence appears to accord with this belief, particularly the *stela* of Aurelius Mucianus, who is depicted holding at least five narrow-bladed, shafted weapons (ibid., fig. 85. 3; Balty 1988, pl. 14. 2): the fact that so many of these weapons were carried implies that they were employed as missiles.

According to Vegetius (2.15), by the fourth century the *pilum* was known as the *spiculum*. It had a triangular iron head measuring 9 Roman inches (20cm/8in) long, attached to a shaft 5.5 Roman feet (162.8cm/5ft) in length.

Fig. 41 *Iron* pilum *head from Richborough, England, believed to date from the third century. (Drawn by K.R. Dixon.)*

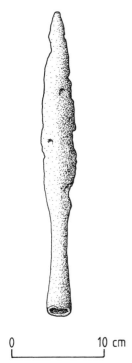

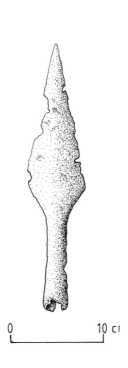

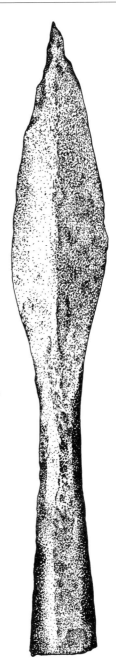

Fig. 42 *Third-century sock-eted iron spearhead of long, thin type from Saalburg, Germany. (Redrawn by K.R. Dixon from Jacobi 1897.)*

Fig. 43 *Third-century socketed iron spearhead of the type widest at the base, from Saalburg, Germany. (Redrawn by K.R Dixon from Jacobi 1897.)*

He further states that in his day a similar type of weapon, the *bebra*, was used by shield-bearing barbarian infantry, who carried between two and three into battle (1.20).

A number of long-shanked iron heads have been recovered. The examples from Carvoran (Richmond 1940) and South Shields (**fig. 45**; Allason-Jones and Miket 1984, fig. 5.90) both have long barbed heads and can be closely paralleled to the German *angon*.

Another form of shafted weapon described by Vegetius is the *verutum*, which was previously called the *vericulum* (2.15). This javelin had an iron head 5 Roman inches (11.4cm/4.5in) long, attached to a shaft measuring 3.5 Roman feet (103cm/3.4ft) in length.

A distinctive type of missile which appeared during the fourth century was the lead-weighted spearhead, called either a *plumbata* (probably a diminutive of *hasta plum-bata*, meaning leaded spear), or, as referred to by Vegetius,

Fig. 44 *Third-century sock-eted iron spearhead, widest in the middle of the blade, from the Künzing hoard. (Drawn by K.R. Dixon.)*

mattiobarbulus, presumed to be a scribal error for *martio-barbalus*, meaning Mars-barb (1.17; 3.14).

The *De Rebus Bellicus* describes and illustrates two types of head. The *plumbata et tribolata* was a javelin with a form of spiked caltrop soldered on just below the head, fitted with flights at the lower end of the wooden shaft (10.1–3). The second type, the *plumbata mamillata* ('breasted javelin'), had a lead weight fitted below a pointed iron head of circular section and flights attached to the opposite end of the shaft (11.1). The epithet 'breasted' presumably refers to the bulbous lead weight.

At present there have been no recognized finds of *plumbata et tribolata*. Examples of the *mamillata* style, however, have been recovered from several British sites: six from Wroxeter (**fig. 46**; Musty and Barker 1974; Barker 1979), two each from Richborough (one without the lead weight) (Bushe-Fox 1949, 152. 295–6, pl. 59) and Carvoran, and one each from Burgh Castle (lacking the weight) and Doncaster (Sherlock 1978; 1979; *Current Archaeology* 3 (1971–2), 274–5).

Until recently, Continental finds of *mamillata* heads consisted of single examples from Augst and Castell Weissenberg, Germany (Cahn 1989, 97–8, Lorch, Austria (Bishop and Coulston 1989, 63) and Intercisa, Hungary (Bennett 1991, 60). In 1991, however, three heads from Pitsunda, Georgia, were published (Bennett 1991). This dearth of examples, particularly from the Continent, may lead one to believe that *plumbatae* were never employed on a large scale. Vegetius, however, states that two Illyrican legions were renamed *Martiobarbuli Ioviani* and *Martiobarbuli Herculiani* by the joint emperors Diocletian

0   5 cm

Fig. 45 *Long-shanked barbed iron spearhead from South Shields, England. This type of spearhead is comparable to the German* angon. *(Redrawn by K.R. Dixon from Allason-Jones and Miket 1984.)*

and Maximianus because of their proficiency with this weapon, and that they were preferred above all others (1.17).

According to Vegetius, five *plumbatae* were carried by a soldier in the concavity of his shield, being used both in offensive actions, when they were thrown at the first charge, or defensively, when employed by the third row of reserves (1.17; 2.15; 2.16). Further information concerning their use comes from the *De Rebus Bellicus*, which states that the *plumbata et tribolata* was designed to be hurled by hand at close-quarters, inflicting injury either by directly penetrating the body of the assailant, or

Fig. 46 Plumbata mamillata *head from Wroxeter, England. (Drawn by K.R. Dixon.)*

by falling towards the ground and possibly becoming impaled in the foot of an unsuspecting soldier (10.1–3). Although the Anonymous fails to mention whether the *plumbata mamillata* (which is believed to correspond with Vegetius' *martiobarbalus*) was thrown by hand or machine, he states that because of the addition of a lead weight, it is sufficiently powerful to pierce shields and similar obstacles (11.1).

Experiments have been carried out with replica *plumbatae* based on the Wroxeter examples. Although it is generally held that *plumbatae* were thrown by hand, doubt still remains as to whether they were of javelin or dart-like proportions. The results gained from tests undertaken by Musty and Barker were based on them being similar to javelins; they used a fletched shaft 1m long, with a leather thong 'stretched over the end of the shaft and wrapped down both edges of it and held in the throwing hand at the shaft's centre of gravity', similar to the Roman *amentum* (1974). After a number of attempts this method produced a throw of about 30m (100ft). More recently further experiments were carried out, but giving the *plumbata* a dart-like appearance, being approximately 50cm (20in) long (Eagle 1989). Many variations were tried, allowing different lengths of shaft behind the flights, and throwing it under- and overarm. The underarm method proved the most effective, achieving distances approaching 70m (230ft) with comparatively little effort. This accords well with Vegetius' statement that soldiers using the *plumbata* take the place of archers 'for they wound both the men and the horses of the enemy before they come within reach of the common missile weapons' (1.17).

The sixth-century mosaic of Justinian flanked by his generals and guards from San Vitale, Ravenna, depicts the latter carrying spears equipped with long, narrow heads, with a broader middle section to the blade (see **fig. 22**). It is interesting to note that the shafts of these weapons appear to be decorated down one side in alternating bands of red, white, red and green. Earlier evidence for this practice in a Germanic context comes from the Kragehul bog deposits (Engelhardt 1867).

Axes

The most characteristic piece of equipment used by the Franks was the throwing-axe (*francisca*). A number of late authors comment on this weapon, including Sidonius and Procopius (respectively, Bk 4.20 and Panegyric on Maiorianus 5; 6.25.12 and 6.28.10–11: for a full list of ancient references see Dahmlos 1977, 161–5). Procopius describes them as follows (6.25.2–4): 'Now the iron head of this weapon was thick and exceedingly sharp on both sides, while the wooden handle was very short. And they are accustomed always to throw

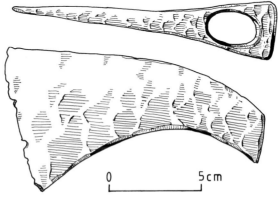

Fig. 47 *Axe head, possibly a* francisca *from Burgh Castle, England. (Redrawn by K.R. Dixon from Johnson 1983b.)*

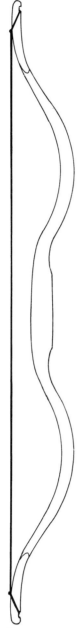

these axes at one signal in the first charge and thus shatter the shields of the enemy and kill the men.' Germanic troops probably introduced this weapon into the Empire by the fourth century (Bishop and Coulston 1993, 165). Two axe-heads recovered from Burgh Castle have been tentatively identified as *franciscii* (**fig. 47**; Johnson 1983b, 73, fig. 32, 26–7).

A tombstone dating to the Tetrarchy depicts a cavalryman carrying a more conventional style of axe (see **fig. 11**; Srejovic *et al*. 1983, fig. 42). The style of the head suggests that it was probably used for hacking at opponents and their shields rather than throwing.

Archery Equipment
Bows

The composite bow was employed during the late period, so called because of the component parts which were used in its construction. A wooden core supplied the basic shape, having bone, horn and sinew adhered to it (**fig. 48**). It was the latter material which gave this bow its great flexibility.

Owing to the high degree of skill required to make quality composite bows, specialist *sagittarii* units were probably supplied by their own *fabricae*. The establishment of centralized factories in the fourth century may simply have provided an additional source of production, possibly supplying the *comitatenses* (Coulston 1985, 259). According to the *Notitia Dignitatum*, three *fabricae* produced archery equipment in the west: Ticinium (Pavia, Italy) made bows (*arcuaria*), whilst Concordia (Portogruaro, Italy) and Matisconia(?) (Mâcon, France) produced arrows (*sagittaria*). No factories, however, are recorded for the east, a possible reason being that this area of the Empire would have had a native tradition in this craft, and it may have proved impracticable or unnecessary to enforce central organization (S. James 1988, 264).

Archaeological evidence comes primarily from finds of bone laths, two of which were attached to both angled ears, and, more rarely, the recessed grip of the bow. The fortress of Caerleon produced one of the finest collections of ear laths (Nash-Williams 1932, fig. 42; Coulston 1985, 227–9, figs 11–12). In total 215 fragments, dating to the late third century, were recovered, including one complete lath, 1.7cm (0.7in) wide and 30cm (11.8in) long. The

Fig. 48 *Illustration to show the basic shape of a composite bow when strung with the bowstring. Note the laths on the tips of the bow. (Redrawn by J.R.A. Underwood from Coulston 1985.)*

longest example, in two pieces, measured 1.9cm (0.7in) wide, by 37cm (14.6in) long. Six complete and two fragmentary laths for grips were also present at this site, ranging in length from 12.4–16.5cm (4.9–6.5in), and 1.2–1.8cm (?) wide (Bishop and Coulston 1993, 139, fig. 96, 2–3).

Pictorial evidence supplements the meagre archaeological remains, particularly mosaics, which depict strung bows in use in numerous hunting scenes.

Arrows

Arrowheads constitute the bulk of archery-related finds from military sites. The size, weight and style of head and type of fletchings employed, were dependent on the size of the archer, the use to which the bow was being put, and the degree of protection the target had (Coulston 1985, 264).

The third century saw the continued use of the tanged, trilobate style, together with a similar, longer socketed, type, examples of which have been found at Corbridge and Caerleon. Flat 'leaf'-bladed heads, socketed or tanged, are found Empire-wide, with the bodkin-head style being particularly prevalent in Germany (**fig. 49**; Bishop and Coulston 1993, 139, fig. 97).

Fig. 49 *Third-century arrow-heads: a: trilobate tanged arrow-head from Saalburg, Germany: b: bodkin-head arrowhead from Saalburg, Germany. (Redrawn by K.R. Dixon from Jacobi 1897.)*

The fourth-century arrowheads recovered from Gornea and Gundremmingen are socketed, with narrow, flat blades (Gudea 1977, figs 47–8; Bersu 1964, pl. 9, 6–9). Approximately 800 tanged, triangular-headed blades were found in a late fourth- or early fifth-century context at Housesteads, Hadrian's Wall (**fig. 50**; Manning 1976, 22–3, fig. 14).

The shafts to which the arrowheads were secured, either by means of a tang or a socket, rarely survive in the west. Some examples of arrowheads from Corbridge, Caerleon and Housesteads, however, still retain remains of wood on their tangs (Coulston 1985, 268). The best-preserved examples come from Dura-Europos, where the lower portions of three reed

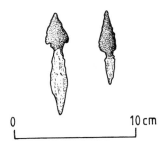

Fig. 50 *Tanged triangular-bladed arrow-heads from Housesteads, England. (Redrawn by K.R. Dixon from Manning 1976.)*

or cane shafts bearing painted markings were found (Rostovtzeff *et al.* 1936, 453–5, pl. 24). The shafts were probably marked to identify their owner, or denote a matching set (Coulston 1985, 266–7).

Bow-cases and quivers

Bow-cases and quivers were essential items of equipment since they protected both the bow and the arrows from the effects of moisture which could cause serious damage to the binding of the stave and string of the bow, together with the glue holding the fletchings to the shaft of the arrows.

There is no direct evidence for the use of bow-cases by the Romans. Some Sassanid and Parthian reliefs, however, depict the use of the Scythian-developed *gorytus*, a combined quiver and bow-case, and it is possible that some archers within the Roman army may have employed this style of case (Coulston 1985, 271).

Roman quivers, according to sculptural depictions, are all of cylindrical form. When used by horse archers, they are usually suspended from the right-hand side of the saddle behind the trooper; for infantrymen, the quiver was hung from a baldric.

Bracers and thumb rings

The method by which an archer drew his bow dictated which one of these items he would use. The Mediterranean release, which used two or more fingers to draw, brought the string close to the left forearm, necessitating the wearing of a leather bracer for protection. If the Mongolian method was employed, whereby the thumb drew back the string, a ring of bone or leather was worn on the thumb for protection and comfort. Although the former release was the most commonly used in the Roman army, the Mongolian method was probably adopted by some men during the fourth century (Coulston 1985, 278).

There is as yet no archaeological evidence for either of these items in the Roman period, although a scene on Trajan's Column does depict archers wearing bracers (Dixon and Southern 1992, 55, fig. 24; Lepper and Frere 1988, pl. 50, Scene 70).

Belts

Belts were an extremely important part of Roman equipment, not purely in practical terms, but also in symbolic terms, since they distinguished the soldier from the civilian.

Several styles of belt were prevalent during the third century, ring-buckled belts being the most commonly featured on tombstones of this period (see **fig. 27**). The latter were broad waist-belts, which were fastened by the tapered ends of the belt being brought through the ring from behind, then pulled outwards over the front to either side of the ring where they were then secured by studs (**fig. 51**). Examples of this type of buckle, which can be of iron or copper alloy, have been found on a number of military sites (**fig. 52**).

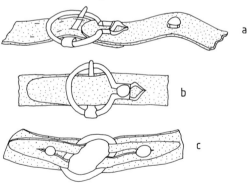

During the fourth and fifth centuries belts became broader, necessitating a greater use of stiffeners. One of the most characteristic belt fittings of the fourth century is the 'propeller' belt stiffener, which consisted of a central roundel with two opposing elongated triangular projections. Stiffeners of this style have been

Fig. 51 *Illustration showing the two methods of fastening ring-buckle belts: a and b demonstrate the method by which Oldenstein believes ring buckles with a tongue and side extension would have been fastened; c: where no tongue or extension exists on the buckle, the tapered ends of the belt are brought through the ring from behind and pulled outwards over it, being secured at either side by studs. (Redrawn by K.R. Dixon from Oldenstein 1976.)*

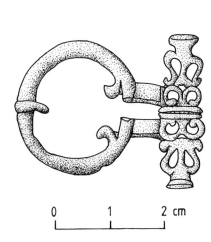

Fig. 52 *Ring buckle from Weissenburg. (Redrawn by K.R. Dixon from Oldenstein 1976.)*

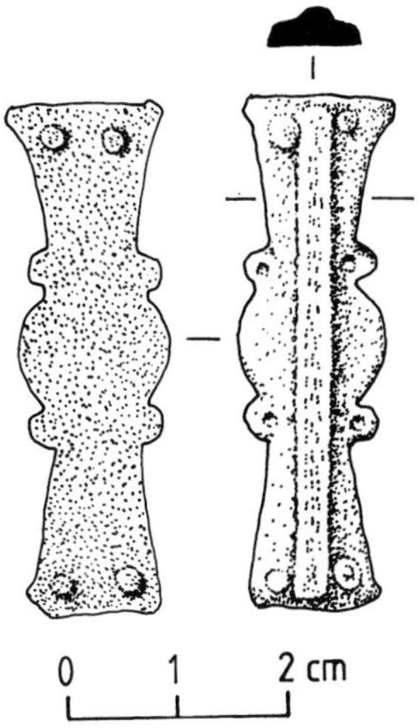

Fig. 53 *'Propeller' belt stiffener from Maryport, England, believed to date to the second or third quarter of the fourth century. (Redrawn by K.R. Dixon from Webster 1986.)*

recovered from various sites, including Maryport (**fig. 53**; Webster 1986, 63–5, fig. 7. 41) and Richborough (Bushe-Fox 1928, pl. 21, fig. 2). Two silver examples were found with the Berkasovo helmets (Klumbach 1973, 25, fig. 10, 3–4). A belt assemblage which included two propeller stiffeners was found at Zenkóvárkony (Bullinger 1969, fig. 62.5). This style continued to be used until the early part of the fifth century (Bishop and Coulston 1993, 173).

By the second half of the fourth century broad belts, ranging from 5–10cm (2–4in) in width, had become highly decorated, with the fittings being ornamented using a technique rather misleadingly known as 'chip-carving', since in reality 'chip-carved' items were cast (**pl. 17**). This style of belt was fastened by a narrow strap, which was attached behind a plate at one end of the belt, being passed through a buckle attached near the other end (**fig. 54**). From various depictions, such as the porphyry statues from Vienna

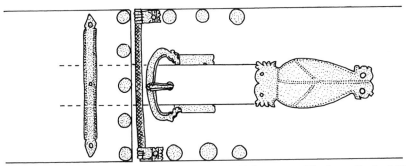

Fig. 54 *Reconstruction of the belt from a grave at the Lankhills cemetery, Winchester, England. The narrow strap end could sometimes be extremely long, being worn dangling downwards, or it could be wrapped over the belt, leaving the end hanging over the right hip. (Redrawn by K.R. Dixon from Clarke 1979.)*

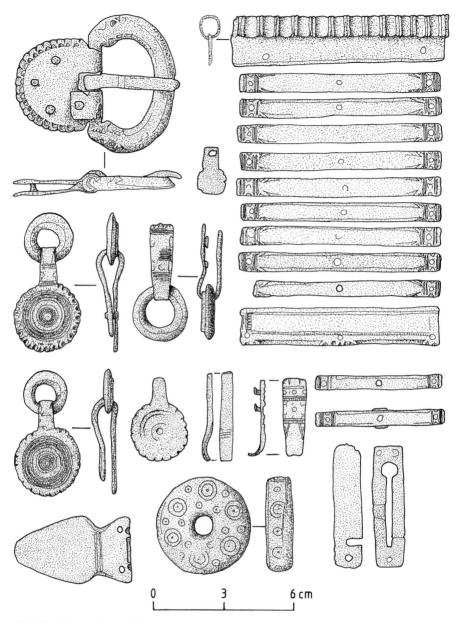

Fig. 55 *Fitments from a belt from Dorchester on Thames. The two rectangular objects (shown bottom right in illustration) represent an unusual suspension system, with the two plates being secured by a single rivet, one on top of the other, the plate with the elongated notch terminating in a circle being placed underneath. The object to be suspended would be provided with a shanked stud, the head of which could fit through the circular opening. The stud would then be moved towards the narrow end of the notch, whereupon the uppermost plate would be swung over, securing the stud in the corresponding gap, and thus preventing the stud from slipping downwards to the circular hole. (Redrawn by K.R. Dixon from Hawkes and Dunning 1961.)*

and Ravenna, it appears that the narrow fastening strap could sometimes be extremely long, being left either to dangle from the buckle, or wrapped over the belt, leaving the end hanging over the right hip. Most late Roman belt assemblages have been recovered from graves, and some appear to have their complete set of fitments. The assemblage from Dorchester on Thames comprises elongated rectangular stiffeners, tubular edging plates, a lancet-shaped strap terminal, various ring suspension fitments and a buckle with confronted animal heads incised on the loop (**fig. 55**; Hawkes and Dunning 1961, fig. 1). This burial also included a very unusual rectangular suspension system, possibly from which to hang a pouch or a small knife, and a bone sword bead. The exact function of the latter object is still uncertain.

From the fifth century onwards broad belts were replaced by narrow examples, and many beautifully decorated gold and garnet belt plates have been recovered from western Germanic graves.

Clothing

Tunics

Third-century tombstones depict soldiers wearing knee-length tunics, usually with long sleeves (see fig. 27). Numerous woollen tunics dating to this period were recovered from Dura-Europos (Pfister and Bellinger 1945). Woven in one piece with a neck slit, they are generally decorated with two bands on the cuff, together with a single, double or triple *clavus* band (occasionally with an ornate terminal) which ran down over both shoulders to the middle of the chest or the hem (ibid., 15). The decoration was woven in reddish-purple wool, with the main body of the garment being undyed. Although true purple dye (*murex brandaris*) is present on this site, cheaper madder-based dyes are more commonly used.

The basic shape and construction of the tunic remained the same throughout the late Roman period, differing only in an increased use of decoration, with large ornate roundels (*orbiculi*) being added to the existing repertoire during the fourth century (**fig. 56**). As mosaics from Piazza Armerina show, these roundels were positioned near each corner of the hem

Fig. 56 *Roundel from a tunic, believed to date from the fourth or fifth century, decorated with a scene from the story of Orestes and Iphigenia. Purple wool on undyed linen. (Drawn by K.R. Dixon.)*

Fig. 57 *Detail of the great hunt mosaic from the Piazza Armerina villa, believed to date to the early fourth century. The man's tunic is decorated with roundels on the shoulders and bottom corners, bands on the cuff and additional strips of decoration* (clavi) *running downwards from the shoulder. Note also the cloak* (sagum). *broad belt and decorated shield. (Drawn by K.R. Dixon.)*

(two on the front and two on the back of the tunic), and one on each shoulder (**fig. 57**). The decoration was either woven into the fabric, or woven separately and sewn on (Trilling 1982, 14).

By the middle of the fifth century, square patches of decoration on the shoulders and lower corners of the tunic became more common than roundels, although the latter continued in use throughout the period. The sixth-century mosaics from the church of San Vitale, Ravenna, depict the Emperor Justinian flanked by generals wearing undyed tunics, decorated with squares of geometric patterns executed in dark brown (see **fig. 22**).

Although white (undyed) tunics with purple decoration were the norm, there is evidence for the use of other colours, particularly red: the Syracuse catacomb fresco, dating to the fourth century, depicts a soldier wearing a red tunic (Bishop and Coulston 1993, pl. 7b), and a passage in the *Scriptores Historiae Augustae* states that two red military tunics were supplied annually to the tribune Claudius (later to become emperor) (Claudius 14). A sixth-century tunic of red wool, decorated with figures and geometric motifs in black wool, is housed in the Washington Textile Museum (Trilling 1982, 77. 74).

The *thoracomachus*

It was necessary for some form of garment to be worn under mail or scale armour, usually a linen or wool tunic, sometimes both. A special garment, the *thoracomachus*, designed for this purpose is described by the Anonymous (*De Rebus Bellicis* 15; Wild 1979, 105–10). It consisted of shirt made from woollen felt, which would protect the wearer's chest against the weight and friction of his armour, and against the cold. He further suggests that in order to stop the *thoracomachus* becoming extremely heavy when soaked with rain, an extra shirt should be worn over it, the armour then being placed on top.

Cloaks

From the third century onwards soldiers are depicted wearing the *sagum*, a type of cloak which finished below the knee, and was often fringed along the bottom hem. It was fastened at the right shoulder, exposing the right side of the body. Many of the fourth-century mosaics from Piazza Armerina depict men wearing *saga*, sometimes decorated with ornate *orbisculi* at the corners (see fig. 57). The sixth-century mosaic from San Vitale, Ravenna, depicting Justinian standing with his generals, shows the latter wearing ankle-length cloaks of undyed cloth, fastened at the right shoulder, and decorated with a single 'rhomboid'-shaped patch or possibly stripe of brown crossing the body from right to left (see **fig. 22**). The decoration and length of these cloaks may have served to distinguish the wearers as men of high rank.

Trousers

Knee-length trousers, probably of leather, were usually worn by cavalrymen. Infantrymen are generally depicted bare-legged, or possibly wearing skin-tight trousers. With the introduction of large numbers of Germanic troops into the army from the third century onwards, the wearing of long, slightly looser fitting wool trousers, such as found in the Thorsbjerg bog deposit, probably became a common sight (Engelhardt 1863, pl. 2). Eastern troops are often depicted wearing long, loose trousers: the Battle of Ebenezer fresco from Dura appears to show two soldiers wearing trousers (Kraeling 1956, pl. 55).

Hats

In late Roman art, soldiers are often depicted wearing the *pilleus*, a hat shaped rather like a fez (**pl. 18**). Originally, according to Vegetius, Pannonian leather caps had been worn by soldiers at all times in order to accustom them to having some weight on their heads in preparation for their helmets (1.20). The *pillei* referred to by Vegetius, however, may have looked more like those of felt worn by charioteers as a form of crash-helmet. These hats were skull- rather than fez-shaped. Furthermore, the Edict of Diocletian lists 'sheepskin with the wool left on for making a *pilleus*', implying that at this time the hats were of a fleecy rather than a smooth nature (*Ed. Diocl.* 9.20a, 21ff.).

Fez-type *pillei* appear to have been particularly popular during the Tetrarchy. The Great Hunt mosaic from the fourth-century Piazza Armerina Villa, Sicily, depicts three individuals wearing *pillei* (**pl. 18**), and the Tetrarchy statue from St Mark's Square, Venice, depicts all four men wearing this style of hat. A tombstone from Gamzigrad, dating from the same period, depicts a cavalryman wearing a fez-type *pilleus* (see **fig. 11**; Srejevic *et al.* 1983, fig. 42).

Footwear

The distinctive nailed military boot (*caliga*) seems to have disappeared from use by the early second century (van Driel-Murray 1986, 140–1). Archaeological evidence tends to suggest that from this time onwards, military footwear differs little from that worn by civilians, implying that standardization had been abandoned in favour of shoes being made to suit local conditions (ibid.).

Many styles of footwear are depicted on late Roman sculptures, including sandals, flat-ended and pointed boots, open and fully enclosed shoes. Three shoes, all from different pairs, were found in association with the Deurne helmet (Klumbach 1973, 73–5, pl. 12, fig. 27).

Miscellaneous Equipment

Brooches

Circular brooches, such as can be seen on the tombstone of Iulius Aufidius (Bishop and Coulston 1993, fig. 101. 2) are the type most commonly depicted for fastening cloaks during the third century. Although cross-bow brooches were used during the third

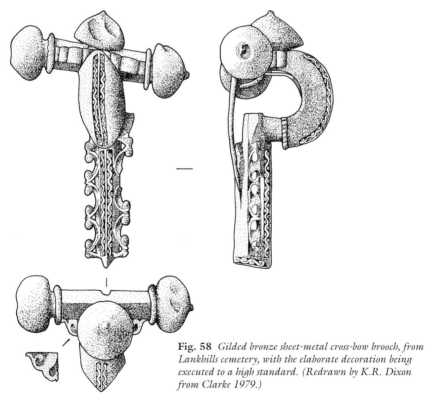

Fig. 58 *Gilded bronze sheet-metal cross-bow brooch, from Lankhills cemetery, with the elaborate decoration being executed to a high standard. (Redrawn by K.R. Dixon from Clarke 1979.)*

century, they are more commonly represented during the fourth century. One of the best depictions of a cross-bow can be seen on the ivory diptych of Stilicho (**pl. 15**). Numerous examples of this type of brooch have been recovered from late Roman sites, including Richborough (Bushe-Fox 1928, pls 17–18; 1949, pls 30–2) and the Lankhills cemetery (**fig. 58**; Clarke 1979, 259–63). As Clarke notes, not all finds of cross-bow brooches can be used to indicate the presence of military or civilian officials (ibid., 262–3).

Standards

The standards were an extremely important piece of equipment in the Roman army. Apart from their religious significance, they served as a rallying point for the troops and a method of communicating signals in the confusion of battle. Ammianus records an instance where some cavalry who were fleeing from the field, heartened by the sight of Julian's standard, returned to the fight (20.4.18). To lose a standard was one of the most disgraceful occurrences which could befall a legion: when a standard was captured by the Persians, the latter taunted the Romans by draping sausages on it, and setting it up on a tower in the city of Nisibis (Procopius 2.18.22–6).

Fig. 59 *Bronze roundel, possibly the badge of an officer, believed to be third century in date, depicting soldiers of vexillations of* Legio XX Valeria Victrix *and* Legio II Augusta. *Note the* vexilla *and oval shields. (Found in France. Redrawn by K.R. Dixon from Casey 1991.)*

The *vexillum* continued in use during the late period. It consisted of a square piece of purple or red material, fringed along the lower edge, and hung from a crossbar attached to a lance (see **figs 21, 59** and **pl. 19**). The only known example, painted with a figure of Victory, was found in Egypt (Rostovtzeff 1942, 92–106).

According to Vegetius, the eagle (*aquila*) was still carried (2.13; 3.5), together with insignia for each century (2.13); it is uncertain whether the latter form of standard existed during the Principate (Zwikker 1937, 7–22).

The most striking type of standard used during the late period was the *draco*. These dragon standards appear to have been introduced into the Roman army by the Sarmatians during the second century, when they were primarily associated with the cavalry. By the fourth century, however, one was apparently carried by each legionary cohort (Vegetius 2.13). They consisted of a hollow, open-mouthed dragon's head, to which was attached a long tube of material. A hole was cut in the underside of the dragon's mouth, through which a pole for carrying the standard was pushed. The fifth-century writer Sidonius describes their appearance when held (*Panegyric on Maiorianus*, 5): 'Now the broidered dragon speeds hither and thither in both armies, his throat swelling as the zephyrs dash against it; that pictured form with wide-open jaw counterfeits a wrathful hunger, and the breeze puts a frenzy into the cloth as often as the lithe back is thickened by the blasts and the air is now too abundant for the belly to hold.' The head from a third-century *draco* was found near the fort of Niederbieber (**pl. 19**; Garbsch 1978, 88, fig. 48.3). The *draco* is depicted on a number of reliefs, including the third-century Great Ludovisi Sarcophagus (Coulston 1991, fig. 8), the Arch of Galerius and the Arch of Constantine, both dating to the early fourth century, and some copper panels from a box from Ságvár, Hungary, dated slightly later (ibid., 102–5, figs 9–11).

Musical instruments

Musical instruments were used to convey commands to troops in battle (Vegetius 3.5): 'By these means through unambiguous sounds the army recognizes whether it should halt, advance or retreat, whether to pursue fugitives into the distance or sound for a withdrawal.'

According to Vegetius, there were three types of musical instrument used in the army (2.5): a straight instrument called the *tuba* (trumpet); a circular type called the *cornu* (bugle); and a type of horn (*bucina*), made from the horn of an auroch, and bound with silver.

A third-century tombstone depicts the soldier carrying a *tuba* (Coulston 1987, pl. 3), whist the Great Ludovisi Battle Sarcophagus, dating to the middle of the third century, shows a man playing a *cornu* (Bivar 1972, pl. 9).

Procopius, writing in the sixth century, states that in the past, the men who blew the instruments could play two different strains on them, one to initiate fighting, the other to denote a withdrawal (6.23.23). According to Procopius, this skill no longer existed, so he urged Belisarius to use the cavalry trumpets to command the men to fight, whilst those of the infantry could be used to sound a retreat, stating that it was impossible for the troops to fail to recognize the difference 'for in the one case the sound comes forth from leather and very thin wood, and in the other from rather thick brass'.

VII

FORTIFICATIONS

Fortifications are, in general terms, related both to perceived threat and internal strength of the state or organization responsible for building them. Forts and fortresses, frontiers marked by running barriers, road posts and watchtowers had always featured strongly in Roman military practice. As the Empire gradually ceased to expand, the army settled down in more or less permanent stations strung out along the frontiers. Many scholars rightly argue that the barriers such as Hadrian's Wall in Britain and the Hadrianic palisade in Germany were never intended to withstand a determined assault; they were not designed to be defended like castles under siege. They were at best a means of population control, of slowing down movement and hindering attackers until the army assembled to meet them in the field. Defence, in the early Roman Empire, meant aggressive response or even offensive pre-emptive strike into enemy territory before there could be any attack on Roman installations.

Although their forts were enclosed by walls and towers, equipped with defended gateways and surrounded by one or more ditches, this was mostly a precautionary measure designed to prevent undesirable elements from approaching or entering the forts. Early Imperial Romans did not sit inside their defences waiting for the enemy to attack. The army met adversaries in the open, often in advance of the frontiers. The whole ethos of military practice was to stay alert, closely observing potentially hostile populations and controlling them so that the situation should never arise whereby the soldiers were attacked in their forts. There were disastrous exceptions to this rule, but it was not the accepted norm. Only in the east was there any danger of meeting forces as well equipped and trained as the Romans were, and whose fortifications were strong enough to demand siege works to overthrow them. In most parts of their empire the Romans were not faced with enemies who could afford to undertake long sieges, mainly because native tribes had no organized commissariat. Food shortages often forced barbarians to move before they had achieved their objective. They could rarely starve a garrison out, and they rarely had equipment to bombard the walls with missiles, or to undermine them. Likewise they rarely built fortifications of their own which were strong enough to repel a Roman army. The Dacians had done so, but only with Roman help. For 200 years, using a mixture of diplomacy and deception, absorption by settlement and control by bestowing subsidies, and if all else failed by fighting, the army managed to keep invaders at bay, on the edges of the Empire. There were disasters, but the army always recovered, even while fighting on more than one front and on occasion embroiled in a civil war as well. But the balance was very fine, and when it tipped, the whole Roman world became aware of how much damage these weak barbarians, who were no good at sieges, could do once they had crossed the frontiers.

In the beleaguered third century, the army still operated in the open, but after the 260s it never really regained the ascendancy that it had enjoyed in the early Empire. Towards the end of the third century, there was a discernible change in the design of fortifications.

Perhaps the most telling sign that the winds of change had begun to blow was Aurelian's decision to build walls round the city of Rome. It implied that though the Emperor had the best interests of the Roman population at heart, he was no longer able to protect the people by using the army alone. Romans of the generation who witnessed the foundation of the walls may well have felt comforted by their presence, but they cannot have failed to reflect deeply on the situation that necessitated fortifying their city, which had proudly eschewed the use of such protection since the time of the early kings.

Offensive defence was now not always possible, and years of devastation alternated with years of reparation whenever there was sufficient respite. The emperors showed by their active building programmes that in fortification they saw at least a partial answer to Rome's problems. The sheer number of surviving remains testifies to their diligence, but does little to elucidate the basic questions of who built them, who garrisoned them, when, for how long and why.

Among others there are three useful works covering a broad range of late Roman fortifications. Johnson (1983a) classifies fortifications by area or region, then by chronology. Lander (1984), more limited in scope for the late Empire since he documents fortifications from the early Empire onwards, follows a chronological plan, classifying mostly by type. Petrikovits (1971) is concerned only with the north-west provinces, and argues that the most sensible means of classifying fortifications is by their function. It could be argued that it is impossible to identify function from ground plans alone, which is often all that remains to be studied, but there are the concomitant factors of position, such as on roads, rivers or hills, and their relation to other forts and fortlets. One major drawback is that it is difficult to prove that sites were occupied simultaneously, and it cannot be reiterated too often that enormous problems arise from the lack of accurate dating materials for many if not most of the large number of late Roman fortifications all over the Empire.

The founders of new forts ought to be more readily identifiable than the authors of repairs to existing buildings, since repair work of any date melds with that of earlier and later rebuilders; but it is not always the case that new buildings can be correctly dated. The surviving ancient literature tends to create an imbalance, since Diocletian, Constantine, Valentinian and, much later, Justinian are marked out as the most energetic builders. Whilst this is probably not untrue, the activities of intervening emperors, not necessarily less energetic than the better documented rulers, are obscured, leading to the assignation of most buildings by modern scholars to one of the aforementioned acknowledged builders whenever the context seems even remotely correct.

The subject is a large one, and lack of space precludes an in-depth discussion of all late Roman forts and fortlets, towers and road posts, cities and citadels. This chapter will summarize the main trends; the next chapter discusses sieges and siege warfare which became such a common feature of late Roman history.

The need for defence in the late Roman Empire extended to every province and every city, town or villa. In the Western Empire, the provinces of Italy, southern Gaul and Spain, peaceful for centuries, were now potentially just as threatened as the Rhine and Danube frontiers. There was internal disorder and unrest, caused by landless men such as the Bagaudae in Gaul, and also the northern barbarians, horrendously and erratically mobile, had shown how quickly they could pillage and destroy their way from the Rhine to the Mediterranean.

An organized invading army would probably aim to capture strategic points and then to dominate the country from strongholds. Therefore, with a knowledge of the local geography, there would be a certain predictability about their movements, thus largely facilitating defence. Barbarians were not predictable; as far as the Romans could understand them, they came and went without ever seeming to know what they wanted, with no long-term plans for settlement. This may not be the absolute truth, but truth is not so important as the way in which the Romans viewed the barbarians. Hence, the barbarian threat as the Romans perceived it meant that ideally, everything, everywhere, required fortification, whether military post or civilian settlement. In parts of the African provinces, fortified farmhouses sprang up, sometimes with such a martial appearance that it is difficult to discern from the remains whether the site was civilian or military. Nothing was safe any more; if the barbarians were quiet, Roman armies recently victorious in civil wars might be on the rampage, and they were not too particular about whose town they sacked as long as it involved carrying off portable wealth and food. This was an even greater hazard than anything that the barbarians could offer, since a Roman army could besiege a city with expertise and appropriate equipment.

New Trends

The outer limits of the Empire, shrunken now, were still protected by forts of various types strung out along river banks, or through terrain not necessarily marked by such natural features or by artificial barriers. Old frontier forts were repaired, rebuilt or altered. Sometimes they were reduced in size, and were often strengthened by the addition of interval and corner towers, usually projecting, to afford a better view of the walls. Gates were sometimes blocked up, often leaving only one usable entrance.

New forts were no longer built to the classic playing-card shape. Now they were often foursquare, with the barracks round the inner faces of the walls. Yet others were quite irregular in plan, no longer resembling the old style forts at all. Walls were much thicker and their towers huge, since some of them now had to support artillery engines. Where the terrain demanded it, for instance on the tops of hills, the walls often followed the natural contours, giving the fortifications a very un-Roman appearance.

Siting of forts also underwent modifications in the late Empire. Early Roman forts were usually laid out in open territory for the purpose of domination and control of the surrounding countryside, while their successors were more commonly built on higher ground with the emphasis on keeping watch and on defence. Many civilian sites now favoured hilltop locations with their better views all around and their difficulty of access. Johnson depicts those areas where hilltops were reoccupied or occupied afresh in the late Empire (1983a, maps 87–8). The occupation of sites that qualify for the name *refugia* began in the middle years of the third century in the Alpine regions, no doubt because of the availability of suitable locations. Those which have been excavated yield coins of the period 260–70, and are thus associated with the Alamannic invasions (Drack and Fellman 1988, 379; 398; 434; 450; 500; 514).

Under the heading 'fortification' can be included several different types of buildings and defensive techniques, besides those qualifying for the label fort or fortlet. The old cordon system, strings of forts and watchtowers with or without running barriers to connect them, had not been entirely abandoned. After the frontiers fell, the idea was revived here and there, though not in exactly the same locations. The Danube–Iller–Rhine frontier (see **fig. 6**) can be included in this category, and also the traces of walls blocking some of the Alpine passes.

More than ever before, interior communications, previously so open, had to be protected by means of road posts and towers, and rivers had to be guarded by bridgehead forts and fortified landing places. Transport and storage of goods became a hazardous occupation, so magazines and storehouses had to be fortified to ensure the survival of supplies and to attempt to distribute them fairly.

Cities too needed defence, and new walls were built or existing walls repaired or completed. Several cities had acquired walls in the early Empire, but usually only in an excess of civic pride, which on occasion expired along with the cash before the walls were completed. These were not usually adequate for the sort of defence which was required in the late Empire. Fortifications of the late third and early fourth century, unlike their predecessors, were built with the tacit assumption that people would try to approach the walls, and may even succeed in their objective. The defenders therefore needed the many towers which feature so largely in late Roman fortifications, not only to be able to keep a lookout at the surrounding territory, but also in order to be able to survey the walls between towers and prevent anyone from approaching too closely by enfilading fire.

The decision to fortify a city may have rested with the local councils, who were presumably responsible for raising the necessary finance and labour force, but it is quite likely that military engineers were called in or even sent by the Emperor to design and build the walls and gateways. It is doubtful that those cities which housed a military presence, whether a garrison, workshops, factories or stores, could have been left to their own devices, given the seriousness of the times. After all, the Tetrarchic bases were in large cities, not at forts, and there would be a vested interest in fortifying these bases at least.

This raises the question of whether there was any central direction from the Imperial courts as to the style and plan of the various fortifications, or whether the emperors simply issued broad general instructions to repair forts and build new ones, leaving the siting, design and layout to the military authorities in the region concerned. Petrikovits (1971, 203–4) argued for the latter, concluding that military architects were given free rein within a set of wider requirements. Lander (1984, 309) disagreed, listing the similarities in fort types from all over the Empire to argue for a coherent strategic plan with the intention of committing long-term resources to a comprehensive fortification programme. Johnson (1983a, 114–16) pointed out that city fortifications do not display signs of indiscriminate haste. They were carefully constructed with no evidence at all that the main aim was speed and penny-pinching, or that the walls were thrown up at the last minute as the barbarians approached. Johnson concluded that the emperors did indeed devise an overall strategic plan which included the fortification of the cities as well as military establishments. Valentinian's programme certainly included cities (Ammianus 28.3.2; 30.7.5).

It is possible to argue for a coherent Imperial policy without entirely disagreeing with Petrikovits' hypothesis that the minor details were worked out locally. An overall strategic plan would make strong sense, but it may not have been possible to execute such a plan in painstaking detail at all times in all regions. Diocletian, Constantine and Valentinian, for instance, may have conceived of sweeping policies for the whole of their sectors of the Empire, but even though they claimed to be gods, they could be in only one place at a time. Therefore some of the Rhine and Danube fortifications may bear the personal stamp of the above-named emperors because they campaigned there and were active in those regions afterwards, but elsewhere they may have been forced to leave even the larger considerations of siting and plan, as well as the multiple smaller matters, to their subordinates. Epigraphic evidence attests that in Africa the *vicarius,* superior to the *praeses* in both military and civil matters, was responsible for siting the small posts known as *centenaria.* Such matters may have been frequently delegated when emperors were unable to appear in person.

The concept of a standard plan, rigidly enforced by a mindless, unquestioning bureaucracy, is difficult to shake off. The editors of the *Abinnaeus Archive* (1962, 21), in considering the fort of *Castra Dionysias* (**fig. 60**), concluded that there was no need for a fort of such strength in this location, so the plan must somehow have been carried through regardless of the level of defence necessary in that area. Their argument is that the main duties of Abinnaeus' unit were police work, collecting the military *annona* and assisting with the enforcement of customs duties and regional administration. Whilst this may be entirely true, the idea neglects the important factor of perceived threat. So often, modern interpreters think they know best, relying on their often very detailed knowledge of the area, which leads them to conclude that the Romans must have made a mistake. This is always an admissible chance in any army, and no one is infallible, but it is worth

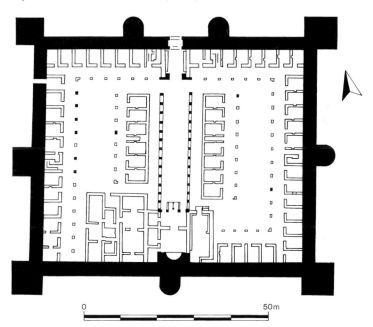

Fig. 60 Castra Dionysias, *the small square fort at Qasr Qarun in Egypt, showing the changes in plan which distinguish such fortified posts from forts of the early Roman Empire. This fort has thick walls and massive towers, only one gate and rooms arranged around all the inner faces of the walls. (Redrawn by G. Stobbs from Lander 1984.)*

emphasizing over and over again that we do not know what motivated the Romans of the third, fourth and fifth centuries, and modern knowledge, even when backed up by documentation, is not enough.

The builders and repairers of the many late Roman forts and towers were invariably military men, using methods carried over from the early Empire, though the sort of buildings they were producing would have looked strange to their forerunners. The brick and tile stamps found on many sites are perhaps fairly reliable indicators of who actually did the work, but not of the units which garrisoned the forts, since the original builders did not necessarily remain in the forts they built. More confusing is the possibility that the bricks and tiles were reused and even transferred to different sites, thus compounding the problem of occupation and chronology. It is therefore most sensible to describe fortifications by function, in so far as this can be ascertained.

Marching Camps

These are hardly a common feature of the late Roman army in action, but they ought to be included in a survey of types of fortification, precisely because of their scarcity, as an indication of changes in procedure. The exact nature and purpose of temporary camps are still hotly debated by modern scholars, but there are enough camps still in evidence to be certain that in the early Empire the Romans built them, perhaps for a variety of reasons. It is usually said that the army on the march built a camp every night, and this perhaps is true in so far as the soldiers carried stakes (*pila muralia*) with which to form a palisade on top of a bank of earth, which would be raised up from digging the surrounding ditch and turning the soil inwards. The banks need not have been very high or very wide. This sort of temporary camp, quite insubstantial in archaeological terms, may have differed widely from a more permanent camp designed to house the army for several days. The camps still in evidence in north Britain may be of this more permanent variety.

Vegetius (1.21.25) complained that soldiers in his day no longer carried the tools for camp construction and were not trained in the methods of erecting them. He went on to explain how such camps should be built, providing modern archaeologists with a wealth of detail on how to cut turves, but probably doing little to effect changes in the late Roman army.

As far as is known, the only example of a late Roman marching camp is the one at Ermelo in Holland (Johnson 1983a, 32). It may be associated with the campaigns of Julian, though the evidence is very slight. However, it is quite possible that there are more examples awaiting discovery, since it was thought at one time that there were few marching camps of early Imperial date in Germany, but with the help of aerial photography and assiduous investigation, more and more have been revealed in recent years. If by the late fourth century the art of camp construction had lapsed, this should not be taken as an implication that all generals neglected to build camps at all times and in all places. A few conscientious military leaders may have acted as exceptions to the rule.

The Byzantine army knew how to erect marching camps, and therefore if the actual practice had lapsed for a time, the knowledge had not disappeared. Maurice's *Strategikon* (12.22) contains a description of a camp with instructions on how to build one. Maurice recommended a square or oblong camp with two intersecting streets running through the middle in the shape of a cross, connecting the four gates, of which there should be one in each side. There should be a ditch all around the camp, and Maurice advised that caltrops should be strewn around outside to prevent the approach of horsemen. He also advocated the digging of pits to trap unsuspecting infiltrators. A legionary of the second century would have recognized this camp, but we can only guess whether a soldier in the armies of Valens or Valentinian would have done so.

Forts and Fortlets

The division between forts and fortlets is a little shadowy, since some of the newly founded late Roman forts were much smaller than their older counterparts, and in the context of the early Empire, modern scholars would have labelled them fortlets. There is also confusion in that some of the smaller forts are comparable in size to some of the larger towers, *burgi* and blockhouses. Sites included under the heading of fortlet in some publications can be categorized as towers and blockhouses in other books and essays.

Late Roman forts do not resemble those of the early Empire in shape or internal arrangements. The classic Roman fort was usually oblong or, less commonly, square, with rounded corners. The administrative buildings were usually placed in the centre range, with barracks, storehouses and workshops grouped in the remaining portions of the fort. This form, not without exceptions in layout and design, survived until more or less the middle of the third century. Little is known of what happened to forts during the years of the Military Anarchy. The first serious reconstructions were carried out under Diocletian and then in sporadic and enthusiastic bursts thereafter, resulting in new forms and altered plans.

Late Roman forts are usually much more strongly built than their predecessors, with thicker walls bristling with towers. The emphasis is on grimly determined defence as opposed to temporary protection. Late forts have a rather more claustrophobic atmosphere than their earlier counterparts, despite the closely packed interiors and narrow streets of the latter. The fort at Deutz (*Divitia*) is quite large, but it still has a closed-in feel about it when one stands in the remains of its gateway, hemmed in by the massive thick-walled towers.

Alterations to existing forts radically changed their appearance. The fort at Eining on the Danube is perhaps the most famous example of a fort much reduced in size. The late Roman fort there is squeezed into the corner of the earlier fort (**fig. 61**), separated from it by its own ditch. The alterations may have been carried out successively over a period of time, and at first the rest of the original fort may still have been occupied. The ditch was added probably in the mid-fourth century. At *Ulcisia Castra*, renamed *Castra Constantia*, situated further down the Danube, all the gates except one were blocked by adding projecting D-shaped towers to the existing square towers flanking what had been the entrance (**fig. 62**). The walls were strengthened by the addition of projecting interval towers, and all four corners received the distinctive fan-shaped towers which projected a little internally as well as externally. The first alterations were probably undertaken by Constantine, but the fort was rebuilt and repaired again in Valentinian's reign, so it is not possible to distinguish who made specific alterations. The towers, particularly the fan-shaped variety, are typical of the Danube forts (**fig. 63**). There were several minor

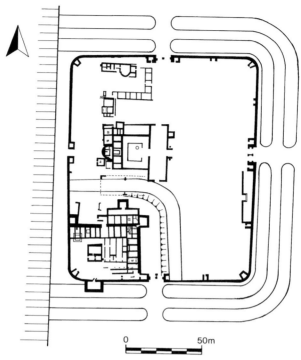

0   50m

Fig. 61 *The auxiliary fort at Eining on the Danube. This fort was much reduced in size during the late Empire, as revealed by the plan showing the late fortlet in the south-west corner, separated from the rest of the fort by its own ditch. (Redrawn by G. Stobbs from Fischer and Spindler 1984.)*

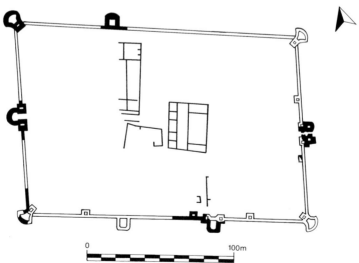

0   100m

Fig. 62 *Plan of* Ulcisia Castra *renamed* Castra Constantia *on the Danube, showing blocked gateways and fan-shaped towers projecting from each corner. (Redrawn by G. Stobbs from Fitz 1976.)*

variations of shape and size of towers, but the purpose of all of them would be the same, namely to facilitate better surveillance of the walls. The same arrangements can be seen at Campona in Hungary (Visy 1988, 89) and at Drobeta (**fig. 64**), where the gates were blocked by oblong towers, and the corner fan towers were sharper angled, like those at Intercisa (Fitz 1976, 101–3).

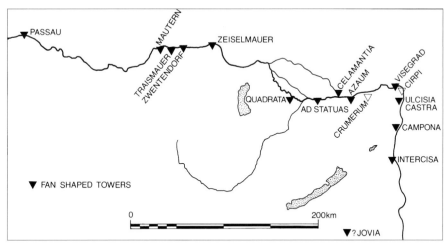

Fig. 63 *Map showing forts and towns on the Danube with fan-shaped towers. (Redrawn by G. Stobbs from Johnson 1983a.)*

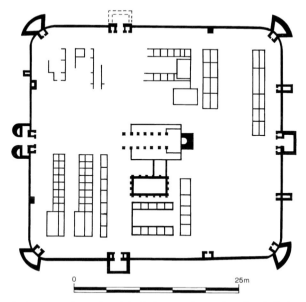

Fig. 64 *Plan of the fort at Drobeta, altered in the late Empire, perhaps by Diocletian, or by Constantine. The plan shows fan-shaped towers added to the corners, and all the gates except one blocked by the addition of projecting towers. The internal arrangements are less certain and the barracks shown here may relate to a different occupational phase. (Redrawn by G. Stobbs from Lander 1984.)*

In Britain, alterations to existing forts were not so far-reaching. The external appearance was not drastically altered, but internally barrack accommodation was changed, as at Housesteads and Wallsend, where the same alignment was used but the long continuous plan was abandoned in favour of the aptly named chalet arrangement of individual dwellings, separated from each other by narrow alleys.

Gates were blocked up in some forts, notably the west gate at Housesteads, perhaps also the west gate at Chesters, the south gate at Lanchester and the east gate at South Shields (Welsby 1982, 114). All these arrangements were probably part of Count Theodosius' restoration of the northern frontier. New buildings were erected in some forts, such as the new granary at Ilkley, and bathhouses which had always been exterior to early forts were often built inside the walls, as though there was too much at risk to allow them to remain outside. The late fourth century was not a phase of complete decline in Britain, as witnessed by the several new buildings inside forts, but it is puzzling that, at the same time, the *principia* at Bainbridge was burnt down and not repaired (ibid., 118). There seem to have been no radical changes in the garrisons of most forts, but after 370 the *vici* probably ceased to be occupied and the inhabitants perhaps migrated to the forts. The building activity of the late fourth century was never surpassed, and thereafter 'little evidence of further work has been found' (ibid., 125). At the beginning of the fifth century, Honorius withdrew the troops and the history of Roman Britain shades off into the history of Dark Age Britain.

Quadriburgia

Newly founded forts unrestricted by the existence of earlier walls and internal buildings were built to innovative designs, displaying a variety of types which some scholars have attempted to classify. A number of small square forts, some of them with square projecting corner towers, used to be collectively labelled the Diocletianic type; the title was possibly applied to them because Diocletian's palace at Split was built to a similarly regimented plan. Lander (1980) challenged this, preferring to label them Tetrarchic which is an even narrower description, one which now requires revision. Small square

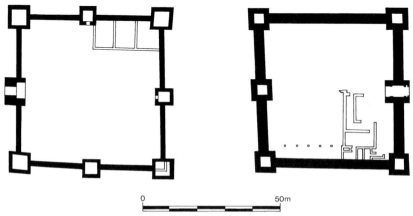

Fig. 65 *Irgenhausen and Schaan in Switzerland, previously dated to Diocletian's reign, but more probably built under Valentinian. (Redrawn by G. Stobbs from Lander 1980.)*

forts of the late third or early fourth century are found in several provinces. The ancient sources sometimes refer to them as *quadriburgia* or in Greek *tetrapyrgia*. A few examples will suffice to indicate how widespread they are, since they include Irgenhausen and Schaan (**fig. 65**) in Switzerland, Qasr Bshir in Jordan, Qasr Qarun (*Castra Dionysias,* see **fig. 60**) in Egypt, and the *centenarium* at Mdoukal (*Aqua Viva*) (see **fig. 2**) in Africa. Some of them are securely dated by inscriptions. Qasr Bshir (**fig. 66**) was built between 293 and 305 (Parker 1987, 468), and *Aqua Viva* in 303, placing them firmly in the Diocletianic category. But as Lander (ibid., 1054) points out, the fort at Bourada (fig. 67) in Numidia is very similar in shape

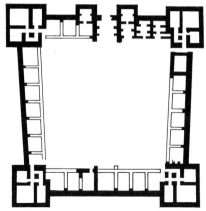

Fig. 66 *Qasr Bshir in Jordan, a small square fort or* quadriburgium *built between 293 and 330. (Redrawn by G. Stobbs from Lander 1984.)*

and is dated to sometime between 324 and 330, which means that it belongs to the reign of Constantine. More important, the evidence of coins, pottery and metalwork from Irgenhausen and Schaan indicates that these forts are more comfortably dated to the reign of Valentinian (Drack and Fellman 1988, 469; 499–500). No one can absolutely disprove the theory that Diocletian had a concerted plan for the fortifications of the whole Empire, but it is perhaps stretching the point too far to suggest that forts of similar shape all spring from the same master plan devised by the same mind. If Diocletian invented the type, its use was not restricted to his reign only. The common occurrence of small square forts with corner towers, interval towers and defended gateways may simply have

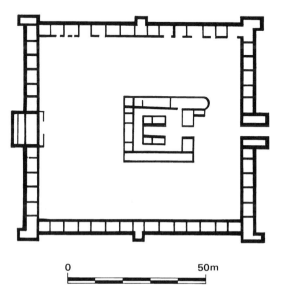

0   50m

something to do with the eminently useful design. To cite only one instance, a glance at the plan of the fort of Theangela, at the western end of the defences of this town in Caria, demonstrates that the Romans did not actually invent or have the monopoly over this type of small square fort. On plan alone, Theangela would at first sight qualify as a fort of the mythical Diocletianic

Fig. 67 *Bourada in Numidia, a* quadriburgium *built between 324 and 330. (Redrawn by G. Stobbs from Lander 1984.)*

type, but it is in fact part of the Hellenistic fortifications and predates the late Roman forts by about 500 years (Lawrence 1979, 179).

Forts of the Saxon Shore

Another group of forts with a collective name is that of the Saxon Shore Forts of the Channel coast, but here the name is indicative of purpose rather than similarity of plan. The forts are probably of different dates and were not planned all at the same time as a concerted series of fortifications. Johnson (1989, 43) places the nine forts in the broad date range 250 to 300, and in an earlier publication (1976, 94–113) he dates five of them more closely, to the years 276 to 285. Reculver and Brancaster may be earlier and Portchester and Pevensey are probably later. A comparison of plans of all the forts in the group gives the immediate impression that Reculver and Brancaster most clearly resemble the old-style forts of the early Empire, being almost square with rounded corners and a gate in each side. On architectural grounds, Johnson (1989, 43) suggests that Burgh Castle and Dover formed a transitional stage between the latter two forts and those at Richborough, Lympne and Portchester (**fig. 68**). The fort at Pevensey (**fig. 69**) is the least Roman in appearance, being an irregular oval, which now houses a Norman castle against its south-east circuit wall. The forts are built with the materials most easily available, and are quite different in external appearance as well as on plan.

After Brancaster and Reculver, Lander suggests that Dover was the next in the building sequence (1984, 173); there is no firm evidence but it would probably be one of the most

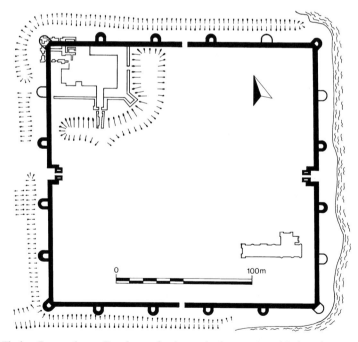

Fig. 68 *The late Roman fort at Portchester, showing projecting towers and indented gateways with narrowed portals. The Norman castle in the north-west corner and the church in the south-east attest to continued occupation of the site after the Romans left. (Redrawn by G. Stobbs from Lander 1984.)*

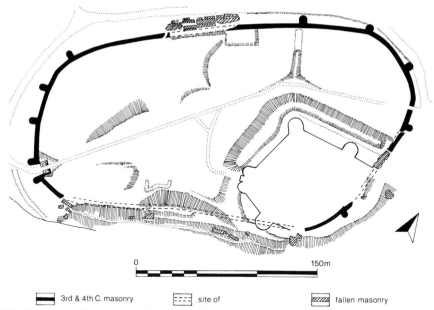

▬▬	3rd & 4th C. masonry	⌐---¬ site of	▨▨	fallen masonry

Fig. 69 *The late Roman fort at Pevensey, probably the latest of the Saxon Shore Forts, irregular in plan with projecting towers, and like Portchester complete with resident Norman castle. (Redrawn by G. Stobbs from Maxfield 1984.)*

important sites as a fleet base and, as Mann emphasizes (1989, 2), the forts of the Saxon Shore are closely bound up with the history of the fleet. Indeed, 'operations by sea were clearly central to the whole functioning of the Saxon Shore' (ibid., 10–11). This does not mean that the system arose fully fledged as part of a single plan, which is an unfortunate and false impression given by the *Notitia*. As the wide variety of foundation dates attests, the nine forts of the Saxon Shore grew up steadily over a period of time. Johnson therefore legitimately asks (1989, 30) when did the system become a unified command, which it clearly is in the *Notitia* (*Not. Dig. Oc.* XXVIII), where the nine forts are listed under the command of the Count of the Saxon Shore. The accumulated evidence resulting from excavations, architectural surveys and documentary research has not as yet furnished the answer to this question.

Internal plans and administration

All over the Empire, standardization was abandoned in many forts. Not even the square shape was paramount, as witnessed by the plans of *Boiodurum* (**fig. 70**) and *Alta Ripa*. There is one similarity between the square and trapezoidal type, in that the barracks and other rooms are arranged round the interior faces of the walls, enclosing an open courtyard, rather like a castle bailey. There are traces of internal buildings inside some of the courtyards, but their function is not obvious, and they need not necessarily be contemporary with the barracks and defences. It is unknown whether the courtyards without traces of buildings housed anything, such as wagon parks or animals, and these uncertainties mean that it is virtually impossible to estimate the numbers of men in garrison or what

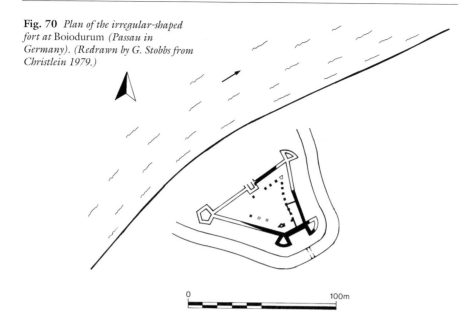

Fig. 70 *Plan of the irregular-shaped fort at* Boiodurum *(Passau in Germany). (Redrawn by G. Stobbs from Christlein 1979.)*

0   100m

kind of unit occupied the fort. Size and plan alone, without dating or epigraphic evidence, are not sufficient to elucidate questions about how the army was deployed. The first problem is that in producing a map of forts along a road or frontier, or in one particular area, it is never certain whether the full complement of sites has been discovered. Secondly it cannot be said with any certainty whether all the forts were occupied at the same time. Even when known sites can be identified in the documentary sources such as the *Notitia*, problems still remain. As Mann points out (1989, 2) the documentary evidence is misleading because taken at face value it seems to indicate that one unit occupied one fort at all times, whereas in reality units were split up, sometimes with different detachments operating in more than one location. The military units listed in the *Notitia* were most probably distributed in detachments in more than one fort, while only one fort is actually noted down because that would be their main headquarters where all the records would be kept. The *Notitia* is probably not a complete list of all the extant forts at the time of its compilation, nor is the archaeological record any more complete.

At some forts, then, the occupying force need not be a whole unit and may even have consisted of a mixture of troops from more than one unit. Further complications arise in that, in trying to estimate numbers of men, fort size is not a reliable guide. Small fort size does not automatically imply reduced numbers of men in comparison with the early Empire. Some of the internal buildings could have been of more than one storey, as they definitely were at Qasr Bshir (Parker 1987, 476). Those forts for which only the foundations survive could therefore have accommodated twice as many men as their ground plans would suggest.

One factor which may have influenced fort size is that a reduced circuit with few gateways is easier to defend. This could be used to support two opposing theories. On the one hand, perhaps manpower was overstretched and the forts housed fewer men because there were not many available, or on the other hand perhaps the forts were deliberately crowded to capacity, with the full appreciation of the fact that since only a few were needed to defend the walls, more men could be released for convoy duty, patrolling, police work and fighting. It is true that the law codes bewail the shortage of men in the *limitanei* and berate the authorities for not training them, but when the forts were planned, these two factors may not have applied. Gichon (1989, 121–42) attempted to work out the strength of the small forts or *quadriburgia* by using evidence from En Boqeq in the Roman province of Palestine. The calculations are complicated because there is not enough evidence about the main functions and the daily routine of the soldiers in such forts, His own military experience and knowledge of the region enabled Gichon to arrive at an estimate of the numbers of men required to defend the walls and towers, employing two shifts, and allowing for some men to go out on patrols and to man outposts, and others to do fatigue duty. But ultimately, as Gichon himself admits, all this is interesting but purely hypothetical.

Lack of knowledge about how the interior buildings were used renders speculation almost useless, but it is worth pointing out that forts in the early Empire were semi-independent installations housing their own clerical administration systems and responsible for the repair and storage of equipment and weapons, as well as food. This necessitated making space for store buildings, workshops and large granaries in all forts. The administrative system of the late Empire changed most of this. Equipment was centrally produced and sometimes repaired in factories, food supply was tightly controlled, and most commodities were kept in fortified granaries and storehouses, only to be issued at strict intervals on production of the relevant authorization. Forts of the late Empire would not need to accommodate these things, except in reduced quantities.

Of administration at individual fort level, very little is known apart from the names of some of the officials and what their duties may have been. The offices where they worked are unidentifiable. There is no obvious *principia* in any of the late forts (Johnson 1983a, 52). The regimented barracks of the fort at Deutz do not appear to include anything like a headquarters building, and in forts where the internal buildings are set against the walls, there is little to distinguish one room from another. This relates to the point made above, that units were often split up, operating away from their main headquarters. In some forts there may have been no need for anything more than a very rudimentary administration, requiring only one or two rooms, thus leaving most of the others for accommodation of the soldiers.

The legionary fortress of El Lejjun possessed a *principia* in the Tetrarchic period (Parker 1987, 203), as did the military quarter at Palmyra, which is incidentally one of the finest and best preserved examples of any such headquarters building anywhere in the Empire (Isaac 1990, 165). Until further discoveries are made, these buildings remain rare.

Road posts

The purpose of some forts is implicit in their position on roads, such as the small square posts on the *Strata Diocletiana*. This route has yielded several Tetrarchic milestones, but the forts along the road are difficult to date since many of them were rebuilt and reoccupied at various times (Kennedy and Riley 1990, 70; 140). Some of them, as at Khan el-Hallabat and Khan el-Qattar, have round towers at the four corners, while others are equipped with square towers. They usually have only one gate. Most of them are identifiable in the *Notitia,* and the garrisons include several *alae,* mounted units which would be able to patrol the surrounding territory. As is only to be expected, the forts are close to reliable water supplies and Khan el-Hallabat is in an area of good pasture (ibid., 203).

The internal roads of most provinces would require protection for the traffic moving along them and to keep communications open. This is a matter of police work rather than the military defence of the frontiers by means of chains of watchtowers and forts. Johnson (1983a, 138) draws a distinction between the internal road posts, with their *mansiones* where officials and soldiers could break their journeys, and the purely military systems characterized by lines of *burgi* and blockhouses strung out along the frontiers. Isaac also makes this distinction (1990. 173–5) in connection with the small post at Qasr Bshir, which Parker (1987) interpreted as a frontier fort guarding against inroads of tribesmen across the road. Isaac interprets it as a police post guarding traffic passing along the road. In the Roman world, the distinction between police forces and military forces did not exist since both functions were undertaken by the soldiers, which means that there are no clues in the official documents to reveal what the functions of individual units would have been.

Forts in some areas may have guarded roads in a slightly different way, for instance in Numidia the small posts at Kikouine, Mdila and Djendel may have watched passes into the Aurès mountains, combining police work with military protection (Fentress 1979,120). Route blocking was an important consideration in the Alps too. This did not always entail the building of forts and towers, but merely the blocking of passes by means of walls with soldiers to guard them. According to Aurelius Victor (*De Caes.* 42.5) in 351–2 Constantius could not get through the Alpine passes because they were manned, and Zosimus is more specific (2.45.3) when he says that because Magnentius had closed the passes, Constantius could not pass Atrans, north-east of Emona. Moss (1973, 718) suggests that Aetius could have stopped Attila if he had fortified the passes and manned them. In the war between Theodosius and Maximus, Theodosius managed to fool the enemy into thinking he was to approach Italy by sea, so the troops were removed from the passes, and Theodosius forced them. Walls have been traced in the Alps, but there is little to date them.

River Fortifications

The larger fortifications along the major rivers include walled towns and cities, bridge-head forts, and fortified landing places and storehouses. The usual dating problems apply to all these types of fortification, with the famous names of Diocletian, Constantine, Valentinian and Justinian once again claiming most attention.

Diocletian was probably responsible for the fort at *Contra Aquincum* (**fig. 71**) on the Danube (Fitz 1976, 123) It has fan-shaped towers at the corners, which feature is sometimes associated with the restructuring of the Danube forts under Constantine. At the bridgehead fort at Deutz opposite Cologne construction work was carried out in the years 312–5 *(CIL* XIII 8502). This may not have been a completely new Constantinian foundation, but the fort properly belongs to Constantine's Rhine fortification scheme. It was a large fort with 18 towers around the circuit of the walls, and 2 defended gateways.

Fig. 71 *The bridgehead fort of* Contra Aquincum *on the Danube. (Redrawn by G. Stobbs from Fitz 1976.)*

The 16 barrack blocks could have accommodated about 1000 men, a figure which attests to the importance of the city of Cologne in Roman times. The fort seems to have been occupied until the fifth century, being given up peacefully at an unspecified date (Horn *et al.* 1987, 514–15).

The rebuilding of the bridgehead fort at Kastel opposite Mainz may also have been undertaken as part of Constantine's rebuilding programme, although the coin evidence allows for only a broad date of about 300. The fort opposite Kaiseraugst is like a small version of Deutz, with round towers defending all four walls, but together with the restucturing of the earlier fortifications and the bridgehead at Zurzach, the evidence of the finds suggests that this fort probably belongs to the restoration programme of Valentinian (Filtzinger *et al.* 1986, 301–2; Hartmann 1980).

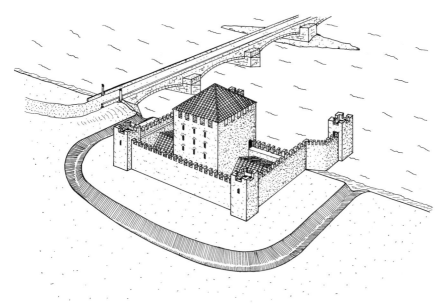

Fig. 72 *Reconstruction drawing of a typical fortified landing place, showing central tower and walls reaching down into the river with terminal towers at the end of each one. (Redrawn by G. Stobbs from Fitzinger* et al. *1976.)*

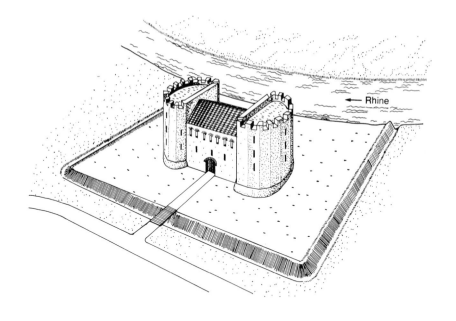

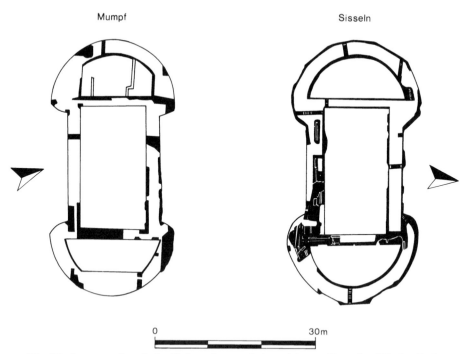

Fig. 73 *Reconstruction of a fortified storehouse and plans of those at Mumpf and Sisseln. (Redrawn by G. Stobbs from Drack and Fellman 1988, and Stehlin 1957.)*

The security of river transport entailed the building of fortified landing places, sometimes called *burgi*, of which there are several examples on the Danube. They are not all identical in plan, but the principle elements consist of a central fortified tower, with walls extending towards the river, each terminating in a smaller tower at the river's edge, providing a protected harbour where ships could land their cargoes (**fig. 72**).

Procopius descibes a fort very similar to this type of harbour, but clearly very much larger than the excavated landing places on the Danube. This was *Circesium*, built originally by Diocletian, at the point where 'the river Abhorras empties into the Euphrates' (*Buildings* 2.6.2.4). 'For Diocletian, when he constructed this fortress, did not surround it with a wall on all sides, but carried out the construction of the circuit wall only as far as the river Euphrates, and he finished off the work at the two ends with a terminal tower, believing, I suppose, that the water of the river would serve as protection for the fort on that side.' Justinian restored the fort, adding a new wall on the river side, thus enclosing it completely.

The landing place at Dunaflava (*Contra Florentiam*) on the Danube in Hungary is probably also Diocletian's work, or possibly Constantine's (Fitz 1976, 125). The Szentendre fortifications seem to date to about 380 (ibid., 79), but this is from tile stamp evidence, which may represent a later rebuilding. On the right bank of the Rhine, Valentinian built fortified landing places at Neiderlahnstein, Zullestein and possibly Wiesbaden-Biebrich (Baatz *et al.* 1982, 222).

Fortified storehouses such as those at Mumpf and Sisseln also feature as part of the river fortifications of the later Roman Empire (**fig. 73**). Traces of a very similar building have come to light at Agerten (Drack and Fellman 1988, 319), and it may be that more await discovery. Coins discovered at Mumpf were all of Gratian and Magnus Maximus (ibid., 481–3). Stehlin (1957, 71) suggested that these buildings were storehouses, largely on account of the existence of cellars at Mumpf.

Watchtowers

No survey of fortifications would be complete without some mention of the many kinds of free-standing towers built by the Romans as part of coastal and frontier defence systems, river fortifications and internal road surveillance. This sort of structure had been employed by the Romans from the earliest times, in Scotland in the Flavian period, and in Germany at about the same time. The inscriptions attesting the building of *burgi* under Commodus provide information that they were designed to keep watch for the approach of robbers (*latrunculi*) and other unauthorized personnel, thus falling into the category of police work rather than military defence.

The term *burgus* was a wide-ranging one, including the larger fortified landing places already described, the substantial towers such as the 13m (43ft) square tower at Basel with walls 1.2m (4ft) thick, and also the much smaller free-standing towers of lesser dimensions.

Chains of towers are known on the Rhine frontier, the Danube–Iller–Rhine *limes*, and on the Danube itself near Aquinicum. They date from all periods, including Diocletian's and Constantine's work, but it is Valentinian who is generally credited with making the fullest use of them. Two inscriptions dating to 371 have been found at towers on the

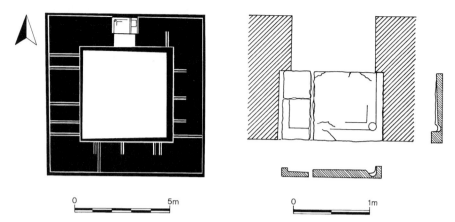

Fig. 74 *Plan of the watchtower at Kleiner Laufen (Switzerland). (Redrawn by G. Stobbs from Drack and Fellmam 1988.)*

upper Rhine, at Rote Waag and Kleiner Laufen (**fig. 74**; Drack 1980, 25–6; 29–30; Drack and Fellman 1988, 483–4; 485–6). Similar towers, without such specific dating evidence, are known all along the upper Rhine, stone built, often not quite square with walls at a slight angle, and often with a ditch around them, which was probably for purposes of drainage rather than defence. At Kleiner Laufen the doorway was still in evidence, complete with socket for the door pivot. These towers were therefore unlike the examples from the earlier frontier of Roman Germany, which are usually thought to have no entrance on the ground floor, but a door on the first floor reached by ladder.

The upper storeys of the towers, the shape of their roofs, and whether or not they had projecting galleries are matters for conjecture. Likewise their true function and method of operation. To label them signal towers begs the question of how signals were transmitted, to whom and why. This cannot be answered by archaeological means or by using maps to measure distances between towers. A notable experiment was carried out by Parker, in transmitting signals at night by means of burning torches from the towers of the *limes Arabicus* (1987, 168–81). It was surmised that the necessary criterion would be to pass messages along the frontier, but this did not prove possible because not all the towers were intervisible. What did emerge was that signals from all the towers could be seen at the small fort of Khirbet el-Fityan, north-west of the legionary fortress of El Lejjun. It was concluded that this was a relay station designed to intercept messages and to pass them on to the fortress, which was too low down to intercept messages itself. This ultimately makes much more sense than the suggestion that the towers merely signalled to each other. It would not help the men in one of the towers to know that those in another tower somewhere along the line had seen intruders approaching, but to inform the garrison at the fortress would mean that help could be sent to deal with the trouble.

This would probably be the only type of simple message that could be sent by using torches or smoke signals. Complicated messages involving the transmission of whole words is assumed to be possible because the ancient sources detail methods of doing so, but in the context of the watchtowers perhaps all that was required was an early warning system that could be used to inform a headquarters fort that there was trouble of some kind at a specific point.

Towers on internal roads would have this same function of policing and surveillance. They would presumably be related to the military establishments along or near the routes that they watched. However, it is possible that not all the towers were used by soldiers. Hopwood (1986, 343–56) suggested that in the eastern provinces the city authorities utilized towers manned by their own retainers in order to subdue the surrounding territory by means of a protection racket. More specifically, he pointed out that archaeologists presented with several ground plans of towers in a region perhaps interpret the collection of remains as a sophisticated corporate organization which would not have been apparent to contemporary Romans.

A string of towers has been identified on the Yorkshire coast, at Scarborough, Huntcliffe, Goldsborough (**fig. 75**) and Ravenscar, dated to the fourth century mostly on pottery evidence. An inscription from Ravenscar (RIB 721) describes the fortification as a tower and a fort, and it is indeed rather like a hybrid of the two. Unfortunately the inscription does not help to date the tower more closely. It has been suggested that these towers were built by Count Theodosius as part of his restoration of Britain, but this is only conjectural, and they could well be later. They are of a more complicated design than the supposedly Valentinianic towers of the Rhine and Danube, consisting of a quadrilateral tower set within an enclosure wall with smaller towers at the corners. Their function of coastal defence is clear but it is not clear

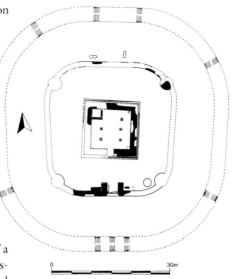

Fig. 75 *The so-called coastal signal station at Goldsborough, near Whitby in Yorkshire. (Redrawn by G. Stobbs from Hornsby and Laverick 1933.)*

how they operated. The suggestion that they all passed signals to the legion at York is possibly correct, but the fortress was at least 40 miles away, and it is more probable that the towers signalled to a fleet base, possibly on the Humber, which has escaped detection up to now.

The Goldsborough tower yielded lurid evidence of a last desperate fight for an unknown cause, which may not have been of a military nature. The two skeletons found there may have belonged to squatters rather than soldiers, and the skeleton of the dog found at the throat of one of the men may have been the pet of the other. Whatever the nature and date of this last battle, it is significant that no one came back to bury the bodies.

VIII

SIEGE WARFARE

According to Zosimus, Constantine destroyed the security of the frontiers by removing most of the troops and stationing them in the cities, 'thus both stripping of protection those being molested by the barbarians and subjecting the cities left alone by them to the outrages of the soldiers' (2.34.1–2). As Tomlin notes (1987, 119–20), however, this was a deliberate misunderstanding of late Roman strategy by a critic of this emperor. From the late third century onwards, it had become increasingly difficult for the frontiers to be held against the numerous, and often concurrent, attacks. A screen of garrisons was therefore provided in the frontier zone, which would in theory 'check minor incursions, and hinder major invasions by holding fortified towns and supply-bases, and strongpoints of all kinds along the lines of communication' (ibid., 119–20). This, in theory, would hinder the enemy's supplies, better defend the civilian population, and grant the mobile troops more time to gather. In practice, however, this theory had several weaknesses since, to a large degree, its effectiveness relied on speed of communication and the ability of the mobile army to respond quickly (ibid., 120); Procopius records numerous occasions where cities were captured either because of a lack of communication between the commanders, or that support was not sent in time, or was simply not available.

This change in strategy resulted in the Roman army becoming increasingly engaged in siege warfare. It may also have provided the impetus for the advancements which occurred in siege equipment at this time (see below), since from the Republic to the early Empire there had been little progression from those machines developed during the Hellenistic period.

The majority of the sieges described by Ammianus and Procopius occurred in cities. Although a reasonable proportion were defended by sufficient numbers of troops, some cities, either because the garrison was too small or inadequate for various reasons, necessitated the military involvement of the civilian population. Procopius describes the situation during the siege of Edessa (2.27.32–7): 'the whole population, even women and children, were going up on the wall. Now those who were of military age together with the soldiers were repelling the enemy most vigorously, and many of the rustics made a remarkable show of valorous deeds against the barbarians. Meanwhile the women and children, and the aged also, were gathering stones for the fighters and assisting them in other ways.' Later on, one of the Roman commanders led a large number of soldiers and civilians into battle outside the walls, and managed to defeat the Persians (2.27.42–3).

Sometimes, however, the population were not as keen to play a part in the proceedings. Such a situation occurred during the siege of Rome when the civilians became dissatisfied with the conditions, being unable to bathe, badly provisioned, and obliged to forgo sleep in guarding the circuit-wall (Procopius 5.20.5). A solution to this unrest was devised by

Belisarius, who mingled the soldiers and citizens together and distributed them to different places, setting a fixed daily wage for unlisted men (5.25.11–12).

The full horror of siege warfare is graphically described by Ammianus in his account of the assault of the city of Amida (19.2.7–9):

> Then heads were shattered, as masses of stone, hurled from the scorpions, crushed many of the enemy [the Persians]; others pierced by arrows, some struck down by spears and the ground strewn with their bodies, while others that were only wounded retreated in headlong flight to their companions. No less was the grief and no fewer the deaths in the city, since a thick cloud of arrows in compact mass darkened the air, while the artillery which the Persians had acquired … inflicted still more wounds. For the defenders, recovering their strength and returning in relays to the contest they had abandoned, when the wounded in their great ardour for defence fell with destructive results; or if only mangled, they overturned in their writhing those who stood next to them, or at any rate, so long as they remained alive kept calling for those who had the skill to pull out the arrows implanted in their bodies.

The archaeological evidence for sieges is even more horrific than Ammianus' description. The excavators of Dura-Europos came across some extremely disturbing finds under, and in the vicinity of, Tower 19 (Rostovtzeff *et al.* 1936, 188–205). The skeletons and associated equipment of approximately 16 or 18 Roman soldiers were discovered, some of which had suffered heavy damage from fire. Some of the skeletons lay in contracted positions, implying that the men had tried to protect themselves from the cave-in of the mine (see below) or had been crushed in defensive positions. Another man appears to have been thrown backwards with his legs wide apart and folded beneath him, suggesting he had made an attempt to get to his feet. One further skeleton, in a better state of preservation, was found some distance away from the above group. He appeared to have fallen backwards after receiving a mortal wound, and had attempted to raise the *lorica hamata* he was wearing, since it was found pulled up and folded back on his chest (ibid., 192–4).

The excavators were able to deduce from the extant remains the possible course of events which led to the deaths of the above soldiers: the Persians had dug a mine from outside of the city, underneath Tower 19, continuing under the circuit wall. The Romans then began a counter-mine, whereupon the two sides clashed, and the Romans, suffering a number of casualties, were driven back into their counter-mine. Those defending the city, seeing the retreat of the Romans out of the mine, decided to hastily block the entrance to prevent the Persian troops getting through. Thus, the wounded Romans, and those slow to escape, were shut up inside. At the same time, the Persians set fire to the counter-mine, and made a hasty withdrawal (*ibid.*, 198).

As Vegetius noted, there were two main types of siege (4.7): the first employs the blockade tactic, in which the defenders are starved into submission, the besiegers having prevented all means of supply, whilst the second relies on the use of siege equipment and constant attacks to force the defenders to surrender. Obviously, these two tactics are not mutually exclusive.

Blockade Sieges

The blockade tactic was utilized whenever possible, since it resulted in fewer casualties for the besieging side and obviously required considerably less effort. Vegetius offers advice on how to minimize the risk of famine during a siege (4.7). He suggests that those animals which cannot be kept enclosed should be cured, so that meat can supplement the grain supply: chickens, he states, can be maintained enclosed without much expenditure. Priority should be given to stockpiling fodder for horses, and any which cannot be stored should be burned to prevent it falling into enemy hands. Similarly, fruits should be collected, in order that they should not provide food for the besiegers. Furthermore, he urges that all available plots of land within the walls should be used for the production of food, including the 'pleasure-grounds of town houses' (4.7). This recommendation was put into practice by Diogenes whilst defending Rome in 549, when he sowed grain in all parts of the city inside the circuit wall (Procopius 7.36.2).

The supply of water was obviously essential if the besieged were to survive. As Vegetius states, it was extremely advantageous if a city contained springs within its walls (4.10). Where they were not a natural feature, however, wells could be dug where feasible. Furthermore, he writes that 'under all public and many private buildings cisterns should be constructed very assiduously to provide reservoirs for rainwater that flows off roofs' (4.10).

Many sieges record instances where sabotaging the water supply was one of the tactics employed to force the defenders to surrender. Procopius records one episode where Belisarius polluted the Gothic water supply by ordering his soldiers to throw dead animals and deadly herbs into the water cistern (6.27.21–2). The Persian king Chosroes, realizing that when the Romans besieged Petra they would undoubtedly attempt to cut off the water supply, devised the following plan. He divided the water being carried into the city into three separate pipelines. Having dug a very deep trench, he laid one pipe on the bottom, covering it with mud and stones, another in the middle section which he again concealed, and finally the third, which was above ground level. When the Romans besieged the city they severed the visible pipeline, believing that by so doing they had destroyed the water supply. During the course of the siege, however, they captured some of the enemy who stated that the city was still drawing water from the aqueduct. Accordingly, the second pipe was found and smashed, but the third remained intact, and it was not until later when the city fell that the Romans discovered the ingenious plan (Procopius 8.12.21–7).

The aqueducts themselves could sometimes provide a means of entry for the enemy. In order to eliminate this possibility, Belisarius, during the siege of Rome, sealed off each of the aqueducts by filling their channels with masonry for a considerable distance (Procopius 5.19.18).

As noted by Vegetius, there was little point in collecting huge amounts of stocks if they were not going to be subject to controlled issuing, since 'men who begin to keep a frugal diet while there is still plenty are never in danger of starving' (4.7). If a shortage of food was imminent, it was sometimes prudent to let the non-combatants leave the city in order to conserve supplies for the soldiers (Vegetius 4.7). Belisarius took such a decision when he commanded all the Romans to send their women and children to a nearby city.

Furthermore, he issued orders to the soldiers to make their attendants do the same (5.25.1–4). Despite these measures, Belisarius was still forced to halve the daily ration of his troops, paying them the remaining portion in silver.

Often, of course, desirable supplies did run out and desperate measures had to be taken. Procopius records several instances where the defenders resorted to consuming less than appetizing products, including sausages made from dead mules (6.3.11–12) and boiled nettles (7.17.13). His references to the consumption of human excrement (7.17.18) and human flesh (7.16.2–3) can probably be discounted, particularly since according to the chronology of events outlined by Procopius, the besieged started eating each other before they tried the nettles!

For some entrepreneurs even famine had an up-side. During the siege of Rome, the commanders made large amounts of money by selling some of their rations to the desperate citizens. Some troops even ventured outside the fortress to hunt, beef being highly sought after by those rich enough to pay the exorbitant prices (Procopius 7.17.10–12).

It should be noted that it was rarely possible for the besiegers to completely prevent the besieged from leaving or re-entering their city or fort. This was, in fact, not the purpose of most sieges, since the besiegers were far more concerned about capturing an enemy stronghold rather than those inside of it. Similarly, defenders did not, in the majority of cases, stay because they were forced, but because they were trying to prevent the place from falling into enemy hands. During the siege of Rome, the Goths realized that to besiege the entire length of the wall effectively a huge force would be required, so they decided to assault specific areas of it. This, Procopius records, afforded abundant opportunities for the besieged to bring in provisions (5.25.7–8). He further states that the great majority of inhabitants left the city, some going to Campania, some to Sicily (5.25.10–11). Obviously, however, the severity of some sieges did force those inside to remain, since they would probably be extremely fortunate to elude capture by enemy patrols and guards, particularly if the city was small enough to be surrounded.

Offensive Sieges

This style of siege relied on the use of military force to bring about the surrender of a city or fort. The equipment listed below was, with some exceptions, employed by both the besieged and the besiegers.

Many of the items used during a siege, such as towers and ladders for example, were constructed 'on site', in order that they could be built to the necessary dimensions. As Vegetius states (4.30), it was advantageous if the besiegers could build these higher than the walls, and he offers two methods by which the necessary measurements could be taken:

> Either a thin, light thread is tied at one end of an arrow, and when it reaches its mark having been aimed at the top of the wall, the height of the walls is found from the length of thread. Or else when the slanting sun casts a shadow of the towers and walls on the ground, the length of the shadow is measured without the knowledge of the enemy. At the same time a ten-foot [3m] rod is fixed up in the ground and its shadow measured in the same way.

During the siege of Rome, the Gothic leader Vittigis, in order to be able to construct the towers to the correct height, calculated the necessary measurements by counting the courses of stones in the city's wall (Procopius 5.21.4).

Artillery

Ancient artillery can be divided into two broad groups: torsion and non-torsion. The former term is applied to those engines which derive their power from the *twisting* of rope springs, generally made from hair or animal sinew. The latter term denotes those which, like a bow, obtain power by the *bending* of a wooden stave.

Torsion engines

THE *CATAPULTA/BALLISTA*

Until the fourth century, the term *catapulta* was used to denote an arrow-shooting engine. From then onwards, however, they were called *ballistae*, a term which had previously been applied to machines which shot stones (Marsden 1969, 188–9).

Literary evidence for this type of twin-armed torsion engine comes from Ammianus (23.4.2–3) and Vitruvius (**fig. 76**). They were powered by two cord springs which were placed under tension. Each spring was wound round an iron lever, the levers in turn being

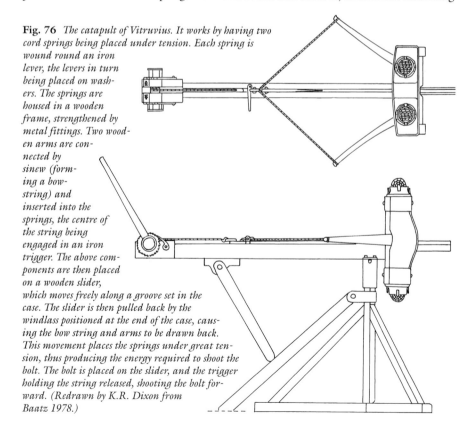

Fig. 76 *The catapult of Vitruvius. It works by having two cord springs being placed under tension. Each spring is wound round an iron lever, the levers in turn being placed on washers. The springs are housed in a wooden frame, strengthened by metal fittings. Two wooden arms are connected by sinew (forming a bowstring) and inserted into the springs, the centre of the string being engaged in an iron trigger. The above components are then placed on a wooden slider, which moves freely along a groove set in the case. The slider is then pulled back by the windlass positioned at the end of the case, causing the bow string and arms to be drawn back. This movement places the springs under great tension, thus producing the energy required to shoot the bolt. The bolt is placed on the slider, and the trigger holding the string released, shooting the bolt forward. (Redrawn by K.R. Dixon from Baatz 1978.)*

placed on washers. The springs were housed in a wooden frame, strengthened by metal fittings. Two wooden arms connected by sinew (forming a bow-string) were inserted into the springs, with the centre of the string being engaged in an iron trigger. The above components were then placed upon a wooden slider which could move freely in a groove set into the case. The catapult was shot by the slider being pulled back by a windlass positioned at the end of the case, which caused the bow-string and the arms to be drawn back. The movement of the arms resulted in the springs being placed under greater and greater tension, thus providing the energy to shoot the bolt. A bolt, with the fletched end in contact with the string, was then placed on the slider. The trigger holding the string was then released, shooting the bolt forward (Baatz 1978, 3).

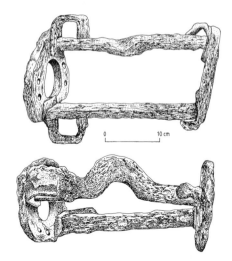

Fig. 77 *Field frame* (kambestrion) *from a late fourth-century arrow-shooting* ballista, *possibly similar to Heron's* cheiroballista, *found in the Roman fort of Orsova, Romania. Two of these items were required, each one holding a torsion spring. (Redrawn by K.R.Dixon from Gudea and Baatz 1974.)*

The remains of a late fourth-century light arrow-shooting *ballista* was found in the Roman fort at Orsova, Romania (ibid., 9–14). The find consisted of two iron rings joined by two beams, which measured 36cm (14in) high (**fig. 77**), and an iron arched rod, forked at either end, 1.45m (4.7ft) in length (**fig. 78**). Although larger in size, in the Orsova artefacts there can be found a parallel with the drawings which accompany Heron's description of a *cheiroballista* (see below). From the text and drawings, it was possible to identify the first find as a field frame (*kambestrion*), two of which were needed, each one holding a torsion spring, whilst the second object (*kamerion*) was required to hold the top of the field frames in position. A ladder strut (*klimekion*) was also needed to secure the bottom of the field frames.

The Orsova find is extremely important since it represents a progression towards all-metal frames, making it superior to Hellenistic timber-framed catapults (Baatz 1978, 13). An all-metal frame would have had two main advantages over a wooden one: the joints of the frame would have had greater shock-resistance when shot, and metal is not prone to

Fig. 78 *Late fourth-century* kamerion. *used to hold the top of the field frames in position. From Orsova, Romania. (Redrawn by K.R.Dixon from Gudea and Baatz 1974.)*

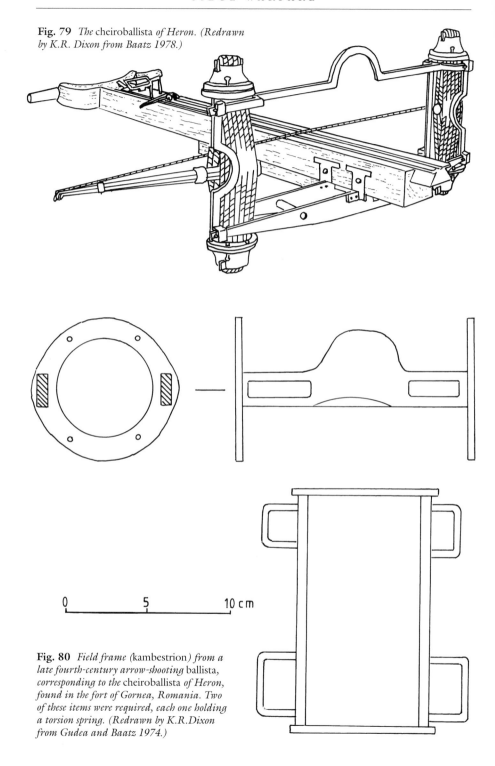

Fig. 79 *The* cheiroballista *of Heron. (Redrawn by K.R. Dixon from Baatz 1978.)*

0   5   10 cm

Fig. 80 *Field frame* (kambestrion) *from a late fourth-century arrow-shooting* ballista, *corresponding to the* cheiroballista *of Heron, found in the fort of Gornea, Romania. Two of these items were required, each one holding a torsion spring. (Redrawn by K.R.Dixon from Gudea and Baatz 1974.)*

the variations of humidity which would cause distortion in wood (ibid., 13). Interestingly, Baatz notes that the curve of the arched strut (*kamerion*) was possibly connected with a sighting device (see **fig. 78** ibid., 13).

Three field frames (*kambestria*) were found in two corner towers of the late fourth century fort at Gornea, Romania (**fig. 79**; Gudea and Baatz 1974; Baatz 1978, 14–17). They are smaller than the frame recovered from Orsova and are believed to represent the remains of machines corresponding to the *cheiroballistra* of Heron (**fig. 80**), and the *manuballista* of Vegetius (4.22). This type of machine was a torsion crossbow, being cocked in a similar manner to the belly-bow (*gastraphetes*) in that the user pushed down on a curved butt of wood with his stomach, forcing the slider and the string back (Bishop and Coulston 1993, 166).

CARROBALLISTAE

Carroballistae were *ballistae* mounted on carriages. According to both Trajan's Column and Vegetius, they were drawn by mules (2.25; Cichorius 1896–1900, pl. 31, scene 40). Those depicted on Trajan's column have only two wheels. The later version, however, may have had four, similar to the *ballista quadrirotis* (four-wheeled *ballista*), described by the Anonymous (*de Rebus Bellicis*[7]).

This machine was designed to provide a mobile *ballista*, employable in open battle situations, where they were sometimes apparently kept at the rear of the army alongside the *manuballistarii* (crossbowmen or catapulters), *fundibulatores* (sling-staff men) and *funditores* (slingers) (Vegetius 3.14).

BALLISTAE BOLTS

The bolts which were shot from all the above machines varied little from the third century to the time of Procopius. They had pyramidic iron heads and have been recovered from sites Empire-wide. Dura-Europos produced numerous socketed examples, including one bolt head which still retained the shaft, together with two of the three wooden (maple) vanes which formed the 'fletchings' of the tail (**fig. 81**) (Rostovtzeff *et al.* 1939, 455–6, pl. 240). These vanes were positioned so that half of the surface of the shaft remained smooth, enabling it to be placed in the groove of the machine. Furthermore, no nock is evident, it being unnecessary when the string of the engine is held by a trigger (see above). The use of wooden vanes instead of feathers is noted by Ammianus (24.4.16) and Procopius (5.21.16): 'However, it [the arrow] does not have feathers of the usual sort attached to it, but by inserting thin pieces of wood in place of feathers, they give it in all respects the form of an arrow.'

The power with which these bolts hit their targets is well documented in the works of Ammianus and Procopius. Several notable instances are recorded. Grumbates, the king of the Chionitae, lost his son to a *ballista* bolt, piercing both his cuirass and his chest (19.1.7), and light *ballistae* were so powerful that they sometimes pierced two men at the same time (19.5.6).

Fig. 81 *Bolt head with wooden shaft and fletchings from Dura-Europos, Syria. (Drawn by K.R. Dixon.)*

Procopius, describing the siege of Rome, states that a Goth who was standing by a tree, was shot by a bolt from an engine mounted on a tower. The missile passed through his cuirass and body, and sank into the tree by more than half its length, pinning him to the spot (5.23.9–12).

FIRE-DARTS

Ammianus describes a type of dart which was employed by the Romans specifically during sieges (23.4.14–15). The head comprised three iron bars which were joined together at both ends, but bowed outwards in the middle to form a cage filled with flammable material. According to Ammianus, these darts were more successful when fired from a loosely strung bow, since it would prevent the fire from being extinguished during flight.

Arrowheads which match the above description have been recovered from two British sites. Bar Hill produced five examples, which ranged in length from 5.2–6cm (2.1–2.4in) (**fig. 82**; Robertson *et al.* 1975, fig. 32, 14). The dart from Wroxeter was about 8.2cm (3in) in length. A similar dart was found at Dura-Europos (**fig. 83**; James 1983). This example, however, was intended to be fired from a *ballista*, rather than a bow. It was socketed (all the British examples were tanged) and had an overall length of 11.3cm (4.4in), with the head measuring 2.7cm (1in). The socket still retained a nail which would have attached the dart to a wooden shaft.

The primary function of these fire-darts was to destroy enemy installations and artillery. Ammianus recalls an incident at the siege of Maiozamalcha in 363, when the Roman besiegers, carrying wicker shields as protection, were assailed by Persian fire-darts (24.4.16). Various methods were devised to minimize

Fig. 82 *Head of a tanged fire-dart from Bar Hill, Scotland. Flammable material was placed inside the 'cage' of the head, set on fire and shot from a bow. (Redrawn by K.R. Dixon from Robertson et al. 1975.)*

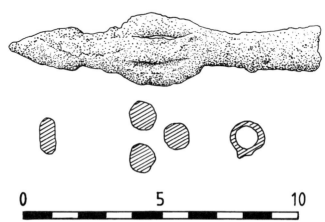

0   5   10

Fig. 83 *Socketed head of a fire-bolt from Dura-Europos, Syria. It is believed that this example would have been shot from a* ballista *rather than a bow. (Redrawn by K.R. Dixon from James 1983.)*

the effectiveness of these darts. During the siege of Bezabde in 360, the attacking Romans covered their wooden ram with wet rags and hides, together with alum, which proved a successful remedy against the Persian fire-darts (20.11.13).

THE STONE-THROWING *BALLISTA*

The stone-throwing *ballista* was constructed in a similar manner to the arrow-shooting type, differing only in it being of larger dimensions, and having a band rather than a bow-string.

Metal fittings from the frame of a third-century *ballista* were discovered at Hatra (Baatz 1978, 3-9). This twin-armed engine was found at the foot of a tower upon which it had originally been placed, possibly having fallen off during the Sassanid capture of the city in *c.* 240/1 (Bishop and Coulston 1993, 139). The find consisted of cast bronze corner plates, torsion counter plates and washers, five rollers, and nailed sheeting which was attached to the front, having two semicircular holes cut out to accommodate the arms of the engine. From both the finds and excavation photographs of the remains *in situ*, it appears that the frame measured about 2.40m (8ft) long, by 0.84m (2.7ft) wide (excluding fittings). Utilizing ancient literature dealing with artillery, Baatz concluded that this *ballista* was possibly of Roman manufacture, and was of medium calibre, shooting stones weighing approximately 10 Roman pounds (3.27kg/7lb).

THE *SCORPIO/ONAGER*

A new piece of heavy artillery, the *scorpio* (later called the onager), was introduced during the late period. Ammianus provides us with a detailed description of this machine (23.4.4–7):

> The scorpion, which is nowadays called the onager, has the following form. Two posts of oak or holm-oak are hewn out and slightly bent, so that they seem to stand forth like humps. These are fastened together like a sawing-machine and bored through on both sides with fairly large holes. Between them, through the holes, strong ropes are bound, holding the machine together ... From the middle of these ropes a wooden arm rises obliquely ... and is twined around with cords in such a way that it can be raised higher or depressed. To the top of this arm, iron hooks are fastened, from which hangs a sling of hemp or iron. In front of the arm is placed a great cushion of hair-cloth stuffed with fine chaff, bound on with strong cords, and placed on a heap of turf or a pile of sun-dried bricks; for a heavy machine of this kind, if placed upon a stone wall, shatters everything beneath it by its violent concussion, rather than by its weight ... a round stone is placed in the sling and four young men on either side turn back the bar with which the ropes are connected and bend the pole almost flat. Then finally the firer, standing above, strikes out the pole-bolt, which holds the fastenings of the whole work ... thereupon the pole is set free, and flying forward with swift stroke, and meeting the soft hair-cloth, hurls the stone.

He further states that it was previously called a *scorpio* because it had 'an upraised sting', whilst later it was known as an onager, derived from a type of wild ass with a powerful kick (23.4.7).

It is difficult to ascertain when this single-armed torsion engine was introduced into the Roman army, eventually coming to replace the stone-throwing *ballista*. An inscription dating to 225 *RIB* 1280) recording the building of an artillery platform at High Rochester, Northumberland (see above), has led Marsden to believe that the onager was in service by the early third century, since he feels that the platform, although described as a *ballistarium*, is of sufficient resilience (outlined as necessary by Ammianus) to accommodate an onager (1969, 191).

The onager was specifically designed for siege warfare rather than open battle, and Ammianus cites many instances where this engine was used to great effect: during the siege of Amida in which the attacking Persians had built four high towers each surmounted by *ballistae*, which were bombarding the Roman defences, the latter retaliated by opposing them with *onagri*, which 'shattered the joints of the towers, and threw down the *ballistae* and those who operated them' (19.7.6–7).

History demonstrates that the life of an artilleryman could be fraught with danger, largely emanating from his own machine! Ammianus, however, records that those simply standing near were also at risk, as occurred at the siege of Maiozamalcha (24.4.28):

> an artificier on our side ... happened to be standing behind a scorpion, when a stone which one of the artillerymen had fitted insecurely to the sling was hurled backward. The unfortunate man was thrown on his back with his breast crushed, and killed; and his limbs were so torn asunder that not even parts of his whole body could be identified.'

Crossbows (non-torsion)

Evidence for the use of crossbows comes from two third-century reliefs depicting hunting scenes, and the mention of a type of crossbow called an *arcuballista* by Vegetius (Espérandieu 1907, 66, pls 1679 and 1683; Coulston 1985, 260; pl. 4.22).

Crossbows consisted of a wooden stave which was secured on to the end of a grooved wooden beam (tiller) which held the arrow. The string, which was attached to either end of the stave, was pulled back down the tiller where it was held by a trigger mechanism.

Crossbows were not particularly suited to open battles, since they took longer to load and were heavier than ordinary bows. They were, however, ideal for siege warfare, since they had a longer range and greater penetrative ability (Coulston 1985, 262). A passage in Ammianus refers to the Emperor Julian being escorted on a journey by *cataphractii* and *ballistarii* (16.2.5). Coulston (ibid., 261) has suggested that this statement would make more tactical sense if the *ballistarii* were *arcuballistarii*, making them much more mobile than the former. It should be noted, however, that Ammianus stated that the types of troops Julian chose were, he believed, far from suitable.

The construction and operation of artillery

A great deal of skill was required in the construction and operation of siege engines. According to Vegetius it was the duty of the legionaries to undertake all those tasks associated with siege warfare. He states that a legion was equipped with *ballista* bolts (*iacula*), each century customarily having its own carriage *ballista* (*carroballista*), with mules designed to draw it and 11 men to arm and aim it (2.25). Fifty-five *carroballistae* were traditionally assigned to a legion, together with ten *onagri*, one for each cohort. Both types of engine were apparently carried around ready-armed on ox-carts 'so that should the enemy come to attack the rampart to storm it, the camp can be defended with darts and rocks' (2.25).

Vegetius states that the *praefectus fabrorum* was in charge of the legionary craftsmen, whose task it was to construct everything the legion required, including siege equipment (2.11; 25). His main responsibility was to ensure that nothing which the army needed was lacking.

At some point during the fourth century specialized artillery units (*ballistarii*) were created. The *Notitia Dignitatum* records that the commander of the eastern field army (*magister militum per Orientem*) had the services of the *ballistarii seniores*, a *legio comitatensis* (Or. 7.8 = 43), and the *ballistarii Theodosiaci*, a *legiones pseudocomitatensis* (Or. 7.21 = 57). The *magister militum per Thracias* could call upon the *ballistarii Dafnenses* (Or. 8.14 = 46) and the *ballistarii iuniores* (Or. 8.15 = 47), both being *legiones comitatenses*. Only one unit, the *ballistarii Theodosiani iuniores* (Or. 9.47), is recorded as being controlled by the *magister militum per Illyricum*. The western field army appears to have had only one unit of *ballistarii*, a *legio pseudocomitatensis* (Oc. 7.97), being placed under the *magister equitum per Gallias*. A prefect of artillery (*praefectus militum ballistariorum*) is, however, mentioned as being based at Bodobrica under the *Dux Mogontiacensis* (Oc. 41.23).

Based on the above evidence, Marsden suggests that originally two artillery legions may have been assigned to each mobile reserve army, being of necessity primarily equipped with *carroballistae* (1969, 196). He further states that, although only one example is recorded, it is possible that many frontier commanders (*duces*) were allotted an artillery legion, which could obviously have been equipped with a wider range of machines, including less mobile ones (ibid., 197).

In line with the centralization of arms production which occurred during the fourth century, artillery was also manufactured in state factories. Although the *Notitia* only records two *fabricae ballistariae*, one at Augustodunum, and the other at Triberorum (both in Gaul), it is likely that more did exist (respectively: Oc. 9.33; 38).

Marsden casts doubt on the ability of late Roman soldiers to construct and operate artillery (1969, 195). Referring to the third century, he writes: 'But I think that the factor most likely to reduce the effectiveness of artillery during this period was the increasing number of infantrymen in the army who were not sufficiently amenable to discipline and not intelligent enough to understand the benefits that artillery support could afford them.' Such a statement appears wholly unjustified, having being based on, as Marsden himself notes 'very little direct evidence'. The foundation for this belief appears to rest on the fact that both the *onager* and the *arcuballista*, which probably both came into service at about this time, were of relatively simple construction, 'suggesting a shortage of good artificers'. Simple construction, however, should not always be equated with inferiority. If the machine still performs to a high standard there is good economic sense in simplifying the design, since it cuts the time and costs of both production and maintenance.

The fourth century fares little better. Marsden cites as his main example the passage from Ammianus, who writes of the unsuitability for siege warfare of two Magnentian legions, recently brought from Gaul (19.5.2): '[These legions are] composed of brave, active men, experienced in battle in the open field, but to the sort of warfare to which we were constrained they were not merely unsuited, but actually a great hindrance; for whereas they were of no help with the artillery or in the construction of fortifications, they would sometimes make reckless sallies ...' Marsden concludes this quote by saying that 'the Magnentian legions were probably not exceptions to the rule in the fourth century' (1969, 196). To generalize in this way is unwise: that Ammianus specifically notes the ineptitude of these particular legions could imply that there was, in general, a higher level of expertise.

Artillery deployment

The two main siege engines, *ballistae* and *onagri*, served slightly different purposes during a siege. The former engine was primarily an anti-personnel weapon, being most efficient when trying to prevent attackers or defenders from carrying out their objectives. As with hand bows, they were particularly effective when shooting into a dense mass. The *onager*, on the other hand, was more adaptable, since not only was it an excellent anti-personnel weapon (although it did have a slower shooting rate), but it was also extremely effective in disabling enemy machines.

The heaviness of the *onager*, and its terrific recoil, made this machine more suited to placement on battlements, the ground, or stone towers, which were sometimes equipped with platforms built specifically for this purpose, such as occurred at High Rochester (see above). *Ballistae*, however, being much lighter in construction, were more adaptable in their positioning. Many of the sieges record the latter machines being placed on mobile towers and siege-mounds (Ammianus 19.5.6–7; 19.7.5; 20.11.20).

According to Ammianus, lighter ballistae were used during the siege of Amida. These machines are believed to equate to the *cheiroballistae* of Heron (see above), which may also have been the type used for the mobile *carroballistae* (Bishop and Coulston 1993, 167).

Siege Equipment and Devices

Battering rams (*aries*)

A detailed description of the ram is given both by Ammianus (23.4.8) and Procopius (5.21.6–13); Procopius says:

> Four upright wooden beams, equal in length, are set up opposite one another. To these beams they fit eight horizontal timbers, four above and an equal number at the base, thus binding them together. After they have thus made the frame of a four-sided building, they surround it on all sides, not with walls of wood or stone, but with a covering of hides, in order that the engine may be light for those who draw it and that those within may still be in the least possible danger of being shot by their opponents. And on the inside they hang another horizontal beam from the top by means of chains which swing free, and they keep it at about the middle of the interior. They then sharpen the end of this beam and cover it with a large iron head ... And the whole structure is raised upon four wheels, one attached to each upright beam, and men to the number of no fewer than 50 to each ram move it from the inside. Then when they apply it to the wall, they draw back the beam ... by turning a certain mechanism, and then let it swing forward with great force against the wall.

The timber frame from which the ram was suspended made this object extremely heavy to manoeuvre into position, and not particularly suited to rough terrain. Procopius records an instance where the Romans were in a quandary during the siege of Petra, due to the unsuitability of the ground for employment of the ram (8.11.22–34). Some Huns in the army devised a contrivance, which, according to Procopius had never been thought of before, neither by Roman nor Persian. Instead of using heavy wood for the frame, the barbarians used 'thick wands' which resulted in the engine being much lighter, enabling it to be carried on the men's shoulders, rather than having to drag and push it towards the target.

The ram was used to devastating effect against installations already weakened by artillery bombardment. During the siege of the city of Singara, the turning point for the besieging Persians came when they employed a huge ram to shatter the stone tower which the Roman defenders had only recently repaired (20.6.6–7). Once the tower had been breached the Persians poured in and the city and its population were captured.

Vegetius offers advice on offensive action employable against rams (4.23): 'Some people let down on ropes quilted blankets and mattresses, putting them in front of the places where the ram strikes, so that the impact of the machine [may be lessened]. Others catch the rams in nooses and ... drag them from the wall at an angle, overturning them sheds and all.' Such a situation occurred during the siege of Bezabde, in which the Persians entangled the head of the ram in long ropes, preventing its movement (Ammianus 20.11.15). He goes on to suggest that if the ram has already shattered the wall, it is a good idea to demolish some of the internal buildings and build another defensive wall inside.

The wooden body of the ram meant that fire caused a serious threat in a siege environment. In order to minimize this risk, wet rags and hides were wrapped around the timber, and on one occasion the Romans coated the wood with alum (Ammianus 20.11.15).

The men who worked the ram were obviously in an extremely vulnerable position, being constantly assailed by enemy missiles. Accordingly, where the terrain permitted, the rams were housed in sheds or huge mobile towers (see below).

The helepolis

The *helepolis* appears to have been a form of battering ram. Ammianus describes this machine in the following manner (23.4.10–3):

> a huge mantlet is constructed of strong planks of great length fastened together with iron nails, and covered with ox-hides and hurdles of green twigs; and over these is spread mud, in order to protect it from fire and falling missiles. On its front side are set very sharp, three-pronged spear-points, of the form which our painters and sculptors give to thunderbolts, made heavy with iron weights, so that whatever it attacks it shatters with the projecting points. This powerful mass is guided by numerous soldiers within by means of wheels and ropes, and by their united efforts is brought up to the weaker part of the walls; and unless the strength of the defenders above is too great, it shatters the walls and opens great breaches.

The machine of Ammianus should not be confused with the *helepolis* of the Hellenistic period, which was a wooden iron-clad siege tower, used to house various engines on different floors.

Siege-hook (*falx*)

Two very different pieces of equipment bore the name *falx* (hook). The larger of these was a form of battering ram with the tip of the beam fitted with an iron hook, used for tearing out stones from walls (Vegetius 4.14).

The name is also applied to hand-held, hooked poles. Procopius states that men carrying these poles stood on either side of the battering ram, pulling out those stones which had been loosened by its thrusts (8.11.33–4).

The tortoise (*testudo*)

The *testudo* was a type of siege shed which was used to protect the ram. It derived its name from the fact that whilst in use, the head of the ram would move in and out of its 'shell', strongly resembling the actions of a tortoise. It was constructed from planks covered with goat's hair mats and fire blankets (Vegetius 4.14).

Sheds (*vineae/musculi*)

Wooden framed sheds were used to protect men engaged in engineering works, such as undermining walls, building mounds, or filling in ditches.

Vegetius describes these as follows (4.15):

> The machine is made of light wood, 8ft [2.4m; 7.9ft] wide, 7ft [2.1m; 6.9ft] tall and 16ft [4.9m; 16.1ft] long. The roof is constructed with a double protective covering of boards and hurdles. The sides also are fenced with wicker against penetration by impact of stones and missiles. To avoid combustion from fire-darts the outside is covered with raw and freshly flayed hides and fire-blankets. When a number have been made, they are joined together in a line, and under their shelter besiegers make openings to undermine the foundations of walls in safety.

Ammianus records the use of sheds by both the Persians and the Romans on several occasions (20.6.3; 21.12.6)

Screens

According to Vegetius screens were semicircular wicker structures covered with goat's hair mats and hides. They were fitted with three wheels, one at either end and another in the middle (4.15). The besiegers would wheel them up to the wall, where, sheltering behind them, they would attack the defenders with various missiles, offering covering 'fire' for those using scaling ladders.

A different type of screen was sometimes employed by the defenders. This consisted of stretching hair-cloth along the top of the battlements. The cloth was not held very tightly in order that some of the force of the missiles might be checked (Ammianus 24.2.10; 20.11.9).

Towers

Towers played an important part in the besieging of installations. They offered not only protection to those men working close to the walls (with rams, for example), but they also enabled artillery and missile-armed troops to be elevated, thus eliminating the height advantage enjoyed by the defenders. Vegetius describes these mobile towers in detail, stating that they had square bases which could range in dimension from 30–50 Roman feet (9–14.9m/29ft 6in–49ft 2in) (4.17). Wheels were fitted to the base of the towers to aid movement: those built by Vittigis for the siege of Rome were wheeled towards the walls by oxen (Procopius 5.21.3–4). The main wooden structure was protected from fire by hides and fire-blankets. The tower itself could contain several storeys, with the lower housing a ram, the middle level holding a drawbridge, and the upper floor being used by missile-bearing troops, including archers and slingers.

The main aim of these towers was to provide a mobile offensive fort which could hold all the components necessary to attack a building in relative safety. As Vegetius states, it was advantageous to build the tower higher than the installation to be attacked, since it enabled the troops within to shoot down on to the defenders (4.17).

Obviously, the men in these towers were not invulnerable to attack, and Vegetius gives some advice on how these towers could be destroyed (4.18):

> First, if there are brave men or a force of soldiers on hand, a sortie is made in which a group of armed men goes out and, violently repelling the enemy, pulls off the hides from the wood-work and burns the huge machine. But if the garrison dare not go out, they shoot from larger catapults lighted fire-darts and fire-spears, so that piercing through the hides and fire-blankets the flame may be planted inside ... Men are also let down on ropes while the enemy are asleep, and carrying lights in lanterns they set fire to the machines and are hoisted up onto the wall again.

Procopius records numerous incidences in which both the towers, and those inside of them, met with disaster. On one occasion a strong wind caught the Persian fire-pans which had been placed close to the tower in readiness for employing against the Romans, resulting in the tower catching fire and those inside it being burnt to death (8.11.59–62).

Both Ammianus and Procopius refer to ocassions where wooden towers were placed on ships. One instance took place at Aquileia, where the ground surrounding the walls made it unsuitable for the normal means of attack. The River Natesio flowed close by the city, however, and Julian therefore built wooden towers higher than the walls, placing one on each of the three ships which had been fastened together. When the defenders saw the ships approaching, however, they shot fire-darts steeped in pitch at the wooden structures. The fire spread rapidly, and the towers toppled over, killing many of the men who were placed in them (21.12.8–10). A similar tactic was used more successfully by Belisarius during the siege of Palermo (Panoromus) (Procopius 5.5.13–7).

Ladders and drawbridges

On reaching the bottom of the enemy walls, wooden ladders were sometimes used as a means of helping the men to gain entry. As Vegetius notes, ladders were also carried inside the mobile towers, the men being able to attempt to scale the walls from whichever level of the tower was appropriate (4.17).

A great deal of bravery was required on the part of those scaling the ladders, since very little protection was possible. Procopius recounts an episode during the siege of Petra in which the Roman general Bessas, who was in his seventies, was the first to mount a ladder, encouraging others to do likewise (8.11.39–51). A heated struggle ensued at the top of the ladders, with both Romans and Persians vying for supremacy. During the fighting, Bessas fell from his ladder, but soon returned to renew the assault. Fortunately, the Romans did not always face such strong resistance: the general Narses, whilst besieging the Goths in Rome, was able to scale the walls without any opposition, the Goths being too few in number to man the entire length of the walls (8.33.21–3).

Drawbridges provided a slightly safer alternative to ladders since they allowed more men to attack at once. They were, however, not as versatile in deposition, being dropped into place from towers, which were obviously more restricted in movement than ladders. Vegetius refers to these drawbridges as *sambuci*, so named because of their likeness (slight as it may be) to a zither in the following manner (4.21): 'For corresponding to the strings on the zither, there are ropes on the beam which is stowed on the side of the mobile tower, and these let the drawbridge down from the upper storey on pulleys, so that it can descend onto the wall.'

The swing-beam(*tolleno*)

This was a type of crane which was used to lift a number of men on to the walls of a city or fort. It is described by Vegetius in the following manner (4.21):

'… a very tall pole planted in the ground, which has attached to its top end a cross-beam of longer dimensions, balanced by the middle so that if you depress one end, the other is raised. On one end is constructed a machine made from hurdles and boards, and in it a few soldiers are placed. Then as the other end is pulled and lowered by ropes, they are lifted up and deposited on the wall.

Wolves (*lupi*)

This was a form of spiked drawbridge, which was dropped by the besieged on to attacking troops. Procopius describes a *lupus* which was placed outside of the gates during the siege of Rome (5.21.19–22):

They set up two timbers which reach from the ground to the battlements; then they fit together beams which have been mortised to one another, placing some upright and others crosswise, so that the spaces between the intersections appear as a succession of holes. And from every joint there projects a kind of beak, which resembles very closely a thick goad. Then they fasten the cross-beams to the two upright timbers, beginning at the top and letting them extend half way down, and then lean the timbers back against the gates. And whenever the enemy come up near them, those above lay hold of the ends of the timbers and push, and these, falling suddenly upon the assailants, easily kill with the projecting beaks as many as they catch.

According to Vegetius this term was also applied to grappling-irons (2.25).

Mounds (*aggeres*)

Vegetius records the use during sieges of mounds constructed from earth and timber from which missiles were shot (4.15). A detailed account of how these mounds could be constructed comes from Procopius, describing the 'artificial hill' built by Chosroes (2.26.23–5):

... accordingly he cut down trees in great numbers ... [and] ... without removing the leaves, laid them together in a square before the wall [of Edessa] ... then he heaped an immense amount of earth right upon the trees and above that threw on a great quantity of stones ... cut at random, and only calculated to raise the hill as quickly as possible to a great height. And he kept laying on long timbers in the midst of the earth and the stones, and made them serve to bind the structure together, in order that as it became high it should not be weak.

During the siege of Bezabde huge mounds were raised by the attacking Romans, from which arrows, sling-shots and fire darts were shot (20.11.17). The mounds were eventually built higher than the walls, and were surmounted at their highest point by two *ballistae* 'through fear of which it was believed that no one of the enemy [the Persians] would be able even to put out his head' (20.11.20).

The city of Amida was besieged by the Persians in 502. They raised a huge mound overtopping the walls, but the defenders managed to hollow out a large part of the interior. The Persians were unaware of this plan due to the mound retaining the same external form, and therefore many men mounted the hill. This sudden weight caused the mound to collapse, killing many of those who had climbed upon it (Procopius 1.7.14–16).

Saps

Saps were a method of undermining the foundations of various structures, particularly the walls of cities and forts, by digging underground tunnels, sometimes supported by beams (Ammianus 24.4.21). According to Vegetius this stratagem enabled two methods of attack (4.24). Firstly, those digging the tunnel could emerge at night without the knowledge of the defenders, open the gates and admit some of their own side, and surprise and kill the enemy, as occurred during the siege of Maiozamalcha in 363 (Ammianus 24.4.21–3; Zosimus 3.21–2). Secondly, when the foundations of the walls are reached, as large a section as possible is excavated, the walls being temporarily held up by dry timber. The gaps are then filled with flammable material which is later set on fire, causing the wooden props to burn, resulting in the walls collapsing (Vegetius 4.24).

During the siege of Daras, a city defended by two circuits of wall, Chosroes ordered the Persian soldiers to dig a tunnel beneath the foundations. The Romans, however, discovered the Persians' plan, and subsequently began to dig a tunnel in a cross-wise direction so that they would not by-pass the enemy sap. Consequently, the Persian tunnel broke through into the Roman one, with the first to emerge being killed by the waiting Romans (Procopius 2.13.20–8).

The noise of the digging was often a problem since it could alert the enemy to underground activity, as occurred during the siege of Edessa when the Persians heard the blows of the Romans beneath who were burrowing into the mound (2.27.1–2). One way of combating this was to instigate some sort of military activity, artillery producing the best results, since both the noise and ferocity of these machines compelled the enemy to respond:

Therefore, although the night was far advanced, the trumpets sounded, and at the given signal for entering battle they [the Romans] rushed to arms. And, as had been planned, the fronts of the wall were attacked on two sides in order that while the defenders were rushing here and there to avert the danger, the clink of the iron tools digging at the parts close by might not be heard, and that with no hindrance from within, the band of sappers might suddenly make its appearance. (Ammianus 24.4.22)

Caltrops (*triboli*)

Caltrops are an iron device, comprising four spikes joined at the base in such a manner that when thrown on the ground, one spike always projects upwards, impeding the movement of both man and beast. Numerous examples dating to the third century were recovered from Caerleon (Nash-Williams 1932, 27–8, fig. 22).

They were usually placed around cities and fortifications, as occurred during the siege of Rome when copious amounts of them were sprinkled in front of the open gateways (Procopius 7.24.15). Herodian, however, records an instance where they were employed in open battle:

> And when the size of the cavalry and the numbers of the camels began to cause them [the Romans] trouble, they pretended to retreat and then threw down caltrops and other iron devices with sharp spikes sticking out of them. They were fatal to the cavalry and the camel-riders as they lay hidden in the sand, and were not seen by them. The horses and the camels trod on them and (this applied particularly to the camels with their tender pads) fell onto their knees and were lamed, throwing the riders off their backs. (4.15.2–3)

Slings and sling-staffs

According to Vegetius (3.14), slings (*fundae*) were made from flax or hair, the latter apparently being the better material for such use. The stones were discharged by the *funditor* whirling the sling above his head and releasing the stone.

The sling-staff (*fustibalus*) consisted of a 1.2m (4ft)-long staff (*fustis*), with a leather sling attached to the top end (Vegetius wrongly says the middle) (3.14), acting very much like a portable *onager*.

Vegetius states that these two weapons were sometimes placed at the rear of the army, alongside *carroballistae* and *manuballistae* (3.14). They were also particularly useful for mural defence, since the walls provided protection to the slinger, and it was easy to maintain a constant supply of stones.

Burning liquids

Various flammable liquids for pouring on assailants and machines were used during sieges. Vegetius lists these as being bitumen, sulphur, liquid pitch and 'burning oil' (4.8): according to Procopius, the latter substance was known as 'naphtha' by the Persians, and 'Medea's oil' by the Greeks (8.11.36). During the siege of Edessa the women and children used olive oil (Procopius 2.27.36). It was poured into numerous basins, heated, and then sprinkled on the heads of the assailing enemy by means of a type of whisk!

Miscellaneous missiles

Various items could be thrown down on the heads and machines of besieging forces. One of the most interesting sequences which occurred during a siege was that undertaken by the commander Constantinus in his defence of Hadrian's tomb (Procopius 5.22.15–25). The Roman archers were unable to prevent the Goths from scaling the walls because they were carrying large shields. Furthermore, the *ballistae* proved useless since it could not be angled to shoot steeply downwards. Constantinus, therefore, decided the only course of action available to them was to break the statues which surmounted the tomb into pieces, and throw them with both hands down onto the enemy.

Ammianus records the use of large jars, millstones and pieces of columns during the siege of Bezabde (20.11.10).

IX

THE MORALE OF
THE LATE ROMAN ARMY

...it has always been a military axiom, that a man's will to fight is the ultimate arbiter of battles and that this is governed by the thoughts however elementary which pass through his head.   Lord Moran 1945, 16

Morale, in its broadest sense, pertains to the manner in which people respond to the situations they encounter. Good morale is essential to the efficient functioning of an army, since it provides men with sufficient mental resilience to face the most arduous and dangerous situations.

The importance of morale in ancient armies has generally been overlooked, with more emphasis being placed on tactics and equipment. Whilst both these aspects of war deserve study, it should be remembered that without good morale, even a superbly equipped force, armed with a brilliant tactical plan, can fail. As Baynes states (1987, 94), where morale is high, however, 'The plan can be bad, the conditions appalling, the task hopeless: a good unit will make something of it.'

The aim of this chapter is to assess the level of morale in the late Roman army, by analysing factors such as cohesion, discipline and leadership, and to ascertain how they affected the performance of the soldiers throughout the period in question.

Cohesion

'Personal bravery of a single individual does not decide on the day of the battle, but the bravery of the unit, and the latter rests on the good opinion and the confidence that each individual places in the unit to which he belongs. The exterior splendour, the regularity of movements, the adroitness and at the same time the firmness of the mass – all this gives the individual soldier the safe and calming conviction that nothing can withstand his particular regiment or battalion.'

Field Marshal François Comte de Guibert

Cohesion, or *esprit de corps*, is that powerful sense of 'family' or 'belonging' which members of any large corporate body feel. It is the close, sometimes almost claustrophobic nature of armies, and thus the interdependence of the men within them, that provides the stimulus for the individuals to 'not let the side down'. Such a feeling is illustrated by an incident recounted by Zosimus, which occurred under Valentinian, in which a unit of Batavi were found guilty of initiating a rout in an engagement against the Germans (4.9.2–4). Valentinian commanded that the Batavi be stripped of their arms and sold as runaway slaves for public deportation. The Batavi pleaded with the Emperor, 'begging that the army should be freed of such shame, promising that they would show themselves men worthy of being called Romans, whereupon he bade them prove this by their actions … and arming themselves as necessary, they left the camp and resumed the battle with such enthusiasm that few barbarians out of their vast numbers got safely home'.

If cohesion is fundamental to the efficient functioning of an army, was it possible for such a disparate army as that existing during the late Roman period to perform effectively? The following passage, attributed by Procopius to the Gothic leader Totila, describes the nature of the late Roman army:

> *But the vast number of the enemy is worthy only to be despised, seeing that they present a collection of men from the greatest possible number of nations. For an alliance which is patched together from many sources gives no firm assurance of either loyalty or power, but being split up in nationality it is naturally divided likewise in purpose.*
> (Procopius 8.30.17–18)

It is wrongly assumed that an army made up of different nationalities cannot possibly form an efficient force. Although cohesion is crucial within the structure of an army, research shows that it is the cohesion which exists within small groups that forms the greatest motivation for the soldier (Dinter 1985, 40–51), since ultimately the safety of comrades is more important to the individual soldier than the safety of the army as a whole. The defence of moral principles rarely drives men to perform acts of bravery in war, but they commonly perform them for the life of a friend.

Distinctions between barbarians and Romans would have blurred considerably during the late Roman period, particularly with the high degree of cultural assimilation on both sides. Greater divisions would, however, have existed between the citizen forces (including Germans etc.,) and Asiatic troops such as the Huns. It is a well-known fact that the further removed in physical appearance, language and culture a race is, the more they are distrusted. The best modern illustration of this comes from the Second World War: Men of the 247th American Infantry Regiment (still unassigned in the States) were asked the following question, 'How would you feel about killing a German soldier?' A possible answer was 'I would really like to', and 6.6% of the men ticked this box. Where 'Japanese' was substituted for 'German', 44% chose this answer' (Ellis 1993, 319).

Evidence conducted on units of the Wehrmacht in the latter part of the Second World War suggests that, provided nationalities are kept in distinct groups, there is no serious effect on the fighting capabilities of the army as a whole; where various ethnic groups are intermixed, there was, however, a detrimental effect on cohesion (Shils and Jonowitz 1948). Thus the Roman army's policy of keeping distinctive ethnic groups separate from the 'regular' force probably ensured a relatively cohesive structure. The real problem with employing such large numbers of barbarian troops, particularly from the late fourth century onwards, was their lack of standardization in training and discipline.

One aspect of military policy, may, however, have had a detrimental effect on cohesion: the billeting of troops within cities. As mentioned in Chapter 5, this policy was increasingly employed from the end of the third century onwards. The soldiers were usually lodged in the suburbs of cities, being placed individually in private houses, inns, etc. When an army is divided up in such a manner, the élitist boundaries which set apart the soldier from the civilian are broken down, resulting in a weakening of the *esprit de corps*. It also hinders the development of strong bonds between fellow soldiers, and soldiers and their officers. Such relationships are essential if the army is to function cohesively.

The billeting of men in cities also appears to have been damaging to the maintenance of discipline within the army, and this aspect is discussed below.

Discipline

No sane man is unafraid in battle, but discipline produces in him a form of vicarious courage which, with his manhood, makes for victory. Self-respect grows directly from discipline ... The sense of duty and obligation to his comrades and superiors comes from a knowledge of reciprocal obligation, and from the sharing of the same way of life. Self-confidence, the greatest military virtue, results from the demonstrated ability derived from the acquisition of all the preceding qualities and from the exercise in the use of weapons.   Patton 1947, 336

Discipline serves two main purposes within the army. Firstly, it ensures that when the soldier is in personal danger, he does not yield to his natural instinct to run, but performs his duty: as Graham remarked (1919, 2), the soldier should feel that 'the avenue to the rear is absolutely closed up in the mind'. Secondly, it is a method of maintaining order within the army itself.

Ill-disciplined troops existed throughout the history of Rome, but the conditions prevailing during the late Empire may have been instrumental in causing a marked increase in the problem.

One of the main ways of preserving discipline within an army is by an organized and thorough training programme. The rigorous training regime practised by the Roman army had been the vital ingredient which had set her apart from the barbarian armies she faced. During the fourth century, however, there is abundant evidence to suggest that military exercises were not being taught as conscientiously as they had been in the early Empire. According to Zosimus (4.23.2–4), the condition of the army in the period leading up to the battle of Adrianople was so poor that the *magister militum* Sebastianus, in readiness for the campaign against the barbarians, chose to train only 2000 soldiers from the entire force, stating that it was not an easy task to take over command of a mass of men used to weak officers, but that it was fairly easy to train a few and restore their manliness. The men he chose were not those that had been inured to luxury and idleness, but those men who had been recently recruited, subjecting them to rigorous training. Thus, the seeds of an untrained, undisciplined force were sown before Adrianople, although the situation was irreparably worsened by this disastrous battle in 378, when approximately two-thirds of the Roman army was wiped out. The fact that the soldiers themselves fought extremely bravely in the most gruelling of conditions (both climatically and militarily) implies that Zosimus' assessment of the functioning ability of the army was an exaggeration, since morale must have been sufficiently strong to enable the men to stand their ground.

Adrianople was, however, a devastating blow, not only in numerical terms, but more importantly in the huge loss of experienced soldiers. When losses had previously been incurred, a core of highly trained men had been available, alleviating the problems caused by an influx of 'green' recruits. Another commodity that was lacking was time. Many armies, including that of Rome, have suffered massive military set-backs, but the difference with the situation that existed after 378 is that there was little respite in which to repair the damage. Had the needs of filling the ranks not been so urgent, it would have been possible to spend the necessary time to train those newly enlisted. Such a situation did not exist after Adrianople, and untrained, undisciplined soldiers filled the ranks of the army in increasingly large numbers. Vegetius, possibly writing only a few years after this disastrous event, stated that:

> In every battle it is not numbers and untaught bravery so much as skill and train-ing that generally produce the victory. For we see no other explanation of the conquest of the world by the Roman People than their drill-at-arms, camp-discipline and military expertise ... A small force which is highly trained in the con-flicts of war is more apt to victory: a raw and untrained horde is always exposed to slaughter. (1.1)

This lack of training would have resulted in the soldiers themselves having little confi-dence in their own abilities, causing greater numbers of men to desert or surrender during combat. Although soldiers generally despise the endless drills they are subjected to, most realize that without such tuition and practice, they are not effectively equipped, either physically or mentally, for battle.

The increasing tendency towards the urban billeting of troops during the late period also affected the standard of training within the army. Such men received little or no instruction in manoeuvres, primarily serving a defensive purpose, and thus were of little value when called upon to engage in open warfare.

Under strict disciplinary control, the billeting or stationing of troops in cities was a suc-cessful and useful policy. During the late Empire, however, many of the commanders were financially rather than militarily motivated, seeking only to acquire greater wealth than maintain a disciplined force. Such an attitude by the commanders was disastrous in an urban environment, since the opportunities for relaxation and extortion by the troops was greater than when stationed in a fort or on campaign. In these circumstances, the soldiers ceased to serve a primarily military function, being increasingly employed as thugs to exact 'payments' from the civilian population on their commander's behalf. The *dux* Cerialis exploited Libya by moving his soldiers from city to city, forcing the residents to pay him to remove the ill-disciplined troops elsewhere (Synesius *Epistulae* 129).

The soldiers themselves bullied the civilian population into supplementing their income, an income which was much reduced by the various deductions extorted by their officers. As MacMullen noted, it was difficult for the civilian to distinguish between illegal and legal exactions, since the military shared the responsibility of the collection and receipt of various taxes with civilian personnel: 'In consequence, when someone in uni-form turned up with a demand for a bushel of wheat or a jug of wine, you couldn't easily say he had no right to it' (1988, 160). Furthermore, the laws regarding what the civilian was obliged to furnish his military lodger with were vague and inconsistent, enabling the soldier to demand whatever he desired, with little fear of punishment.

Zosimus, Ammianus and Procopius all comment on the deplorable lack of discipline exhibited by soldiers stationed in cities: most civilians appeared to fear their own soldiers more than those of the enemy (Zosimus 2.34.2; 4.16.5; Procopius 7.9.1–5). Libanius records the following money-making scheme by the soldiers (*Oration* 47.4-5):

> There exist large villages ... These have recourse to the soldiery stationed in them, not so as to avoid trouble but so as to be able to cause it. And the payment comes from the produce of the land ... or else bullion or gold coin. So protected by their arms, the donors have purchased for themselves complete licence. And now they inflict toil and trouble upon their neighbours by encroaching on their lands, cutting down their trees, looting, slaughtering and butchering the cattle ... with the result that if any of the victims loses his temper or defends himself, and one of the soldiers happens to be hit too, then it is death for the one who struck him, and not the slightest chance of an excuse for him. He must knuckle under to a soldier, however drunk, and put up with anything; and the laws in this instance are a dead letter.

The lures of urban decadence were so strong that garrisons were often otherwise engaged during enemy attacks: Zosimus (1.33.2) recounts one episode where the Scythians, on reaching the city of Trapezus and 'observing that the soldiers were given over to laziness and drinking and that finally they did not even go up onto the walls for fear of missing an opportunity for pleasure or carousing', could attack without any opposition. The commanders, who should have provided a steadying influence on their men, and severely punished those who failed to do their duty, were also, unfortunately, occupied elsewhere: '... meantime the commanders of the Roman army, as well as the soldiers, were plundering the possessions of their subjects, and they did not shrink from any act of insolence and licentiousness whatsoever, but the commanders, for their part, were revelling with mistresses inside the fortresses, while the soldiers, showing themselves more and more subordinate to their commanders, were falling into every form of lawlessness' (Procopius 7.9.1).

Few men are sufficiently self-disciplined not to succumb to the pleasures of relaxation, or the opportunity for acquiring wealth, particularly when no one is bothered if you perform your duties well, badly or not at all. Procopius records an instance of such indifference by officers (7.20.2): 'but any of the soldiers who so wished were allowed to neglect their duties; meanwhile there was only an insignificant garrison on the walls, and even this received very little attention. For those who chanced from day to day to be assigned to guard duty were freely permitted to sleep, since no one was put in command of them who might possibly take some notice of such an act; nor did any officers consent to go the rounds of the fortifications ... and inspect the guards to see what they were doing ...'. As Baynes noted (1987, 186–7), soldiers often prefer to be subjected to strictly imposed discipline, since tolerance of poor performance implies that both themselves and their actions are unimportant and of no consequence. Thus, the motivation for undertaking any task ceases to exist.

Ultimately, therefore, the blame for such a lack of discipline and direction lies with the commanders. When those in control have lost, or perhaps never had, the motivation to function efficiently, the effects obviously trickle downwards through the ranks. The quest for booty and lasciviousness by the officers, which is fully discussed below, appears to have been the *raison d'être* of many. Late Roman sources record numerous examples of appalling behaviour by the officers, including many instances in which the lives of both officers and men where sacrificed for the above reasons. On one occasion the Scythians, having been severely harassed by the Huns, plead with Valens to be granted permission to settle on the Roman side of the Danube:

Valens allowed them to enter the Empire if they first give up their arms. The tribunes and other commanders therefore crossed over to escort the unarmed barbarians into Roman territory, but all they did was select good-looking women, pursue mature boys for disgraceful purposes, and seize slaves and farmers. By devoting themselves only to these activities and neglecting whatever was conducive to public good, they carelessly allowed most of the barbarians to cross with their arms undetected. (Zosimus 4.20.6–7)

With the officers behaving in such a manner, it is easy to understand why the men also conducted themselves in an ill-disciplined way. As Patton stated, discipline can only be obtained when all officers are imbued with a sense of obligation to their men and the state they serve: 'Officers who fail to correct errors or to praise excellence are valueless in peace and dangerous misfits in war' (1975, 402).

Where punishments were implemented by strict commanders, the morale of the army was obviously higher, although this was only true if the penalties inflicted were considered commensurate with the misdemeanour: excessive cruelty by those in authority could have the opposite effect on the men. In this regard, Theodosius was particularly renowned for his extremely severe forms of punishment, which usually revolved around the amputation of hands (Ammianus 29.2.22–4; 29.5.31; 29.5.49). The cruelty of Theodosius was apparently so notorious that Valentinian's enemy Firmus used this factor to urge the Roman soldiers to desert from him (Ammianus 29.5.49).

If the troops knew that they would be punished if they committed an offence, then the threat of castigation was often deterrent enough to maintain discipline. Julian, in a peptalk to his troops before the Persian campaign, stated that if anyone showed reluctance to engage in battle, they would be hamstrung (Ammianus 23.5.21).

Making a public spectacle of those who had failed to do their duty or misbehaved was one method of ensuring that others would not follow their example. Zosimus records one incident where Julian, appalled by the cowardice of some of his cavalry, ordered them to be dressed in women's clothing and paraded through the camp, 'thinking this a punishment worse than death for manly soldiers' (3.3.4–5). On this occasion, the troops in question, when next in battle, fought extremely bravely in order to try to extinguish the disgrace of their previous behaviour and the shameful punishment awarded them. It must be wondered whether it was possible for the same form of corporate 'camp-discipline' to be maintained when troops were stationed in cities, particularly with the men being dispersed and intermingled with the civilian population. This relative isolation of soldiers from their comrades may have resulted in a detrimental effect on the impact of punishment. If a man is disciplined individually, and without an audience, then only the man concerned will have benefited from his punishment; if, however, that man is castigated before the eyes of his fellow soldiers, many will presumably benefit from the exercise.

The influx of such large numbers of barbarians into the army, particularly after Adrianople, may have caused severe disciplinary problems, since the emergency of the situation and the prevailing conditions were ill-suited to the enforcement and maintenance of strict behavioural control. Furthermore, many of the barbarians now served under their native leaders, and were no longer subjected to the same disciplinary standards as the citizen troops. Many comments by ancient authors imply that the barbarians felt themselves to be exempt from the code of ethics which governed the regular army. Zosimus records the following incident (4.31.1):

> but while the Egyptians marched quietly through the cities and bought what they needed at a fair price, the barbarians proceeded in disarray and behaved selfishly in the markets. When the two detachments met at Philadelphia in Lydia, the Egyptians, who were much fewer than the barbarians, observed discipline, while the barbarians began to be arrogant. And when one of the traders in the market-place asked payment for the goods he had sold, the barbarian used his sword on him. He shouted and another man who tried to help was struck also. The Egyptians took pity and urged the barbarians in reasonable terms to refrain from such offensive behaviour, saying that this was not the action of men who wished to live under Roman law.

A fight between the barbarians and the Egyptians ensued, in which the latter won, resulting in the barbarians curtailing their outrageous behaviour.

If some sections of an army are apparently living under different rules to others within the same force, trouble is bound to ensue. Whilst the Egyptian troops dealt with this problem in an extremely commendable manner, other soldiers may not be sufficiently motivated or disciplined to resist succumbing to the desires of following their baser instincts, particularly if other men are seen to be doing so, and, more importantly, getting away with it. As a commander of the modern American army stated (Nye 1986, 42): 'If a few soldiers are allowed to remain in the unit while they refuse to clean weapons, smoke pot and get stoned while on guard duty, and push dope to new soldiers, the borderliners will join them and the good soldiers will become cynical and quit working.' Despite the manpower shortage the American army was suffering at this time (the 1970s), this particular commander believed that the only remedy was to discharge any worthless men from service. The manpower shortage was even greater in the late Roman period, however, so the utilization of this approach may not have been practicable. If the barbarians had continued to serve under 'Roman' commanders the problem would no doubt have been alleviated to some degree.

Leadership

> *There are no bad regiments; there are only bad colonels.*
> Napoleon Bonaparte

This remark by Napoleon could undoubtedly be applied to the late Roman army. Unquestionably, the men themselves were as courageous and potentially effective as their counterparts had been in the preceding centuries of Rome's history, but an apparently greater proportion of their commanders were militarily inadequate, leading Ferrill (1986, 65) to state that the defeats suffered in Persia and at Adrianople, 'were the result of a failure in leadership, not a lack of training, discipline or *esprit*.'

There are numerous comments by late Roman authors on the incompetence of those in command. Valens was apparently depressed by the poorness of his commanders, feeling unable to dismiss them because of the unsettled state of affairs (Zosimus 4.22.4). Ammianus cites several examples of commanders displaying cowardice during battle (24.3.1–2; 25.1.7–9; 27.2.6–7), whilst Procopius (8.16.19–20) records one incident where the 'commanders of the Roman army … refusing to withstand the enemy's attack … dispersed and saved themselves as each found it possible'.

During the late period the primary motivation behind men wishing to attain high rank within the army appears to have been for financial gain. Any man who controlled the army, or at least a section of it, had under his command a ready means of extorting personal revenue from the civilian population, particularly if the soldiers were actually stationed in the cities. Furthermore, the extortion of money and goods from their own troops was also a lucrative method of subsidising their income (see Chapter 5). Whilst the latter means of acquiring funds had been prevalent during the early Empire, it had usually only been utilized by lower ranking officers such as centurions; during the later period, however, it was those in the highest positions who subjected their men to this treatment. Libanius laments on the state of the commanders (*Or.* 47.28–9):

> As for the generals of today – what ruins them is precisely this life of plenty, which causes them to have more regard for their lives than for their reputations, and induces them to shun noble ventures and to make for what provides the means of loose living. Hence you should not all present the commanders with opportunities for making money, but you should show yourselves as desiring great deeds from them. As it is, they have eyes for one thing only – money …

He proceeds in his attack by castigating the commanders for their extortionate behaviour towards the troops (31.2):

> Then there is what they [the commanders] can get from the regimental ration returns: here they can keep the dead alive and themselves draw rations in the dead man's name … the gold that should properly stay in the hands of the men … finds its way into those of the commander. As a result the fighting man is pauperized, his morale lowered, as he wears his scraps of boots and his ghost of a uniform. And quite often the contribution he makes is from his belly, so that they lead into action starving bodies.

If such a deplorable state of affairs was as prevalent as the ancient authors would have us believe, it is little wonder that the troops were ill-disciplined and, bereft of morale, themselves being forced into extorting from others in order to survive. Thus, a chain of extortion was created, leaving a deep sense of loathing between the civilians and the military, and amongst the different ranks within the army itself.

In defence of the officers, the pay awarded them by the government was paltry, and this factor must surely have had some bearing on their preoccupation with money-making schemes, most of which appear to have been sanctioned by the state. Numerous astounding incidences of this financial motivation are recorded in the sources, particularly Procopius. On one occasion, the Armenian commander Artabazes had volunteered to enter the city of Verona under cover of darkness with a number of troops, hoping to surprise the Goths into flight. The plan worked, but due to the commanders haggling over what share of the booty each should get once they entered the city of Verona, the Goths were able to return to the city, and prevent its capture. Artabazes and his men were left in a desperate situation, and many failed to escape (Procopius 7.3.6–22).

There were, however, many fine generals and officers during the late Roman period, with the Emperor Justinian being particularly blessed in this area. When the soldiers were led by militarily capable men, who had a reasonable moral code of behaviour which they enforced, the army proved to be as effective in combat as it had been during the days of the Principate. The achievements of men such as Belisarius, Narses, Julian and Theodosius were all the product of ensuring that strict discipline was maintained, together with the possession of all those qualities which make men want to follow, despite the possible consequences. Zosimus states that Generidus trained the soldiers with continual exercises and distributed their rations in full without allowing any deductions, giving rewards to those who performed well from his own pay (5.46.5).

One of the most respected attributes a commander could possess was his willingness to endure the privations of the common soldier.

> 'In carrying out very critical operations the general ought not set himself apart as though such labour was beneath him, but he should begin the work and toil along with his troops as much as possible. Such behaviour will lead the soldier to be more submissive to his officers, even if only out of shame, and he will accomplish more.'
>
> Maurice's *Strategikon* 8.1.1

Both Zosimus (3.9.1) and Ammianus recount how Julian scorned the trappings of his position, preferring to live like a common soldier: 'For their [the Roman soldiers] affection, warmer after their experiences with him, prompted them to follow willingly one who was a fellow-soldier in every task, a leader brilliant in his prestige, and accustomed to prescribe more drudgery for himself than for a common soldier …' (Ammianus 17.1.2). Libanius, in his *Lament over Julian*, records how through this behaviour, Julian gained the respect of the troops, and therefore their courage in battle.

Commanders who possessed this quality could bring out the very best in their men, since a stronger bond would be formed, resulting in the soldiers feeling a greater sense of personal, rather than professional, obligation towards their officer and the aims he wished to achieve. It must be stated, however, that even the best leaders of the period had disciplinary problems: Julian was continually forced to deal with the cowardice of his cavalry (Ammianus 16.12.37-41; 18.8.2-3; 24.5.10; 25.1.7–9), whilst Belisarius faced the formidable task of trying to control troops who had not received their pay and were generally ill-supplied (Procopius 7.12.10). It is testimony to the ability of both these men that they achieved so much in the face of such logistical and disciplinary problems. When similar difficulties were encountered by leaders of a weaker nature, or less military ability, the consequences were disastrous, frequently leading either to mutiny or mass desertion.

War Weariness

War weariness was undoubtedly a major problem during the late period. Many of those involved, both civilian and military, appear to have despaired of the constant aggression required to defend the Empire. When Justinian proposed a campaign against the Vandals in Libya, 'the soldiers, also, having recently returned from a long, hard war, and having not yet tasted the full blessings of home, were in despair' (Procopius 3.10.5–6). Whilst only a proportion of the army would have been engaged in combat at any one time, and some men would possibly have escaped the horrors of battle completely, many unfortunate soldiers would have staggered from one engagement to another. Subjecting men to the pressures produced by combat causes many to suffer psychological damage, resulting in desertion, mutiny, cowardice and insubordination: to force men to endure such immense strain over prolonged periods, without adequate rest and relaxation, is to risk a total collapse in morale, and thus combat efficiency. By the end of the Second World War, many allied units had fought in more than one demanding offensive, resulting in the men stating that they were 'dog tired, and our spirits were sinking lower and lower. Every day seemed to be the same … There seemed to be no end to it and little hope … Pervading everything … was a feeling of endless tiredness and a gloomy sense of growing depression, like a man walking home on a foggy night, who had lost his way, and finds himself floundering weary and aimless, ankle-deep in a muddy bog' (Stirling 1946, 91).

During prolonged periods of active service, late Roman commanders were faced with the extremely difficult task of maintaining control over groups of deeply demoralized troops. Furthermore, it is often forgotten that the officers themselves were not only subject to the terrific strains of command responsibility, but were also affected by the same combat pressures and weariness which afflicted the ordinary soldiers. Thus the stress felt by leaders was enormous, and as Dinter points out, such men tend to 'burn out' at a faster rate than their subordinates: 'Leading is more difficult than being led' (1985, 58). It may be possible to identify a case of commander 'burn-out' from the late Roman sources: Ammianus refers to Severus, a master of the horse, who had previously been a warlike and energetic officer, but suddenly had lost heart, '… and he that had often encouraged one and all to brave deeds, now advised against fighting and seemed despicable and timid' (17.10.1–2). The vast majority of the citizen population of the late Roman Empire were undoubtedly suffering from a deep malaise regarding war. Citizens were embittered and exasperated, being continually asked to fund an army which rather than protecting them, appeared to cause more hardship than the supposed enemy. Ammianus records one telling incident in which the state-treasurer Ursulus, on seeing the state of the city of Amida after it had been besieged and destroyed by the Persians, cried, 'Behold with what courage the cities are defended by our soldiers, for whose abundance of pay the wealth of the Empire is already becoming insufficient' (20.11.5).

Conclusion

It should be noted that caution needs to be applied when using evidence from writers such as Zosimus and Libanius to assess the level of morale within the late Roman army, since both had personal grievances and biases which no doubt tainted their views, although more reliable sources do, on the whole, paint a similar picture.

Obviously the level of morale existing within the late Roman army fluctuated. It is undoubtedly true that where leadership was good and strict discipline and training maintained, the soldiers of this period could be just as courageous and efficient in battle as their earlier counterparts. Unfortunately, however, many of the factors discussed above which engender combat efficiency were deficient, resulting in many of the units becoming nothing more than bands of well-armed thugs.

The population of the Empire as a whole suffered from low morale during the late period, and the army should not be viewed in isolation. Many of the problems which afflicted the civilians impacted on the functioning ability of the military. The gulf between these two sections of society grew wider and wider, as the officers of the soldiers increasingly used the men under their control to exploit the citizens. In general the soldiers were loathed by the citizens, and such animosity must to some degree have had a detrimental effect on the morale of the army.

The disparate nature of the late Roman army brought with it many problems, although due to the reticence of the citizen population to enlist, the state had little alternative but to resort to the policy of large-scale barbarian recruitment. In such an army the maintenance of discipline was crucial to its functioning ability. Where control was allowed to falter for even a short period of time, the results could be disastrous. The fact that the machinery which could have ensured the working order of the army, i.e. the officers, was often considerably lacking in both skill and motivation, meant that the preservation of a constant, efficient force was virtually impossible. Commanders of great military dexterity managed to keep checking the disintegration of discipline, but such men were not sufficiently constant in supply to ensure the continuance of any recently acquired proficiency.

What is utterly remarkable about the army of this period is the fact that the men stood and fought at all. The sources record hundreds of examples of the extraordinarily brave behaviour of both leaders and soldiers, and as Ferrill notes (1986, 65), it should be remembered that despite the unmitigated horror of Adrianople, the army stood its ground. Sadly, however, many troops were ill-equipped, both physically and mentally, for war. The training regime which had made the early Roman army a force to be feared, had ceased to be maintained with any consistency. Many motivated emperors and leaders managed to halt the deterioration of discipline, but such respites were too short in duration, and too infrequent to allow the army to build on any regeneration of efficiency.

X

THE END
OF THE ARMY

A history of the late Roman army is inextricably bound up with the fate of the Empire and the reasons why the western half fragmented and the eastern half survived into and beyond the early Byzantine era. Probably no single satisfactory explanation will ever be formulated to answer the question why the Empire fell, nor even how, nor exactly when.

It is currently fashionable to describe the fall of Rome as merely a transformation rather than a cataclysmic collapse. Cameron (1993a, 10) points out that modern retrospective views of the problems of the late Empire have always tended towards the negative, whereas contemporaries may not have seen their lives in quite the same negative way. She also suggests (1993b, 36) that the fall of the Western Empire, overwhelmed by unstoppable hordes of barbarians, has been overstated and overdramatized.

None the less, overstated or not, the Western Empire turned into the Frankish, Visigothic and Ostrogothic kingdoms, and the Roman army disappeared. The east retained its army, but it was only partially recognizable as a Roman army.

The dilemma of the emperors *vis á vis* the army became apparent very early. A military force strong enough to protect the state was also strong enough to place usurpers on the throne. Anyone intending to become (and possibly remain) emperor needed to cultivate the army, thus letting the soldiers into the secret of their power. To fail to reward the soldiers was self-defeating and made recruitment difficult, whilst to reward them too liberally made them unpopular, sometimes greedy for more, and above all it gave them an inflated sense of their own worth and fractious if thwarted. This was of little consequence when the state was wealthy, but of enormous and dangerous consequence if the state was bankrupt, whether or not war threatened at the same time.

The evolution of static frontiers has been blamed for the decline of the army, in that frontier troops became too attached to their homes and idle through lack of occupation and training. This is to ignore the fact that the frontier armies did not always perform unsuccessfully, and units from some frontiers were transferred to the field armies. Whilst this does not entirely disprove the theories about lack of effectiveness and narrow local interests, it suggests that, potentially at least, the *limitanei* were capable of fighting just as well as the troops of the field armies.

Manpower shortage has also been advanced as a major contributary factor in the decline of the army, despite the fact that population figures are notoriously difficult to estimate. Naturally, shortage of soldiers is not quite the same as shortage of population. Economic factors also play a part. The bureaucracy of the late Empire swallowed up large numbers of men who might otherwise have followed a military career. The administration of the *annona* put a heavy strain on production, and more and more men were tied to the land. Only very rarely, and usually as a last resort, did Rome employ armies made up of slaves, which indicates either that class prejudice and snobbery were too instinctively deep-seated to be overcome, or that the slaves were considered as the Roman equivalent of the men and women who worked in reserved occupations during the Second World War.

Shortage of suitable provincial manpower, however it may have been caused, may have led to extensive employment of barbarians in the army, but even this was merely a continuation of the procedure already well-established in the early Empire. It has been suggested in this book that shortage of actual numbers of men was not necessarily a problem, and that there were hosts of barbarians willing to serve in the army. The major problem was lack of trained manpower, because there came a point when it was no longer possible to integrate the barbarians into existing units, or to train them as Roman soldiers, or to Romanize them sufficiently so that Roman traditions and fighting methods could be passed down to succeeding recruits.

Whatever the truth about the disappearance of the army, the effect was most cruelly felt by the generations of people who witnessed the transformation, as it is now commonly called. This eventual recovery has been exploited by some historians, who argue that the intervening period between collapse and resurgence was transitory, and that the crisis has been overstated.

The beginning of the fifth century was the nadir of the West. Britain was abandoned, and in 410 Alaric sacked Rome. Yet this did not lead directly to immediate collapse. Aetius managed to assemble armies to take the field against successive invasions of Alans, Burgundians and Huns, but his were not 'Roman' armies in the strict sense of the word. Lack of Romanitas need not imply that the armies were ineffective; the Huns were stopped in their tracks by Aetius at the battle of the Catalaunian Fields in 451. But the respite was only temporary. There was never enough time to re-establish long-term peace and prosperity, without which there could be no economic recovery. The East did not share this problem: having purged itself of barbarians, the Eastern army enjoyed the fruits of increased wealth and selective recruitment, while the Western army was forced to rely on whatever manpower it could obtain. Lack of consistent success in the field led to a corresponding lack of faith in its performance, and a growing disunity which resulted in the establishment of the separate barbarian kingdoms.

Occasionally, the experiences of an entire country can be epitomized by purely localized events. In Gaul, the lack of faith in the ability of the army to protect the citizens is perhaps succinctly expressed in the reoccupation of the prehistoric cave at l'Hortus in southern France (Chapelot and Fossier 1985, 69). Towards the end of the fourth century this site was occupied twice, at first only temporarily and then, judging from finds, on a more permanent basis at the end of the century. The material from the second occupation of the late fourth century is of a high, even luxurious, quality, but the contemporary finds of wild animal bones indicate that the occupants had to resort to hunting for food. The fifth-century occupation provides a contrast, in that the wealth of the inhabitants had obviously declined. Material finds are of a much lower quality, but the bones of domestic animals associated with this phase indicate that a return to a settled economy had begun.

As for the late fourth-century occupants of l'Hortus, surrounded by luxury goods but forced to live in a cave and hunt for food, the suggestion that they were merely undergoing a transformation might have been greeted with a rather hollow laugh.

MAPS I–IV

THE EMPIRE FROM
THE MID-SECOND CENTURY TO THE
FIFTH CENTURY AD

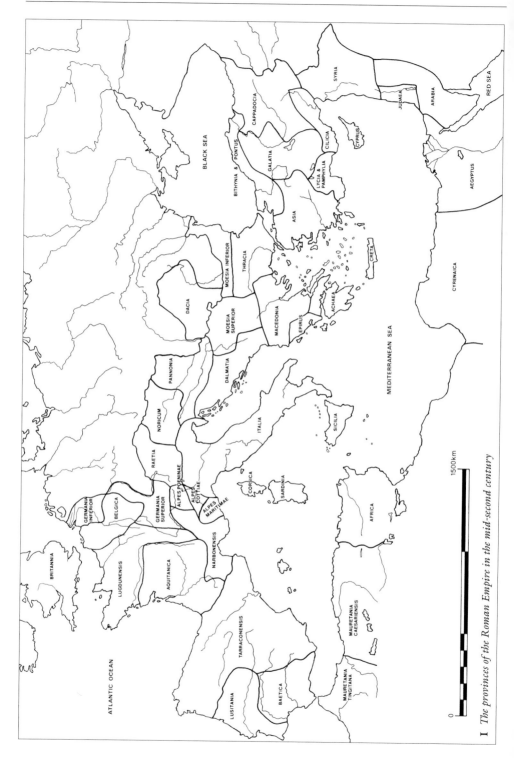

I *The provinces of the Roman Empire in the mid-second century*

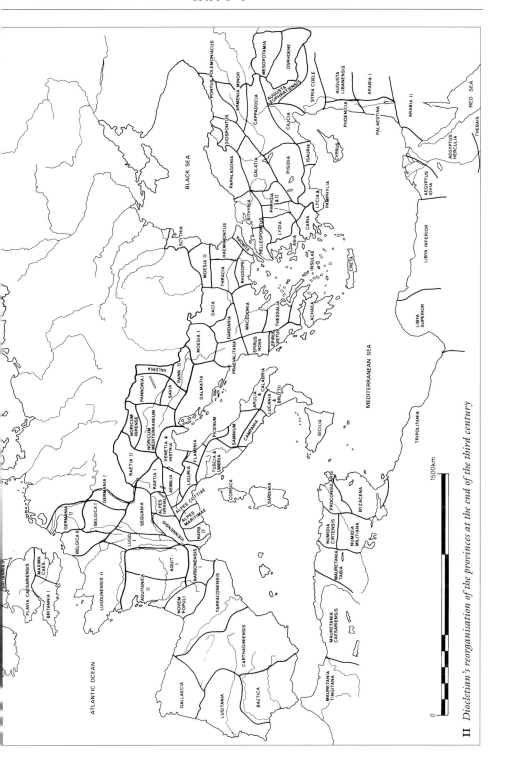

II *Diocletian's reorganisation of the provinces at the end of the third century*

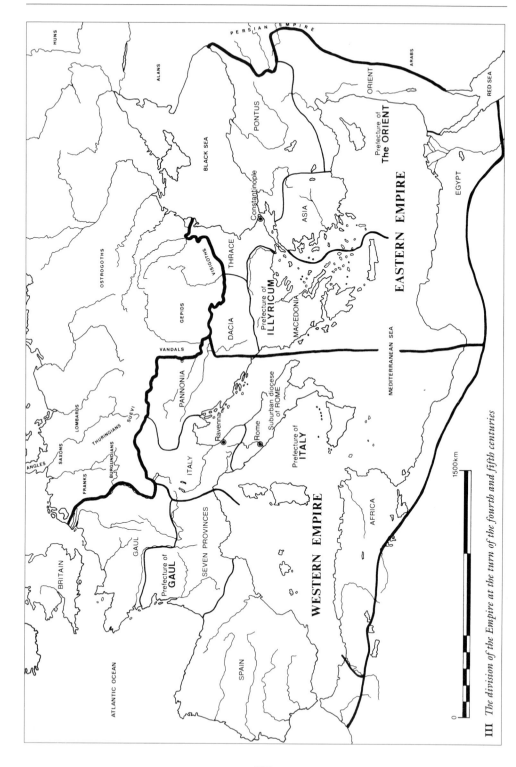

III *The division of the Empire at the turn of the fourth and fifth centuries*

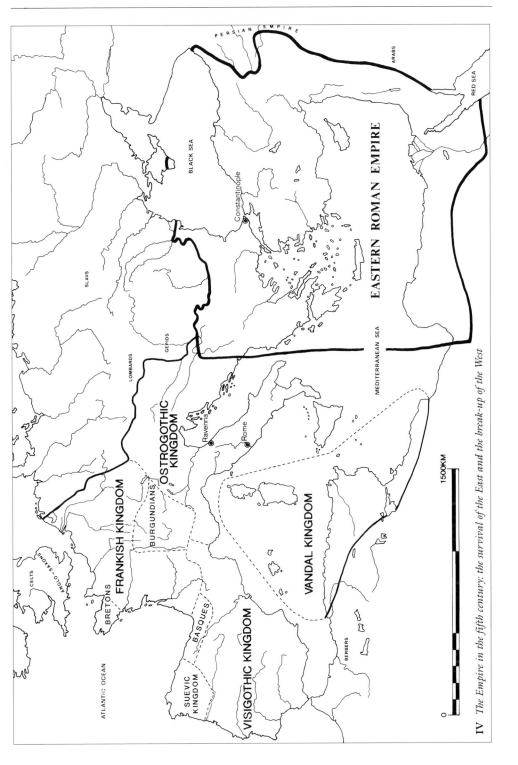

IV *The Empire in the fifth century: the survival of the East and the break-up of the West*

PERSIAN EMPIRE

ARABS

RED SEA

BLACK SEA

Constantinople

EASTERN ROMAN EMPIRE

SLAVS

GEPIDS

LOMBARDS

MEDITERRANEAN SEA

OSTROGOTHIC
KINGDOM

Ravenna

Rome

FRANKISH KINGDOM

BURGUNDIANS

CELTS

ANGLO-SAXONS

BRETONS

BASQUES

ATLANTIC OCEAN

SUEVIC
KINGDOM

VISIGOTHIC KINGDOM

VANDAL KINGDOM

BERBERS

1500KM

GLOSSARY

aerarium militare military treasury

ala milliara cavalry regiment *c.* 1000 strong in the Early Empire, later reduced

ala quingenaria cavalry regiment *c.* 500 strong in the Early Empire

annona militaris supply of provisions for the army

aquila eagle standard of a legion

aquilifer bearer of the eagle standard

as basic unit of Roman coinage made of bronze; two and a half asses made one *sestertius* (q.v.)

aureus gold coin, one of which was equivalent to 25 *denarii* (q.v.)

auxilia cohorts and *alae* (q.v.) raised in the provinces from non-citizens; used later for infantry regiments raised in the fourth century to serve in the field army

barding armour covering body of a horse

bucellarii literally 'biscuit eaters'. The private retainers of a landowner or government official

burgus watchtower or fortified landing place

capitatio a poll-tax, paid in cash

capitum literally 'fodder'. In the later empire, the term was used for supplies of food for army horses, equivalent to *annona* (q.v.), or supplies for the men

caput (pl. *capita*) literally 'head'; used as a basis for assessing the *capitatio* (q.v.)

cataphractarii heavy-armour cavalry. They may have differed from *clibanarii* (q.v.) by being equipped in a more western manner, carrying a lance and shield

centenarium small fort, usually square, found in Africa. The name appears on inscriptions and should indicate a garrison of *c.* 100 men, but some of the forts are too small to accommodate so many men.

centuria infantry unit, nominally *c.* 100 strong, but more usually *c.* 80 strong

centurion commander of a *centuria* (q.v.)

clibanarii heavy-armoured cavalry. The term derives from *clibanus* which means 'baking oven'. These troops may have been equipped in an eastern fashion, employing bow and lance

cohors equitata auxiliary unit of infantrymen with cavalry added to it, either *quingenaria* or *milliaria* in the Early Empire, but reduced in size, like the *alae*, in the Late Empire

colonus tenant of a landowner

comes (pl. *comites*) literally 'companion', usually translated as count. The *comites* were originally in the immediate entourage of the emperor, forming a sort of court. From Constantine's reign the title *comes* was given to military commanders and provincial governors. There did not seem to be any specific rank implicit in the title, or function. Eventually there were three grades of *comites* distinguished by the terms: *ordinis primi, secundi,* and *tertii*; meaning first, second and third rank

comitatenses the late Roman field army, consisting of both cavalry and infantry units, the vexillations and *legiones comitatus* (1) from *comes*, meaning literally 'escort', applied to the entourage of the emperor. Eventually the *comitatus* came to mean the field army, consisting of cavalry and infantry units, collectively called the *comitatenses*

comitatus (2) field army of the fourth century

constitutio antoniniana legislative enactment of the Emperor Caracalla in AD 212, which admitted free-born inhabitants of the Empire to Roman citizenship

contarii cavalry units in the Roman Empire equipped with the *contus* (q.v.)

contubernium tent party, or the number of soldiers sharing the same barrack room; usually eight men

contus heavy lance approximately 3.6m (12ft) long, which was held two-handed

cuneus literally a 'wedge'; used for cavalry formations of the Later Empire and for some units in Britain from the third century

curiales members of the city councils

decurio commanding officer of a *turma* (q.v.)

denarius Roman silver coin worth four *sestertii*

diocese administrative groupings of several provinces, instituted by Diocletian

dona militaria military decorations

draco dragon standard believed to have been introduced into the Roman army by the Sarmatians

draconarius bearer of the draco (q.v.)

dux title given to a high-ranking officer in the third century, usually when he was performing duties normally above his rank. Later the title was given to equestrians with military commands, usually in frontier zones; *duces* were elevated to senatorial rank under Valentinian

equites (1) cavalry vexillations (q.v.) of the Late Empire

equites (2) men of the equestrian order or middle classes, who rose in influence under Severus and Diocletian who bestowed of them most of the administrative posts and many of the higher military commands

equites singulares mounted bodyguard of a provincial governor, or the emperor

excubitores bodyguard instituted by the Emperor Leo to replace the *scholae* (q.v.)

exploratores scouts

fabrica workshop

foederati from *foedus*, a treaty (q.v.); meaning literally those who are allied. After a war, tribes would contribute troops to the army by terms of their treaty. In the sixth-century army the *foederati* were regular troops.

foedus a treaty between Rome and another state, or a tribe. The treaty could be made in times of peace, but was enacted more commonly after a war.

frumentum grain; a term used for the corn supply in general

gentiles non Romans, free tribes living outside the empire, or tribal units settled on Roman territory

gladius short, stabbing sword of Spanish origin used by legionaries

hasta spear

hiberna winter quarters

hippika gymnasia cavalry tournament of the Roman army in which both the men and horses were richly adorned *honesta missio* honourable discharge from the army

honestiores upper classes, whose status was not so clearly defined as, for instance, that of the *equites*, whose qualifications for rank rested on wealth. The *honestiores* enjoyed greater legal privileges than the *humiliores* (q.v)

horrea granaries

humiliores lower classes, a status not strictly defined by law

imaginifer bearer of the *imago*, a standard which bore the image of the emperor

iugum a unit of land

laeti people settled on lands inside the Empire obliged to provide recruits for the army

legiones infantry units in both the frontier and field armies. In the Early Empire they were *c.* 6000 strong, but in the Late Empire some legions were probably only 1000 strong, while the larger units of 6000 men were often split up into detachments.

limes frontier

limitanei frontier troops

magister equitum Commander-in-Chief of the cavalry

magister militum Commander-in-Chief of the army

magister officiorum head of the secretarial offices

magister peditum Commander-in-Chief of the infantry

palatini administrative palace staff, regimented like soldiers

praepositus not strictly a rank. A title bestowed on a military officer serving on special missions, temporarily in command of vexillations (q.v.)

praeses (pl. *praesides*) provincial governor, usually of equestrian status.

protectores a title instituted by Gallienus, given to high ranking officers; a staff college of men loyal to the emperor, but not strictly a bodyguard

pseudo-comitatenses troops taken from the *limitanei* (q.v.) to serve in the field army

quadriburgium a small square fort

ripenses frontier troops on river frontiers

scholae palatinae units of the imperial bodyguard

scrinia department of the secretarial services in the administration of the Empire

sestertius a Roman silver coin; a fourth of a *denarius* (q.v.) and equal to two and a half asses (q.v.)

symmachoi allies; a Greek word used for specific troops in the sixth-century army

territorium land outside a fort on which military or tenant farmers could graze livestock and grow crops

tirones recruits

turma cavalry unit in an *ala* or *cohors equitata*, probably containing *c.* 32 men, commanded by a *decurio* (q.v.)

valetudinarium hospital

vexillarius bearer of the *vexillum* (q.v.)

vexillation detachment of troops drawn from an auxiliary unit or legion

vexillationes cavalry units of possibly 500 men, although some authorities consider that they may have been 1000 strong. They may have originated under Gallienus.

vexillum cavalry standard consisting of a square, red or purple tasselled flag which was hung from a cross bar attached to a lance

vicarius governor of a *diocese* (q.v.) responsible to the praetorian prefect

BIBLIOGRAPHY

Abbreviations

BAR	*British Archaeological Reports*
Brit	*Britannia*
CAH	*Cambridge Ancient History*
CIL	*Corpus Inscriptionum Latinarum*
Cod. Just.	Codex Justinianus (*Corpus Iuris Civilis* 2). Berlin 1877. Repr. 1967
Cod. Th.	*The Theodosian Code and Novels and the Sirmondian Constitutions.* Translated by C. Pharr. New York: Greenwood Press
Chr. I	*Chrestomathie.* U. Wilcken. Berlin 1912
Chron. Min.	*Chronica Minora saec. IV, V, VI, VII.* Edited by Th. Mommsen, Berlin 1892–8.Three vols
Digest	*The Digest of Justinian.* Translated by A. Watson. Philadelphia: University of Pennsylvania
Ep. Stud.	*Epigraphische Studien*
FIRA	*Fontes Iuris Romani Ante Justiniani*
ILS	*Inscriptiones Latinae Selectae.* H. Dessau. Berlin. Three vols
JRMES	*Journal of Roman Military Equipment Studies*
JRS	*Journal of Roman Studies*
Migné	J.P. Migné (ed.) *Patrologia Graeca.* Belgium. 161 vols
	J.P. Migné (ed.) *Patrologia Latina.* Belgium. 221 vols
Not. Dig.	*Notitia Dignitatum.* Edited by O. Seeck. Berlin 1876
Nov. Th.	*Novellae of Theodosius II.* In *Codex Theodosianus* (*Cod. Th.*)
Pan. Lat.	*Panegyrici Latini. Panégyriques Latines.* Text by E. Galletier. Paris: Société d'Edition Les Belles Lettres, 1949–55. Three vol
P. Oxy.	*The Oxyrhynchus Papyri.* B.P. Grenfell, A.S. Hunt and H.I. Bell *et al.* London (1898–)
P. Ryl.	*Catalogue of the Greek Papyri in the John Rylands Library, Manchester.* A.S. Hunt *et al.* Manchester 1911–52
RE	*Real Encyclopädie der Klassischen Altertumswissenschaft.* Pauly-Wissowa. 1893–
RIB	*Roman Inscriptions of Britain*, vol. 1 R.G. Collingwood and R.P. Wright. Oxford, 1965
SJ	*Saalburg Jahrbuch*
SPP	*Studien zur Palaeographie und Papyruskunde.* C. Wessely. Leipzig 1901–
Symm. *Ep.*	Symmachus *Epistulae*
V. Pach	*Vita S. Pachomii.* F. Nau and J. Bousquet, *Patrologia Orientalis* IV.V

Zach. Myt. Chron.   *Chronicles of Zacharias of Mytilere*
ZPE   *Zeitschrift für Papyrologie und Epigraphik*

Ancient sources

The Abinnaeus Archive: Papers of a Roman officer in the reign of Constantius II. Collected and re-edited by H.I. Bell, *et al*. Oxford: Clarendon Press. 1962.

Aineias the Tactician *How to survive under siege*. Translated by D. Whitehead. Oxford: Clarendon Press. 1990.

Ammianus Marcellinus. Loeb.

Anonymous *De Rebus Bellicis*. M.W.C. Hassall and R.T. Ireland (eds) 1979. Oxford: BAR S63.

Cassiodorus *Variae*. Translated by S.J.B. Barnish. Liverpool Univ. Press. 1992.

Chronicon Paschale 284–628 AD Translated by M. and M. Whitby. Liverpool Univ. Press. 1989.

Claudian *De Consulatu Stilichonis*. Loeb.

Claudian *De Bello Gildonicus*. Loeb.

The Digest of Justinian Translated by A. Watson. Philadelphia: University of Pennsylvania Press.

Dio *Roman History*. Loeb.

Eugippius *Vita Sancti Severini*. In *Patrologia Latina*. Edited by J.P. Migné. Vol. 62. 1863.

Eutropius *Breviarum*. Teubner 1887.

Herodian. Loeb.

Lactantius *De Mortibus Persecutorum*. In *Patrologia Latina*. Edited by J.P. Migné. Vol. 7. 1844.

Libanius *Orations*. Loeb.

Lydus *De Magistratibus Populi Romani*

Malalas

Maurice *Strategikon: Handbook of Byzantine Military Strategy*. Translated by G.T. Dennis. University of Pennsylvania Press. 1984.

Notitia Dignitatum. Edited by O. Seeck. Berlin. 1876.

Pacatus *Panegyric to the Emperor Theodosius*. Translated by C.E.V. Nixon. Liverpool Univ. Press. 1987.

Panegryrici LatiniPanégyriques Latines. Text by E. Galletier. Paris: Société d'Édition Les Belles Lettres. 1949–55. Three vols.

Procopius *History of the Wars*.

Scriptores Historiae Augustae

Sidonius *Poems and Letters*

Synesius *De Regno* & *Epistulae* in *Patrologia Graeca*. Edited by J.P. Migné. Vol. 66. 1859.

The Theodosian Code and Novels and the Sirmondian Constitutions. Translated by C. Pharr. New York: Greenwood Press 1969.

Aurelius Victor *De Caesaribus*. Translated by H.W. Bird. Liverpool Univ. Press. 1994.

Vegetius *Epitoma Rei Militaris*. Translated by N.P. Milner. Liverpool Univ. Press 1993.

Victor of Vita *History of the Vandal Persecution*. Translated with notes and introduction by J. Moorhead. Liverpool University Press 1992.

Zonaras

Zosimus *New History*. Translation and commentary by R.T. Ridley. Sydney: Australian Association for Byzantine Studies. 1982.

Modern works

Allason-Jones, L., 1985. 'An eagle mount from Carlisle', *Transactions of the Cumberland and Westmorland Archaeological and Natural History Society* 85, 264–6.

Allason-Jones, L., 1986. 'An eagle mount from Carlisle', SJ 42, 68–9.

Allason-Jones, L. and Miket, R., 1984. *The Catalogue of Small Finds from South Shields Fort*. Newcastle upon Tyne.

Alföldy, G., 1974. *Noricum*. London: Routledge.

Anstee, J.W. and Biek, L., 1961. 'A study in pattern-welding', *Medieval Archaeology* 5. 71–93.

Arnheim, M.T.W., 1972. *The Senatorial Aristocracy in the later Roman Empire*. Oxford: Clarendon Press.

Austin, N.J.E. and Rankov, M.B. *Exploratio*. London: Routledge.

Baatz, D., 1978. 'Recent finds of ancient artillery', *Brit* 9, 1–17.

Baatz, D., Herrmann, F.-R. *et al.*, 1982. *Die Römer in Hessen*. Stuttgart: Theiss.

Balty, J.-C., 1988. 'Apamea in Syria in the second and third centuries AD', *JRS* 78, 91–104.

Barker, P.A., 1979. 'The *plumbata* from Wroxeter', in Hassall and Ireland (eds) 1979, 97–9.

Baynes, J., 1987. *Morale: A Study of Men and Courage* (reprint of 1967 edn). London: Leo Cooper.

Baynes, M. 1953. Review of W. Hartke *Kinderkaiser: eine Strukturanalyse Römischen Denkens und Daisens*. Berlin 1951. *JRS* 43, 137–8.

Baynes, N.H., 1925. 'Three notes on the reforms of Diocletian and Constantine', *JRS* 15, 195–208.

Behmer, E., 1939. *Das zweischneidige Schwert der germanischen Völkerwanderungszeit*. Stockholm.

Bennett, J., 1991. '*Plumbatae* from Pitsunda (Pityus), Georgia, and some observations on their probable use', *JRMES* 2, 59–63.

Bersu G., 1964. *Die spätrömische Befestigung 'Burghle' bei Gundremmingen*. Munich: Beck'sche Verlag.

Birley, A., 1988. *The African Emperor Septimius Severus*. London: Batsford.

Birley, E., 1969. 'Septimius Severus and the Roman army', *Ep. Stud.* 8, 63–82.

Bishop, M.C. (ed.) 1985. *The Production and Distribution of Roman Military Equipment: Proceedings of the Second Roman Military Equipment Seminar*. Oxford: BAR S275.

Bishop, M.C. and Coulston, J.C.N.,1989. *Roman Military Equipment*. Princes Risborough.

Bishop, M.C. and Coulston, J.C.N., 1993. *Roman Military Equipment*. London: Batsford.

Bivar, A.D.H., 1972. 'Cavalry tactics and equipment on the Euphrates', *Dumbarton Oaks Papers* 26, 273–91.

Boak, A.E.R., 1955. *Manpower Shortage and the Fall of the Roman Empire in the West*. Connecticut: Greenwood Press.

Britt, A S., 1985. *The Wars of Napoleon*. Wayne, New Jersey: Avery Publishing.

Bullinger, H., 1969. *Spätantike Gürtelbeschläge. Typen, Herstellung, Trageweise und Datierung*. Bruges.

Burns, T.S., 1984. *A History of the Ostrogoths*. Bloomington: Indiana University Press.

Bury, J.B., 1958. *History of the Later Roman Empire from the Death of Theodosius to the Death of Justinian*. New York: Dover Publications. 2 vols. Reprint of original edn.

Burgoyne Diaries 1985. London: Thomas Harnsworth Publishing.

Bushe-Fox, J.P., 1928. *Second Report on the Excavation of the Roman Fort at Richborough, Kent*. Society of Antiquaries of London Research Report no. 7. Oxford.

Bushe-Fox, J.P., 1949. *Fourth Report on the Excavations of the Roman Fort at Richborough, Kent*. Society of Antiquaries of London Research Report no. 16. Oxford.

Cahn, D., 1989. *Waffen und Zaumzeug*. Basle.

Cambridge Ancient History 1939. Volume XII: *The Imperial Crisis and Recovery A.D. 193–24*. Cambridge: Cambridge University Press.

Cameron, A. 1993a. *The Later Roman Empire*. London: Fontana.

Cameron, A. 1993b. *The Mediterranean World in late Antiquity*, AD 395–600. London: Routledge.

Campbell, B., 1978. 'The marriage of soldiers under the Empire', *JRS* 68, 153–66.

Casey, J., 1991. *The Legions in the Later Roman Empire*. Fourth Annual Caerleon Lecture. National Museum of Wales.

Chapelot, J. and Fossier, R. 1985. *The Village and House in the Middle Ages*. London: Batsford.

Christlein, R., 1979. 'Das spätrömische Boiotro zu Passau-Innstadt', in Werner, J. and Ewig, E. (eds), *Von der Spätantike zum Frühen Mittelalter*. Singmaringen: Thorbecke, 90–132.

Cichorius, C., 1896–1900. *Der Reliefs der Traianssäule*. Berlin.

Clarke, G., 1979. *The Roman Cemetery at Lankhills*. Winchester Studies 3. Oxford.

Collins, R., 1991. *Early Medieval Europe, 300–1000*. London: Macmillan.

Coulston, J.C.N., 1985. 'Roman archery equipment', in Bishop (ed.) 1985, 220–366.

Coulston, J.C.N., 1987. 'Roman military equipment on 3rd century AD tombstones', in Dawson (ed.) 1987, 141–56.

Coulston, J.C.N., 1988. *Military Equipment and the Identity of Roman Soldiers*. Proceedings of the Fourth Roman Military Equipment Conference. Oxford: BAR S394.

Coulston, J.C.N., 1990. 'Later Roman armour, 3rd–6th centuries A.D.', *JRMES* 1, 139–60.

Coulston, J.C.N., 1991. 'The "draco" standard', *JRMES* 2, 101–14.

Crump, G.A., 1973. 'Ammianus and the Late Roman army', *Historia* 22, 91–103.

Cüppers, H. *et al.*, 1990. *Die Römer in Rheinland-Pfalz*. Stuttgart: Theiss.

Dabrowski, K. and Kolendo, J., 1972. 'Les epées romaines découvertes en Europe centrale et septentrionale', *Archaeologia Polona* 13, 59–109.

Dahmlos, U., 1977. 'Francisca-bipennis-securis. Bemerkungen zu archäologischem Befund und schriftlicher überlieferung', *Germania* 55, 141–65.

Daly, L.J., 1972. 'The Mandarin and the Barbarian: the response of Themistius to the Gothic challenge', *Historia* 21, 35179.

Daniels, C., 1987. 'The Frontiers of Africa', in Wacher 1987, 223–65.

Dauge, Y.A. 1981. *Le Barbare: recherches sur la conception romaine de la barbarie et de la civilisation*. Coll. Latomus, vol. 176.

Davidson, H.R.E., 1962. *The Sword in Anglo-Saxon England*. Oxford.

Davies, R.W., 1969. 'Joining the Roman army', *Bonner Jahrbuch* 169, 20832.

Davies, R.W., 1971, 'The Roman military diet', *Britannia*, vol. 2, 122–42.

Dawson, M. (ed.), 1987. *Roman Military Equipment: the Accoutrements of War*. Proceedings of the Third Roman Military Equipment Research Seminar. Oxford: BAR S336.

De Blois, L., 1976. *The Policy of the Emperor Gallienus*. Nederlands Instituut te Rome.

Delbrück, H., 1921. *The Barbarian Invasions. History of the Art of War*, vol 2. Univ. Nebraska Press, repr. 1990.

Dill, S., 1905. *Roman Society in the Last Century of the Western Empire*. London: Macmillan.

Dinter, E., 1985. *Hero or Coward: Pressures Facing the Soldier in Battle*. London: Frank Cass.

Dittman, K., 1940. 'Ein eiserner Spangenhelm in Kairo', *Germania* 24, 54–8.

Dixon, K.R., 1990. 'Dolphin scabbard runners', *JRMES* 1, 17–25.

Dixon, K.R. and Southern, P., 1992. *The Roman Cavalry*. London: Batsford.

Domaszewski, A. von, 1910. 'Gürtelzierat aus Aegypten in der Sammlung Golenischew', *Römisch-Germanisches Korrespondenzblatt part* 3, 9–10.

Drack, W., 1980. *Die Spätrömische Grenzwehr am Hochrhein*. Archäologische Führer der Schweiz. No. 13, Zurich.

Drack, W. and Fellman, R., 1988. *Die Römer in der Schweiz*. Stuttgart: Theiss.

Drew, K.F., 1991. *The Laws of the Salian Franks*. Philadelphia: Univ. of Pennsylvania Press.

Driel-Murray, C. van, 1986. 'Shoes in perspective', in Unz (ed.) 1986, 139–45.

Driel-Murray, C. van, 1989. *Roman Military Equipment: The Sources of Evidence*. Proceedings of the Fifth Roman Military Equipment Conference. Oxford: BAR S 476.

Drinkwater, J. and Elton, H., 1992. *Fifth-Century Gaul: A Crisis of Identity*. Cambridge Univ. Press.

Duncan-Jones, R., 1978. 'Pay and numbers in Diocletian's army', *Chiron* 8, 54160.

Durry, M., 1938. *Les Cohortes Prétoriennes*. Paris: de Boccard.

Eagle, J., 1989. 'Testing plumbata', in Driel-Murray, C., van (ed.) 1989, 247–53.

Ellis, J., 1993. *The Sharp End: The Fighting Man in World War II*. London: Pimilico.

Elton, H., 1992. 'Defence in Fifth Century Gaul', in Drinkwater and Elton 1992, 167–76.

Engelhardt, C., 1863. *Thorsbjerg Fundet*. Copenhagen.

Engelhardt, C., 1865. *Nydam Mosefund*. Copenhagen.

Engelhardt, C., 1867. *Kragehul Mosefund*. Copenhagen.

Engelhardt, C., 1869. *Vimose Fundet*. Copenhagen.

Ensslin, W., 1939. 'The reforms of Diocletian', Chapter 11, *CAH* XII, 1939, 383–408.

Espérandieu, E., 1907. *Recueil Général des Bas-Reliefs de la Gaule Romaine*. Paris.

Fentress, E., 1979. *Numidia and the Roman Army*. Oxford: BAR S53.

Ferrill, A., 1986. *The Fall of the Roman Empire: The Military Explanation*. London: Thames and Hudson.

Filtzinger, P. *et al.*, 1986. *Die Römer in Baden-Württemberg*. Stuttgart: Theiss.

Fink, R.O., 1971. *Roman Military Records on Papyrus*. American Philological Association. Monograph 26.

Fischer, T. and Spindler, K., 1984. *Das römische Grenzkastell Abusina-Eining*. Stuttgart.

Fitz, J., 1976. *Der Römische Limes in Ungarn*. Székesfehévàr: Taschenbuch für die Teilnehmer XI Int Limeskongresses.

Freeman, P. and Kennedy, D. (eds), 1986. *The Defence of the Roman and Byzantine East*. Oxford: BAR S297 (2 vols).

French, D.H. and Lightfoot, C.S. (eds), 1989. *The Eastern Frontier of the Roman Empire*. Oxford: BAR S553 (2 vols).

Garbsch, J., 1978. *Römische Paraderüstungen*. Munich: C.H. Beck.

Garbsch, J., 1984. 'Ein romisches Parakenhemd von Bertoldsheim, Ldkar. Neuburg-Schrobenhausen', *Neuburger Kollektaneenblapp* 136, 239–53.

Garnsey, P., 1970. 'Septimius Severus and the marriage of soldiers', *California Studies in Classical Antiquity* 3, 45–53.

Genser, K., 1986. *Der Österreichische Donaulimes in der Römerzeit: ein Forschungsbericht*. Der Römische Limes in Österreich Heft 33. Vienne: öst. Akademie der Wissenschaften.

Gichon, M., 1989. 'Estimating the strength of Quadriburgia garrisons, exemplified by En Boqeq in the Negev', in French and Lightfoot 1989, 121–42.

Gilliam, J.F., 1961. 'The plague under Marcus Aurelius', *American Journal of Philology* 82, 225–51.

Goffart, W., 1980. *Barbarians and Romans* AD *418–584: Techniques of Accommodation*. Princeton University Press.

Goodburn, R. and Bartholomew, P. (eds), 1976. *Aspects of the* Notitia Dignitatum. Oxford: BAR 515.

Graham, S., 1919. *A Private in the Guards*. London: Macmillan.

Grigg, R., 1983. 'Inconsistency and lassitude: the shield emblems of the Notitia Dignitatum', *JRS* 73, 132–42.

Grosse, R., 1920. *Römische Militärgeschichte von Gallienus bis zum Beginn der Byzantinschen Themenverfassung*. Berlin: Weidmannsche Buchhandlung.

Gudea, N., 1977. *Gornea. Asezari din Epoca Romana si Romana Tirzie*. Resita.

Gudea, N. and Baatz, D., 1974. 'Teile Spätrömischer Ballisten aus Gornea und Orsova (Rumänien)', *SJ* 31, 50–72.

Hanson, W.S. and Keppie, L.J.F., 1980. *Roman Frontier Studies 1979*. Oxford: BAR S71.

Hartmann, M., 1980. *Das Römische Kastell von Zurzach-Tenedo*. Schweiz. Gesellschaft für Ur-und Frühgeschichte.

Hassall, M.W.C. and Ireland, R.T. (eds) 1979. *De Rebus Bellicis*. Oxford: BAR S63.

Hawkes, S.C. and Dunning, G.C., 1961. 'Soldiers and settlers in Britain, fourth to fifth century', *Medieval Archaeology* 5, 1–70.

Heather, P., 1991. *Goths and Romans 332–489*. Oxford: Oxford Historical Monographs.

Heather, P. and Matthews, J. 1991. *The Goths in the Fourth Century*. Liverpool University Press. Translated Texts for Historians Vol. 11.

Herrmann, F.R., 1969. 'Des Eisenhortfund aus dem Kastell Künzing', *SJ* 26, 129–41.

Herrmann, F.R., 1972. *Die Ausgrabungen in dem Kastell Künzing/Quintana*. Limes-Museum Aalen.

Hoffman, D., 1969–70. *Die Spätrömische Bewegungsheer und die Notitia Dignitatum*. Epigraphische Studien 7. Düsseldorf: Rheinland Verlag. 2 vols.

Hopwood, K., 1986. 'Towers, territory and terror: how the East was held', in Freeman and Kennedy 1986, 343–56.

Horn, H.G. *et al.*, 1987. *Die Römer in Nordrhein-Westfalen*. Stuttgart: Theiss.

Hundt, H.J., 1953. 'Die spätrömischen eisernen Dosenortbänder', *SJ* 12, 66–79.

Isaac, B., 1990, rev. ed. 1992. *The Limits of Empire: The Roman Army in the East*. Oxford: Clarendon Press.

Jacobi, H., 1897. *Das Römerkastell Saalburg*. Germany.

James, E., 1988. *The Franks*. Oxford: Basil Blackwell.

James, S., 1983. 'Archaeological evidence for Roman incendiary projectiles', *SJ* 39, 142–3.

James, S., 1986. 'Evidence from Dura-Europos for the origins of Late Roman helmets', *Syria* 63, 108–34.

James, S., 1988. 'The fabricae: state arms factories of the Later Roman Empire', in Coulston, J.C.N. (ed.) 1988, 257–332.

Johnson, S., 1976. *The Roman Forts of the Saxon Shore*. London: Elek 2nd edn.

Johnson, S., 1980. 'A Late Roman helmet from Burgh Castle', *Brit* 11, 30312.

Johnson, S., 1983a. *Late Roman Fortifications*. London: Batsford.

Johnson, S., 1983b. *Burgh Castle, Excavations by Charles Green 1958–61*. East Anglian Archaeology Report No. 20. Norfolk Archaeological Unit.

Johnson, S., 1989. 'Architecture of the Saxon Shore forts', in Maxfield 1989, 30–44.

Jones, A.H.M., 1964. *The Later Roman Empire 284–602*. Oxford: Basil Blackwell. 2 vols.

Jones, A.H.M., 1966. *The Decline of the Ancient World*. Harlow: Longman.

Jones, F.P., 1987. '*Stigma*: tattooing and branding in Graeco-Roman antiquity', *JRS* 77, 139–55.

Kennedy, D. and Riley, D. 1990. *Rome's Desert Frontier from the Air*. London: Batsford.

Klumbach, H., 1973. *Spätrömische Gardehelme*. Munich: C.H. Beck'sche Verlag.

Kraeling, C.H., 1956. *The Excavations at Dura-Europos, Final Report VIII.1, The Synagogue*. New Haven.

Lander, J. 1980. 'Typology and late Roman fortification: the case of the "Diocletianic Type"', in Hanson and Keppie 1980, 105–60.

Lander, J. 1984. *Roman Stone Fortification: Variation and Change from the First Century AD to the Fourth.* Oxford: BAR S206.

Lawrence, A.W., 1979. *Greek Aims in Fortification.* Oxford: Clarendon Press.

Lee, A.D., 1993. *Information and Frontiers.* Cambridge Univ. Press.

Lengyel, A. and Radan, G.T.B., 1980. *The Archaeology of Roman Pannonia.* University Press of Kentucky/Akademiai Kiado.

Lepper, F. and Frere, S.S., 1988. *Trajan's Column.* Gloucester: Alan Sutton.

Lewis, N. and Reinhold, M., 1966. *Roman Civilization: Sourcebook II: The Empire.* New York: Harper and Row. Revised edn.

Liebeschuetz, J., 1986. 'Generals, federates and buccelarii in Roman armies around AD 400', in Freeman and Kennedy 1986, 463–74.

Liebeschuetz, J., 1991. *Barbarians and Bishops.* Oxford: Clarendon Press.

Liebeschuetz, J., 1992. 'Alaric's Goths: nation or army?' in Drinkwater and Elton 1992, 75–83.

Lot, F., 1931. *The End of the Ancient World and the Beginnings of the Middle Ages.* London: Kegan Paul.

Luttwak, E.M., 1976. *The Grand Strategy of the Roman Empire.* Baltimore: John Hopkins Univ. Press.

MacMullen, R., 1963. *Soldier and Civilian in the Later Roman Empire.* Harvard University Press.

MacMullen, R., 1988. *Corruption and the Decline of Rome.* Yale University Press.

MacMullen, R., 1990. *Changes in the Roman Empire.* Princeton Univ. Press.

Mann, J.C., 1953. ' "Honesta missio" and the Brigetio Table', *Hermes* 81, 496–500.

Mann, J.C., 1989. 'Historical development of the Saxon Shore', in Maxfield 1989, 1–11.

Mann, J.C. and Roxan, M.M., 1988. 'Discharge certificates of the Roman army', *Brit* 19, 341–7.

Manning, W.H., 1976. *The Romano-British Ironwork in the Museum of Antiquities, Newcastle upon Tyne.* Newcastle upon Tyne.

Marsden, E.W., 1969. *Greek and Roman Artillery: Historical Development.* Oxford: Clarendon Press.

Maxfield, V., (ed.), 1989. *The Saxon Shore: A Handbook.* University of Exeter for 15th Int. Congress of Roman Frontier Studies 1989.

Maxfield, V. and Dobson, M.J. (eds), 1991. *Roman Frontier Studies 1989: Proceedings of the XV International Congress of Roman Frontier Studies.* University of Exeter.

Milner, N.P., 1993. *Vegetius: Epitome of military science.* Liverpool Univ. Press.

Mócsy, A., 1974. *Pannonia and Upper Moesia.* London: Routledge.

Mommsen, T., 1889. 'Das römische Militärwesen seit Diocletian', *Hermes* 24.

Moran, Lord, 1945. *The Anatomy of Courage.* London: Constable.

Moss, J.R., 1973. 'The effects of the policies of Aetius on the history of the western Empire', *Historia* 22, 711–31.

Musset, L., 1975. *The Germanic Invasions: The Making of Europe A.D. 400–600.* London: Elek Books.

Musty, J. and Barker, P.A., 1974. 'Three plumbatae from Wroxeter, Shropshire', *Antiquaries Journal* 54, 275–7.

Nash-Williams, V.E., 1932. *The Roman Legionary Fortress at Caerleon in Monmouthshire: Report on the Excavations Carried out in the Prysg Field 1927–9*. Part II: the Finds. Cardiff: National Museum of Wales.

Nischer, E.C., 1923. 'The army reforms of Diocletian and Constantine and their modifications up to the time of the Notitia Dignitatum,' *JRS* 13, 1–55.

Nye, R.H., 1986. *The Challenge of Command: Reading for Military Excellence*. New Jersey: Avery Publishing Group Incorporated.

O'Flynn, J.M., 1983. *Generalissimos of the Western Roman Empire*. Alberta: University of Alberta Press.

Okamura, L., 1991. 'The flying columns of Emperor Gallienus: "legionary" coins and their hoards', in Maxfield, V. and Dobson, M.J. (eds), 1991, 387–91.

Oldenstein, J., 1976. 'Zur Ausrüstung römischer Auxiliereinheiten', *Bericht der Römisch-Germanischen Kommission* 57, 49–284.

Parker, H.M.D., 1933. 'The legions of Diocletian and Constantine', *JRS* 23, 175–89.

Parker, H.M.D., 1935. *History of the Roman World AD138–337*. London: Methuen.

Parker, S.T. (ed.), 1987. *The Roman Frontier in Central Jordan: Interim Report on the Limes Arabicus Project 1980–1985*. Oxford: BAR S340 (2 vols).

Patton, General L.J.S., 1975. *War as I Knew It*.

Petrikovits, H. von, 1971. 'Fortifications in the North-Western Roman Empire from the third to the fifth centuries AD', *JRS* 61, 178–218.

Pfister, R. and Bellinger, L., 1945. *The Excavations at Dura-Europos, Final Report IV.2. The Textiles*. New Haven: Yale Univ. Press.

Planck, D., 1983. *Das Freilichtmuseum am rätischen Limes im Ostalbkreis*. Stuttgart.

Rémondon, R., 1964. *La Crise de L'Empire Romain de Marc-Auréle à Anastase*. Paris: Presses Universitaires de France.

Richmond, I.A., 1940. 'The barbaric spear from Carvoran', *Proceedings of the Society of Antiquaries of Newcastle upon Tyne* ser. 4.9, 136–8.

Robertson, A., Scott, M. and Keppie, L., 1975. *Bar Hill: A Roman Fort and its Finds*. Oxford BAR 16.

Robinson, H.R., 1975. *The Armour of Imperial Rome*. London: Arms and Armour Press.

Rosenquist, A.M., 1967–8. 'Sverd med klinger ornert med figurer i kopperlegeringer fra eldre jernalder i Universitetets Oldsaksamling', *Universitetets Oldsaksamling Arbok*, 143–200.

Rostovtzeff, M.I., 1942. '*Vexillum* and victory', JRS 32, 92–106.

Rostovtzeff, M.I., 1957. *The Social and Economic History of the Roman Empire*. Oxford: Clarendon Press, 2nd ed.

Rostovtzeff, M.I., Bellinger, A.R., Hopkins, C. and Welles, C.B. (eds) 1936. *The Excavations at Dura-Europos. Preliminary Report of the Sixth Season of Work, October 1932 – March 1933*. New Haven: Yale Univ. Press.

Rostovtzeff, M.I., Brown, F.E. and Welles C.B. (eds) 1939. *The Excavations at Dura-Europos: Preliminary Report of the 7th and 8th Seasons of Work: 1933–34 and 1934–35*. New Haven: Yale University Press.

Ruhlmann, A., 1935. 'A propos d'une plaquette de caractère militaire trouvée à Thamusida', *Comptes Rendus Academie des Inscriptions et Belles-Lettres* 67–78.

Saxer, R., 1967. 'Untersuchungen zu den vexillationen des römischen Kaiserheeres von Augustus bis Diokletian', *Ep. Stud.* 1.

Schönberger, H. and Herrmann, F.R., 1967–8. 'Das Römerkastell Künzing-Quintana', *Jahersbericht der Bayerischen Bodendenkmalflege* 8–9, 37–86.

Scorpan, C., 1980. *Limes Scythiae: Topographical and Stratigraphical research on the late Roman fortifications on the lower Danube.* Oxford: BAR S88.

Seston, W., 1946. *Dioclétien et la Tétrarchie.* Paris: Boccard.

Sherlock, D., 1978. 'A Roman "Mars-barb" from Burgh Castle', *Proceedings of the Suffolk Institute of Archaeology* 34 (2), 141–3.

Sherlock, D., 1979. 'Plumbatae – a note on the method of manufacture', in Hassall and Ireland 1979, 101–2.

Shils, E.A. and Jonowitz, M., 1948. 'Cohesion and disintegration in the Wehrmacht in World War II', *Public Opinion Quarterly* 12, 280–315.

Sinnigen, W.G. and Boak, A.E.R., 1977. *A History of Rome to AD 565.* 6th edn. London: Collier Macmillan Publishers.

Smith, R.E., 1972a. 'The army reforms of Septimius Severus', *Historia* 21, 481–99.

Smith, R.E., 1972b. '*Dux, praepositus*' *ZPE* 36, 263–78.

Srejovic, D., Lalovic, A. and Jankovic, D., 1983. *Gamzigrad: kasnoanticki carski dvorac.* Belgrade.

Stehlin, K. 1957. *Die Spätrömischen Wachttürme am Rhein von Basel bis zum Bodensee I.* Untere Strecke: von Basel bis Zurzach. Basle.

Stewart, N.K., 1991. *Mates and Muchachos.* London: Brassey's.

Stirling, J.D.P., 1946. *The First and the Last.* Art and Educational Publishers.

Stjernquist, B., 1954. 'Runde Beschlagplatten mit Befestigungöse', *SJ* 13, 59–68.

Stoll, H., 1938. 'Ein schwert spätrömischer zeit aus Vrasselt bei Emmerich', *Germania* 22, 247–50.

Syme, R., 1971. *The* Historia Augusta. Bonn: Rudolf Habeit.

Teall, J.L., 1965. 'The barbarians in Justinian's armies', *Speculum* 40, 294–322.

Thomas, E.B., 1971. *Helme, Schilde, Dolche. Studien uber römisch-pannonische Waffenkunde.* Budapest: Akadémiai Kiado.

Tomlin, R., 1987. 'The army of the Late Empire', in Wacher (ed.) 1987, 107–35.

Trilling, J., 1982. *The Roman Heritage: Textiles from Egypt and the Eastern Mediterranean 300 to 600 AD.* Washington: The Textile Museum.

Unz, C. (ed.), 1986. *Studien zu den Militärgrenzen Roms III.* Stuttgart.

van Berchem, D., 1952. *L'Armée de Dioclétien at La Réforme Constantienne.* Paris: Geuthner.

van Berchem, D., 1977. 'Armée de frontière et armée de manoeuvre: alternative stratégique ou politique?' *Studien zu den Militärgrenzen Roms II: Vorträge des 10 Int. Limeskongresses in der Germania Interior.* Köln: Rheinland Verlag, 541–3.

Várady, L., 1961. 'New evidence on some problems of the Late Roman military organization', *Acta Antiqua* 9, 333–96.

Visy, Z., 1988. *Der Pannonische Limes in Ungarn.* Stuttgart: Theiss.

Wacher, J. (ed.), 1987. *The Roman World.* London: Routledge and Kegan Paul. 2 vols.

Walbank, F.W., 1969. *The Awful Revolution: the Decline of the Roman Empire in the West.* Liverpool: Liverpool Univ. Press. Repro.

Warmington, B.H., 1953. 'Review of van Berchem 1952', *JRS* 43, 17–35.

Watson, G.R., 1981. *The Roman Soldier* (repr. of 1969 edition). London: Thames and Hudson.

Webster, J., 1986. 'Roman bronzes from Maryport in the Netherhall Collection', *Transactions of the Cumberland and Westmorland Antiquarian and Archaeological Society* 86, 49–70.

Welsby, D., 1982. *The Roman Military Defence of the British Provinces in its Later Phases.* Oxford: BAR 101.

Werner, J., 1966. 'Spätrömische Schwertortbänder vom Typ Gundremmingen', *Bayerische Vorgeschichtsblätter* 31, 134–41.

White, P., 1967. 'The authorship of the *Historia Augusta*', *JRS* 57, 115–33.

Whittaker, C.R., 1994. *Frontiers of the Roman Empire: A Social and Economic Study.* Baltimore: James Hopkins Univ. Press.

Wild, J.P., 1967. 'The gynaeceum at Venta and its context', *Latomus* 26, 648–76.

Wild, J.P., 1976. 'The Gynaecaea', in Goodburn and Bartholemew (eds) 1976, 518.

Wild, J.P., 1979. 'Fourth-century underwear with special reference to the thoracomachus', in Hassall and Ireland (eds) 1979, 105–10.

Wild, J.P., 1981. 'A find of Roman scale armour from Carpow', *Brit* 12, 305–8.

Williams, S., 1985. *Diocletian and the Roman Recovery.* London: Batsford.

Wilson, R.J.A., 1983. *Piazza Armerina.* London: Granada.

Wolfram, H., 1988. *History of the Goths.* University of California Press. Revised edition.

Wuilleumier, M.P., 1950. 'La bataille de 197', *Gallia* 8, 146–8.

Yorck von Wartenburg, Count, 1902. *Napoleon as a General.* London: Kegan Paul, 2 vols.

Zahariade, M., 1991. 'An early and late Roman fort on the lower Danube limes: Halmyris (Independenta, Tulcea County, Romania)', in Maxfield and Dobson (eds) 1991, 311–17.

Zwikker, W., 1937. 'Bemerkungen zu den römischen Heeresfahnen in der älteren Kaiserzeit', *Bericht der Römisch-Germanischen Kommission* 27, 7–22.

INDEX